Revered and Reviled

A Complete History of the Domestic Cat

L.A. VOCELLE

Great Cat Publications

Revised Edition July, 2017

ISBN-13: 978-0692759820
ISBN-10: 0692759824

www.thegreatcat.org

DEDICATION

This book is dedicated to all my cats, past and present, and especially to my little love Beseechy. They have given me the inspiration to write and complete this book in honor of the cat's universal influence upon our history, art and literature.

CONTENTS

List of Illustrations

ACKNOWLEDGMENTS

A very special thanks to my friends, James Kennedy and Leslie Livingood, who have read through parts of the book and have given me their opinions and constructive criticisms. In addition, many thanks to those who have read portions of the book on my website and have left their valuable comments. Much gratitude must go to Tabassum Ali Kazmi for helping me keep my sanity during our many cathartic lunches as well as to Laureen Quick for offering ideas on social media and publication. Finally, I must thank all my cats, my muses, Beast (RIP), PCMa (RIP), Beseechy (RIP), Sphinx, Nero, Ruby (RIP), Neechia, and Tibby, for keeping me going and focused, without whom this book would never have been completed.

INTRODUCTION

"What sort of philosophers are we, who know absolutely nothing of the origin and destiny of cats?" Henry David Thoreau

Cats are the most popular pets in the world. As both social and cultural icons, their feline influence has even spread to the world of the internet and social media. Approximately 85.8 million cats are owned in the United States, (National Pet Owners Survey APPA for 2015-2016), and it is estimated that more than 600 million are owned worldwide. However, this was not always so. Just a few centuries ago, after the cat's reign as the ancient Egyptian goddess Bast had just barely been forgotten, cats, based on a long history of religious beliefs and superstitions, were deemed to be the epitome of evil. The mass killing and torture of cats were common place activities in a world where they were seen as uncontrollable devils, and feared simply because of their indomitable independent nature. Only in the 17th century did the cat's status in society begin to improve, with artists, writers and intellectuals befriending the free-minded feline. As a representation of rebellious independence, the cat aptly served social reformers as a symbolic reflection of man's own society. Bohemian anti-establishment artists and writers would soon portray the cat as a metaphor of mystery, magic, and evil, as well as domesticity and motherhood, and solidify the cat's ancient bond with women. Throughout history the cat's aloofness and unpredictable nature have been its blessing and its bane. Revered as goddesses and reviled as magical creatures with fearful powers, cats have been an enduring part of man's history for thousands of years.

A complete history of the cat is lacking in today's literature, and the purpose of this book is to fill that void. Some books may address certain segments (eras) of the cat's history, such as Engle's *Classical Cats, The Rise and Fall of the Sacred Cat* which focuses on the cat in Egypt, Greece and Rome, or Malik's *The Cat in Ancient Egypt.* Some, such as Carl Van Vechten's *Tiger in the House*, address the cat's influence in differing areas of interest, but no published book within the past ten years presents the complete history of the cat from its domestication up to the present day. Following the cat's path through history is necessary in order to understand its place in today's society as a social and cultural icon, and it is also essential to fully comprehend the unbreakable bond it has shared with women. This book focuses on the integral part the cat has played in history, art and literature as both symbol and inspiration.

There are various theories regarding the exact place and date of the cat's domestication, which are still being contested by scholars today. The cat, *Felis sylvesterus libycus*, is indigenous to Egypt and, after ingratiating itself into ancient Egyptian homes as a welcomed protector of food stores, it soon rose to become a beloved goddess of fertility, motherhood and domesticity. Even though a crime, cats were smuggled out of Egypt and thus, gradually, spread to the very edges of the Roman Empire. With the rise of Christianity under Theodosius I in AD 394, pagan rituals and worship were proclaimed illegal throughout the Roman Empire, of which Egypt, by that time, was a part. Ancient Egyptians clinging to the old faith were punished, and temples destroyed. With the slow conversion to Christianity, the old gods and goddesses disappeared, and with them the cat goddess Bast. Because of the cat's past association with the goddess Isis, the Greeks came to see it as a symbol of magic, an omen of evil, and eventually the inevitable embodiment of Satan. The other-worldliness of the cat and its identification with Isis and the feminine moon led to its association with mysticism and the occult.

From the very beginning of history the cat has been associated with women. The ancient female cat goddess Bast represented fertility, motherhood, and the home. The Greeks and Romans established a firm foundation for this bond between women and cats in Western Civilization by associating the Egyptian goddesses Bast and Isis with their own goddesses Artemis/Diana and Hecate. Hecate, goddess of the underworld, had the ability to change form and so, during the Dark and Middle Ages, witches were accused of having the power to change into cats. Fearful of pagan traditions, Christians struck out against the old beliefs and punished women for their association with cats and witchcraft (paganism).Vulnerable women who showed any kindness towards cats were soon persecuted and accused of having cat familiars. For better or for worse, the duality of woman and cat forged an unbreakable bond that would forever link them in history, art and literature.

Christianity, preoccupied with the hunt for witches and their familiars, would not come to know of and admit to Jesus's compassion towards cats until much later in history. According to *The Gospel of the Holy Twelve*, several instances of Jesus' kindness towards cats are documented, but yet there is no reference, good or bad, to the cat in the Bible except in the *Letter from Jeremiah.* On the other hand, Islam has always respected the cat. Prophet Mohammed's behavior towards his cat, Muezza, is mentioned in the *Hadith.* It is also stated in the *Hadith* that causing a cat to suffer unnecessarily will deprive the offender of his place in paradise. Conversely, the Jewish holy book, The Talmud, mentions the cat simply as a magical creature. In the East, Chinese and Japanese mythology viewed the cat ambivalently. Some stories portray the cat as a vicious vampire, biting necks and sucking blood, others give testament to its devotion and faithfulness as in the Edo period folktales of the *Maneki-neko.*

In the Dark and Middle Ages the cat plummeted to its lowest depths, ostracized, tortured and killed for its supposed association with pagans, witches and devils. Even though the Christian hierarchy demonized the cat, not all would accept such beliefs. Some saints, intellectuals and artists found the cat a valuable inspiration, if not simply a useful rat killer.

Among the first illuminated manuscripts, *The Lindisfarne Gospels* and *The Book of Kells* contain lovely drawings of cats, not as demons, but as highly decorative creatures going about their cat business. For example, a cat slithers down the side of a page in *The Lindisfarne Gospels,* its stomach visibly containing a just-eaten cormorant. Depictions of cats spread to other holy books such as Bestiaries, Psalters, and Books of Hours as well as to church architecture and interiors. Carvings of cats would even decorate misericords in the 14th and 15th centuries.

Cat lovers would begin to immortalize their pets in poems, and laws were even instituted to protect them. Already initiated into literature in AD 550 in a poem by the Greek Agathias, the cat would next appear in a 9th century poem penned by a lonely monk describing his cat, Pangur Ban. Also, in the 9th century, the Welsh King Howell the Good (880-950) instituted laws to protect cats because they were so important for keeping rodents in check. Later, Henry I of England (1068-1135) enacted laws to ensure the cat's welfare just as Howell the Good had done.

In contrast, the church continued to focus on the cat's imagined propensity for evil. Both the Cathars and the Knights Templar would be accused of heresy founded on their supposed worship of a demonic cat. These charges were, most likely based on the fact that the church was threatened by the idea, supported by both the Cathars and Knights Templar, that individuals had the power to communicate with God on their own and not through a priest. To further condemn all its enemies, the church commissioned paintings of Jews that included the cat as a symbol of heresy.

Although cats served man by keeping large numbers of rodents at bay, man repaid them with torturous deaths by burning and even throwing them from belfries and towers, as was done in Ypres, Belgium from Cloth Hall up until 1817. Most of these abominable actions took place during Christian religious festivals or to celebrate Saints' birthdays. These festivals were a constant reminder that the cat was part of the pagan belief system and should be feared and loathed.

Even though the great artist and inventor, Leonardo da Vinci said, "The smallest feline is a masterpiece," the cat's place in society was little improved during the Renaissance. Instead, it became a symbol of political rebellion, and the discontented rabble used cats in political and religious protests where hundreds of innocent felines suffered horrible deaths. During the Reformation, it was the cat that represented Catholicism, and in one instance, Protestants dressed a feline victim as a priest and ceremoniously hanged it in Cheape, England. Later, Catholics used shaven headed cats to symbolize Roundheads in order to illustrate their being less than human. Perhaps fittingly, the first novel in English, *Beware the Cat* by William Baldwin (1515-1563), uses cat characters to illustrate the undying power of the Catholic Church.

However, by the 17th century the cat's situation began to improve. Dutch genre painters found the cat the perfect example of domesticity and included cats and kittens in their works. Commissioned by well off Dutch merchants, these works captured the cat in energetic Baroque paintings of domestic settings, sometimes conveying a message for proper social behavior.

Many societal changes occurred that positively impacted the cat during the Enlightenment. With the new discoveries of Louis Pasteur, sanitation and cleanliness became more important, and the cat, albeit never seen as a dirty animal, now took the fore as an example of cleanliness. A renewed interest in pagan beliefs by philosophers led to a rekindled respect for nature and animals. Consequently, new laws were instituted to lessen their suffering and abuse. Even though not quite eradicated, the old superstitions of witchcraft were slowly fading away and opening the door to more scientific thinking.

Les Chats published in 1727 was the first book written entirely about cats. François-Augustin de Paradis de Moncrif (1687-1770), a member of the *Académie Française* and the royal historiographer to Louis XV, was highly ridiculed at the time for writing such a book. However, other great thinkers and writers also expressed their fondness for their cat companions. Samuel Johnson, the creator of the first English dictionary, was just one of many who pampered their cats. Johnson was known to feed his cat Hodge oysters. Today you can see a statue of the cat with an oyster at his feet near Johnson's home commemorating his love for his feline Hodge.

Victorian pet-keeping, begun in the early 1800's, influenced both domestic acceptance of the cat as well as its appearance in well-known artists' and writers' paintings and poetry. The cat continued to be placed in paintings of domestic scenes and was often seen in portraits of women. Lengthy poems mourning the loss of dearly departed cats would become the fashion. Stricter laws were instituted to protect the cat and other domestic animals from abuse, and the first shelters for homeless and unwanted cats and dogs were founded in Paris. But the cat continued to be equated with women in a negative manner. For example, Alphonse Toussenel (1803-1885), a French naturalist and writer, was one of many who equated women with cats based on their lustful appetites.

Even so, it was during the Victorian age that the first cat show took place at the Crystal Palace in London in 1875. In addition, the first pet cemetery, *Cimetière des Chiens et Autres Animaux Domestiques*, in the small city of Asnières-sur-Seine just outside Paris, was founded as another example of the newborn respect and love for animals.

During the latter part of the 18th century and the beginning of the 19th, prolific artists that drew and painted primarily cats, such as

Louis Wain and Théophile Steinlen grabbed the public's attention by portraying the cat as either an anthropomorphic representation of man, or as an exotic, sensuous, miniature leopard.

As the foundations laid for the cat's welfare begun in Europe spread to the United States, the 19th century cat became even more ubiquitous. With its new-found notoriety, the cat began to appear even more in literature and art. Writers such as Poe, Twain, and many others used cats as potent symbols in their literature and fondly kept them as pets. Edward Lear, both an artist and writer, captured his beloved Foss in his drawings and perhaps thought of him while he composed the poem *The Owl and the Pussy Cat.*

Cats, especially black ones, had become seafaring animals from their days in ancient Egypt because of their association and assimilation with the goddess Isis Pharia, and thus, beginning with the Romans, became a necessary accompaniment on ships as a symbol of good luck. Both Robert Scott and Ernest Shackleton took cats along when they ventured to the South Pole in the early 20th century. During war, cats kept ships free of rodents, and during trying times they provided much needed affection to distraught sailors. Cats were even awarded medals for their bravery and ability to survive the terrors of battle. In the 20th century, the cat's charms were even thought to extend to provide safety to aircraft as well. The airship *America* carried Kiddo, and Charles Lindbergh took a *Felix the Cat* doll with him on the first transatlantic flight. During WWII fighter pilots proudly displayed drawings of Felix on the sides of their planes as a symbol of courage, cunning and the ability to overcome all odds. Ideals taught in the cartoon first aired in 1919 had influenced a whole generation.

Today the cat is as close to regaining its rightful place as a worshipped goddess as it has ever been at any other time in history. Cats are everywhere and most importantly on the internet and social media. Facebook, Pinterest, and Twitter are bursting with pictures of cute cats, some even dressed in clothing not much different from the photos taken by the 19th century photographer Harry Pointer. Cat celebrities such as Grumpy Cat and Lil Bub appear on the TV with news anchors and in advertisements uttering words of disdain about having to deal with people. YouTube videos feature the French existential cat Henry and his ongoing boredom with being a cat. Hello Kitty, based on the Japanese folktales of the cat *Maneki-neko,* produces fashionable apparel and trendy accessories sporting the ancient beckoning white cat motif.

Throughout history the cat has been an indomitable influence on societies and cultures, first as goddess, then as demon, and now as hero and social media empress. Man's view of the cat has come full circle. As both mascot and muse to great adventurers, writers, artists and statesmen, the cat has offered comfort and inspiration. Never obsequious or ordinary, always elegant and inscrutable, the cat has played a fundamental role in civilization through the centuries, and this is its story.

Chapter One

THE RISE OF THE CAT

Evolution/Ancestry

The ancestors of the first cats appeared at some point during the Early Pliocene to the Eocene period between 65-33 million years ago, and are descendants of the Miacid species *(figure 1.1),* small marten-like carnivores which mainly inhabited forests.

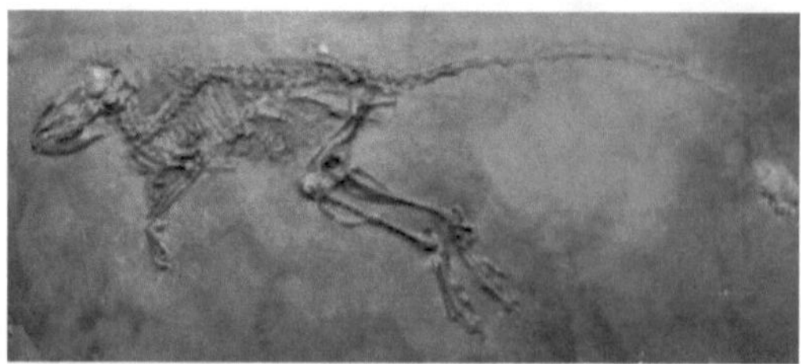

Figure 1.1. Miacid fossil

Descended from the Miacids, the Proailurus or Leman's Dawn Cat appeared about 30 million years ago *(figure 1.2).* Fossils of the Leman's Dawn Cat found in France are considered to be the remains of the first true cat. After the discovery of the Leman's Dawn Cat, there are no fossil records of cats for the next 10 million years. This time period is referred to by paleontologists as the *cat gap* and is believed to have been caused by hyper-carnivorousness and climate change.

Figure 1.2. Proailurus

The next notable cat fossil record is of Pseudaelurus, which appeared during the middle of the Miocene period around 20 million years ago. Pseudaelurus, regarded as the ancient ancestor of all modern cats, originated in the area of South East Asia and crossed over the Bering land bridge, which connected Siberia and Alaska, at around the same time as the cat's appearance on the evolutionary timeline. Throughout this period, crossing the world to inhabit all continents except Antarctica and Australia, cats migrated back and forth from Asia to the Americas not less than 10 times, evolving into a variety of species and lineages. Some species, such as the cheetah and lynx, migrated from the New World back to the Old, where we find them today. Amazingly, fossils of cats dating back to 12 million years ago resemble our small house cats.

The 37 species of cats living today belong to the family Felidae and are divided into three main subfamilies: Panthera, Acinonychinae and Felinae. The cat subfamily Panthera originated around 5 million years ago and includes cats that roar: lions, tigers, leopards and jaguars; while the subfamily Acinonychinae only includes cheetahs. The final subfamily, Felinae, comprises the majority of cats, including the domestic, and appeared about 1 million years ago. Each cat has two names: the first for the genus and the second its own. For example, in the name *Felis catus*, *Felis* is for the group genus and *catus* is the individual's name, meaning *Domestic.*

Just as the ancestors of humans have been traced to just seven women through their mitochondrial DNA (DNA passed from mother to child), all the world's small cats belonging to the genus *Felis* have been found to be descended from just five females (Driscoll, 2007). The five subspecies descended from the original five matriarchs are: the Chinese Desert cat, European, South African, Central Asian, and Near Eastern Wildcats. However, it is the Near Eastern Wildcat, also known as the African Wildcat or *Felis sylvestris libyca,* from which all of the world's 600 million domesticated cats belonging to over 40 different breeds are descended.

Felis sylvestris libyca (figure 1.3) is still found roaming wild today around the Nile Delta valley in Egypt where it is quite common. These ancestors of the domestic cat have characteristics similar to those of our modern day house cats. They are nocturnal and feed upon mice, rats, birds, reptiles and insects. Larger than everyday house cats, they typically grow to a length of between 61 and 93.5

cms, with their tail measuring 23.7 to 39 cms. They have longer legs and bodies than domestic cats, but have similar tabby markings.

Figure 1.3. Felis Sylvestris Libyca, Edward Howe Forbush (1858-1929)

Characteristics of Domestic Cats

Through the millennia cats have developed into lean carnivorous predators that have adapted to varying environments across the world. With domestication, cats' physical characteristics changed. Both body size and brain size shrank and the size of their jaws was affected as well. "By the Middle Ages, the European cat brain was 10 percent smaller still, the same as the average cat brain of today---except for Siamese cats whose brains are yet another 5-to-10 percent smaller" (Hubbell, 2001, p. 92). Skull and jawbone sizes are the most notable difference between a domestic cat and a wild cat (American Genetic Association, 1917).

Cats' bodies are designed for agility, stalking, hunting, and killing. With about 250 bones and 500 muscles in their bodies and no collar bones, they perform the amazing feats of balance, jumping and landing on their feet as well as manipulating their bodies through tiny openings that we as cat owners observe every day. Both males and females tend to be very similar, though tomcats tend to be physically bigger.

Cats have five toes on the front feet and four toes on the back feet. Sometimes cats are born with more than 5 toes and are called polydactyl. The descendants of Hemingway's cats are famous for this abnormal inherited trait. Cats walk on their toes and have extremely sensitive soft pads that help them camouflage any noise they might make while stalking prey. All cats except the cheetah have retractable claws that are embedded into the last joint of the toe. It is important to note that when people want to declaw a cat, it is like cutting off the last joint of a finger where the nail lies.

Feline dental traits are similar to those of all carnivores. Cats have four large canine teeth at the front of the mouth which are used to clutch and kill prey. These fangs fit neatly between the vertebrae of small rodents enabling cats to easily severe their spinal cords. The molars in the backs of their mouths are used to gnaw and tear apart meat to swallow rather than chew.

With a sense of smell 14 times more acute than that of humans, cats obviously have a highly keen sense of smell. They use the Jacobson's organ, or vomeronasal organ, located at the top of their mouths just behind their front teeth to filter interesting scents. This is why the cat will often open its mouth after smelling a particularly tantalizing aroma.

Cats' sense of hearing is far superior to that of humans and dogs. Cats' ears contain 32 muscles and can be rotated up to 180 degrees allowing them to locate the source of a sound 10 times faster than a dog. They can hear frequencies of 45,000 Hz to 64,000 Hz, while dogs can hear only to 45,000 Hz, and humans hear from just 64,000 Hz to 23,000 Hz.

Compared to their body size, cats have the largest eyes of any carnivore. In bright light the cat's eye is seen as just a slit, but in the dark it opens wide so that the pupil is totally round. The *tapetum lucidum*, the reflective part of the eye located behind the retina, enables cats to see six times better than a human at night and also makes cats' eyes look like glowing orbs, which have for centuries conjured up emotions of fear and superstition. The inner eyelid, also called the third eyelid or nictitating membrane, protects the eye from dryness and damage. Even though they can only see the colors blue and green, cats are very sensitive to movement, and their peripheral vision gives them a field of sight of about 285 degrees.

Because of their desert origins, cats are able to endure high temperatures of up to 56C/ 133F. Their normal body temperature is from 100.5F/38C to 102.F/38.8C and they have no sweat glands.

Their hearts beat from 140 to 220 times a minute. Their kidneys are able to concentrate urine more than any other domestic species; therefore, they do not need as much water and can retain water for long periods of deprivation.

Man's Earliest Relationship with Cats, Domestication

The major force behind any type of domestication or relationship between man and animal is that there be some sort of benefit to both. As Neolithic man turned away from a nomadic hunter gatherer lifestyle and began to settle in small villages, agriculture became important. With the knowledge that certain crops such as wheat, rye, and barley could be stockpiled, early man constructed granaries. Naturally, these stockpiles of grains attracted rats and mice, and in turn these vermin prey attracted cats. This working partnership of sorts was of benefit to both man and feline, and so the first relationship between man and cat began as a mutual, symbiotic one.

Based on evidence of terracotta and clay cat figurines found in Syria, Turkey and Israel, some scholars believe that this relationship between man and cat, if not domestication, began in the Fertile Crescent, the cradle of civilization, some 10,000 years ago. Other proof dating back 7,000 years gives evidence of the cat's domestication in Haçilar, Turkey, where archeologists found 22 figurines of women in various poses playing with cats. In addition, in Haçilar and Jericho the bones of small cats have been found among the archeological sites of early farming villages dating back to 6,000 and 5,000 BC (Yurco, 1990).

Other noted scholars, however, disagree on the exact location of the first domestication of the cat. They believe that it was *Felis sylvestris libyca* which was first domesticated in Egypt rather than the Fertile Crescent. It is believed that from Egypt the cat spread to other surrounding Mediterranean countries on board Phoenician trading ships undoubtedly laden with cargoes of grain. French archeologists suspect that this was how the first cat landed in the stone age village of Shillourokambos, Cyprus where they found a grave of a cat and its master dating to 9,500 years ago (Rincon, 2004). The eight-month old cat had been killed and then buried only 40 cms away from its human companion aged around 30 years. What was this person's relationship to the cat? Could it have been religious? Was the cat simply a pet? Because the grave also included the highest number of ceremonial ornaments and shells, more than any other grave found as of yet for the whole Preceramic and Aceramic Neolithic ages in Cyprus, the person was most probably of important social status (Vigne, Guilaine, Debue, Haye, & Gerard, 2004). Both the head of the cat and that of the person were facing West with their backs to the South indicating some sort of special or perhaps religious relationship between them. In addition, there are no cat species native to Cyprus; hence, cats had to have been brought via ships from a nearby Mediterranean country. However, another theory is that domesticated cats were brought from Turkey by farmers; thus, strengthening the theory that cats had already been domesticated in the Fertile Crescent (Wade, 2007).

Recently, however, an African wildcat, *Felis sylvestris libyca,* was discovered in an Egyptian Pre-Dynastic burial pit dating to around 3,700 BC or to approximately 5,700 years ago. The cat had been buried along with a man curled into a fetal position, and wrapped in cloth surrounded with items of jewelry and pots not unlike the Cyprus find. The Mostagedda tomb at Hierakonpolis, near modern day Asyut, was the capital of Upper Egypt from approximately 5000-3100 BC (Linseele, Van Neer, & Hendrickx, 2007). Evidence from this tomb refutes claims that the cat had not been domesticated prior to the 11th Dynasty, a theory based on the fact that there had not been any representations of cats found in the Pre-Dynastic periods.

Because of the cat's importance in protecting food stores and its ability to ingratiate itself with its human keepers, it began to be more widely domesticated by the ancient Egyptians sometime during the 5th Dynasty (2750-2625 BC). A frieze of a cat sitting under a chair with a collar around its neck is depicted on a tomb wall in Saqqara dating from the 5th Dynasty. Once the cat established its rightful place as protector of the granaries, farmers and villagers must have welcomed it into private homes in order to rid them not only of the usual vermin of rats and mice, but also of the more deadly threats of snakes and scorpions. Therefore, in the beginning, cats established themselves as protectors of food stores and subsequently became pets as well.

In all probability cats were domesticated more than once and in various locations at differing times (Mott, 2006). New evidence even indicates that cats had been domesticated earlier than 3,000 BC in China. This would not be unlikely since *Felis sylvestris libyca,* the ancestor of all domesticated cats, ranged from Arabia and the Near East to Southern USSR east to China, Afghanistan, Pakistan, northern and central India; Sardinia, Corsica and Majorca; North Africa, as well as savannah regions south of the Sahara (Ewer, 1997). However, as archeologists continue to unearth more ancient villages, a more exact date and place for the first domestic relationship between cat and man may be discovered and proven. What is indisputable is that man's bond with cats has been a long one.

Chapter Two

THE CAT AS GODDESS

"Thou art the Great Cat, the avenger of the gods, and the judge of words, and the president of the sovereign chiefs and the governor of the holy circle; thou art indeed the Great Cat."
Inscription on a royal tomb in Thebes

Beginnings of the Cult of the Cat

It took hundreds of years from the first evidence of the cat's domestication for it to become worshipped as a goddess during the Middle Kingdom reign of Mentuhotep III. Being a pet and being worshipped were not mutually exclusive. The ancient Egyptians had cats as household pets, and at the same time kept sacred temple cats for worship and sacrifice. Observing their behavior in their households, the Egyptians saw what they perceived to be the divine characteristics of God within the cat. Thus, the cat rose from an ordinary pet to become the goddess Bast. Ancient Egyptians, however, did not believe that God was literally a cat. Instead, they worshipped the characteristics of God that they believed to be manifested in the cat. Humans, animals and even plants had equal status and were a part of the great all, spirit, or God Amun. Animals were the earthly representations of the Gods because animals had powers that man lacked: flight, speed, and a keen sense of sight, smell and hearing.

It is easy to see why the ancient Egyptians considered cats to be godlike. With five more senses than humans have, cats, by their very nature, are much more sensitive to their surroundings than man. As mentioned in Chapter One, cats' acute sense of smell allows them to sense pheromones in their environment through the vomeronasal organ located at the top of their mouths. In addition, all cats seem to have a certain homing sense. How many stories have we all heard about cats traveling great distances to find their lost families? Their ability to predict the weather through an organ located in their ears was creatively mentioned in folklore, suggesting that every time a cat moves its paw up and over its ear there is likely to be rain. Also well documented, is their ability to predict imminent earthquakes based on numerous stories of cats behaving in an agitated manner right before the tremors started. And last but not least, cats have an uncanny way of predicting death. The case of Oscar, a Rhode Island nursing home feline companion that curls up next to people who are about to die, has been widely reported. Oscar has been so correct in his predictions, 50 to date, that nursing home personnel call relatives when Oscar indicates that someone's time is near, as usually only a few hours remain. Because of these uncanny abilities, the ancient Egyptians, understandably awed, deemed the enigmatic cat a goddess.

The cult of the cat did not spread throughout ancient Egypt quickly or at an even pace. Because of the diversity of tribes and their differing beliefs, and primarily due to geographical location and social status, new religious ideas traveled slowly through Pre-Dynastic Egypt. With the gradual unification of Upper and Lower Egypt around 3150 BC, ideas and beliefs were exchanged more readily. Due to this unification, the cult centers for the goddess Bast spread from Lower Egypt to Upper Egypt. Even though ancient Egypt was animist and pantheistic, not all cities had temples erected to all gods. Instead, citizens of some cities worshipped specific gods such as Neith, the goddess of war in Sais; Hathor, the goddess of childbirth and dance in Serabit; Mut, the goddess of all in Thebes; and eventually Bast, the cat goddess in Bubastis. This did not mean that these goddesses were not worshipped elsewhere, but that they were the primary goddesses in the cities mentioned above.

The Goddess Bast's Evolution and Relationship with other Maternal Goddesses

The evolution of the goddess Bast took place gradually over the entire span of the ancient Egyptian kingdom. The gods and goddesses were continually changing, sharing and combining attributes. Because of the complexity of the Egyptian pantheon, various theories of the origin of the goddess Bast have emerged. Archeologists believe that in the Old Kingdom Bast was first combined with the goddesses Nut and Hathor; in the Middle Kingdom Bast merged with Mut, the mother and creator of all; in Memphis, Bast was blended with her evil sister Sekhmet, the lion goddess; in Heliopolis, Bast was identified with Tefnut, daughter of Atum; and at Edfu she was called the "Ba," or soul of Isis (Redford, 2003).

Nut and Hathor

Some archeologists and researchers think that Bast merged into the sky goddess Nut, as well as into the deities Bes and Neith. "At the ancient shrine of Denderea she (the Sky Goddess Nut) was the cow-goddess Hathor; at Sais she was the joyous Neit; at Bubastis in the form of a cat, she appeared as Bast, while at Memphis her genial aspects disappeared and she became a lioness, Sekhmet, the goddess of storm and terror" (Breasted, 1908, p. 60).

The sky goddess Nut was one of the oldest deities of Egypt. Originally the goddess of the night sky, she also appeared as a cow; and thus, a crossover to Hathor, and hence like Hathor, a protector of children and childbirth. Hathor was the cow goddess whose horns contained stars linking her to the sky. She was also a goddess protector of motherhood, childbirth, children, music, dance and fertility. She and Bes were two of the few deities that in statuary looked straight forward, which was symbolic of their ability to be all-seeing protectors. Flinders Petrie, a renowned ancient Egyptian archeologist, noticed that "The cat seems to have been specifically related to the worship of Hathor at Serabit. We find ….also flat tablets with figurines of cats" (Petrie & Currelly, 1906, p. 148). "The cats are sometimes on pedestals...Hence it seems as if it were treated as a sacred animal." In addition, the cat is also evident on faience plaques at the temple of Hathor at Serabit El-Khadim in Sinai. A glazed ring stand shows the head of Hathor with two cats posed as guardians at each side (Petrie & Currelly, 1906, p. 10).

Sekhmet

Sekhmet the lion goddess *(figure 2.1)*, who had her own cult, was Bast's evil sister or alter ego. She is often portrayed as a woman with the head of a lion above which a solar disk with a uraeus sits. Sometimes she holds a scepter and sometimes a knife.

Figure 2.1. Sekhmet, Author's Photograph

Likewise, Bast often has the head of a cat and the body of a woman *(figure 2.2)*. She is the sweet, nurturing smaller feline, while Sekhmet is the fierce bloodthirsty lion imbued with all the warlike destructive powers of the sun god Ra. Translated, the goddess Sekhmet's name means: *Powerful One, Evil Trembles before Me, Dread, and Queen of Death and Destruction.* Ra, the sun god, in a myth about an annually celebrated festival in honor of Sekhmet, created the lion goddess for the purpose of destroying those people who rebelled against him. Sekhmet set about her task with such enthusiasm that she destroyed almost all of mankind. To stop her bloodthirsty killing, Ra had to devise a plan to trick her. So, he turned the Nile the color of blood in order to have her drink it. Ra did not actually turn the Nile into blood, but instead made it into a mix of pomegranate juice and beer which made her drunk and unable to continue her slaughter of humanity. Needless to say, Sekhmet's formidable nature was well known amongst the ancient Egyptians and mindfully celebrated in order to placate her terrorizing ways.

Figure 2.2. Statue of Bast, 400-250 BC, Permission of Walters Museum

Because of the cat's reputation for being a good mother, the primary goddesses and gods, excluding Sekhmet of course, that associated with Bast also protected motherhood, children, fertility and the home. Hence, Tefnut, goddess of water and fertility and the mother of Nut; Neith, the goddess of war and also the protector of women and marriage at Thebes; and the god Bes, the protector of homes, were all associated with protecting motherhood, children and fertility. Since the average age of death was around 35, the need to increase the birth rate was of great importance. The focus on fertility, motherhood and the protection of the home was a constant priority, and thus, the cat, as a symbol of fertility and motherhood, became an essential deity.

The God Bes

Prior to Bast's association with Hathor, the cat goddess might have originated from the god Bes, whose name in Nubian means cat. Bes, a short dwarf-like figure with a cat face, sometimes wearing a cat skin with a tail hanging down to his feet, came from ancient Nubia and perhaps represents a Sudanese dancer from the Dinka tribe. Bes, known as the god of dance, also protected infants from evil. Perhaps the fact that Bes was a champion of children and dance crossed over to the cat goddess Bast. Bast, the ultimate mother figure, is often represented holding a sistrum, a musical instrument based on the form of the ankh.

The sistrum *(figure 2.3)*, a type of rattle called a "shaker" made of bronze, gold or silver, was most probably of African origin. It was held in the hand and shaken to emit a loud shrill sound during dances, music festivals and rituals for Isis/Hathor. However, according to Virgil in the *Aeneid*, the army used it much as a trumpet is used to sound reveille today, to call troops together (Virgil, trans. 1910, 8: 696). The rounded top represents a woman's womb, while the bottom handle symbolizes of the male phallus. The rounded loop has four bars representing the four elements of nature: fire, water, air, and earth that shake when moved upon the bend of the sistrum. According to Plutarch, the body of a cat with a human face often decorated sistrums.

Sometimes one side of the sistrum had the face of Isis, symbolic of birth, and on the other side, the face of Nephthys, symbolic of death (Oldfield, 2003, p. 28). Both represented man's eternal journey from birth to death. Isis, herself, would later be depicted holding a sistrum *(figure 2.4)*.

The Goddess Mut

Bast continued to be associated with other goddesses that were protectors of motherhood and children, such as the ancient Egyptian mother or creator goddess Mut. "In the temple of Koptos the goddess Mut of Thebes was called onetime Bast..."(Erman, 1907, p. 59). Mut's sacred animal was the cat, as jars and vases used in rituals for Mut found at the temple of Luxor at Thebes were decorated with cats (Lesko, 1999). Mut was at one point assimilated into Hathor

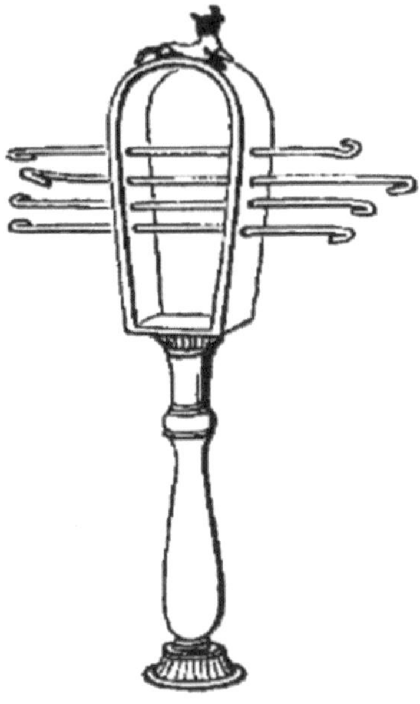

Figure 2.3. Egyptian Sistrum with cat on top, Encyclopaedia Biblica, 1903

when the power of Thebes was in decline. Then Mut, Hathor and Isis merged. However, during the reign of Hatshepsut in the 18th dynasty, Mut once again found her rightful place amongst the gods and goddesses. During this dynasty, Hatshepsut identified herself with Mut and thus rebuilt her temples, only later to have the worship of Mut banned by Akhenaton. However, under the reign of Tutankhamen the creator goddess was brought to life once again and worshipped until the end of the 3rd century AD. Farther down the Nile from Thebes at Beni Hasan, Hatshepsut also built temples to Pakhet, meaning she who scratches, another minor cat goddess.

The Goddess Isis

The relationship between Bast and Isis, the goddess of sun and moon, is a pivotal one that reaches far into the future history of the cat, influencing the symbolism of the black cat and other important aspects, which will be explored later. However, some of the f irst

Figure 2.4. Isis holding a sistrum, Musei Capitolini, Italy

evidence of this Bast/Isis connection is on the walls of the New Kingdom Temple of Isis at Philae where the sun and moon goddess is summoned as Bast *(figure 2.5).*

In addition, word of the city Bubastis had traveled as far as the Greek Isles where an inscription there states that the city of Bubastis, the city that we all believe was dedicated to the cat goddess Bast, was actually built in honor of Isis. The inscription, referring to Isis, states, "…I am she who is called the goddess of women. The town of Bubastis was built in my honour" (Erman, 1907, p. 244).

Another example of Isis/Bast merging is a small figure of Bast under the throne of Isis in *The Turin Table*, also known as *The Bembine Table of Isis (figure 2.6).*

Figure 2.5. Temple of Isis at Philae

Figure 2.6. Cat under Isis's Chair, Bembine Table of Isis, Reprint from Manly P. Hall's, The Secret Teachings of All Ages, 1928

Named after Cardinal Bembo, who bought the table from a Roman in 1527, it is a fine example of metallurgy, as it comprises gold, silver, bronze, tin and copper. Even though thought to have been made in Rome, its style is quite Egyptian.

Furthermore, there are many terracotta statuettes of Bast with an Isaic knot (Clarysse, 1998). The Isaic knot, known in the Egyptian language as *Tyet*, resembles an ankh and like the ankh represents eternal life.

The cult of Isis continued on the Egyptian island of Philae even after paganism was outlawed. It was the Emperor Justinian, in an effort to completely eradicate the cult, who ordered the destruction and defacement of the sculptures at the large temple of Isis. Despite Justinian's efforts to end the cult once and for all, due to the ever persistent onslaught of Christianity, the cult of Isis survived and still exists today as *The Fellowship of Isis,* with its center located in Clonegal Castle in Northern Ireland.

The Goddess Bast is Worshipped

The cat goddess was a very important deity to the ancient Egyptians, confirmed by their unfailing devotion to her not only in one part of the kingdom, but also at various locations in both Upper and Lower Egypt. Saqqara, Thebes, Beni Hasan and finally Bubastis are sites that provide us with ample evidence of the worship of Bast and the cult of the cat.

SAQQARA (Memphis)

Saqqara, located not far from the pyramids of Giza, is famous as the home of the great step pyramid of Zozer, and it is at Saqqara that one of the earliest tomb paintings of a domesticated cat with a collar around its neck dates to the 5th dynasty (2500-2350 BC). Though Pre-Dynastic Saqqara was originally a burial place for royalty, it slowly became a burial site for high officials of the royal court when the kings and queens abandoned it for Thebes and Fayoum during the Middle Kingdom. Later, however, Saqqara again served as a burial site for royalty equaled to that of the Valley of the Kings in Thebes (Zivie, 2008).

The Saqqara plateau is not only the last resting place of important officials and viziers of the royal court, but it is also home to two main animal burial grounds.The first site, located north of the step pyramid has burial evidence of cows and ibises as well as falcons and baboons nearby. The second site, east of the pyramids of Teti and Weserkaf (Bard & Schubert, 1999), has cats, dogs and jackals dating back to the 5th dynasty (2750-2625 BC)*(figure 2.7).* The entrance to the necropolis of cats is called the *Bubasteion* (Door of Cats), in Egyptian Arabic *Bab el Quttat,* or the Greek name for this area, *temenos*, meaning an area dedicated to a God or a place of worship.

These cat burials are among the tombs of officials from other dynasties. Some New Kingdom tombs were even reused for cats; an

Figure 2.7. Animal Necropolis at Saqqara, Photograph by Hajor, December 2002

example is that Vizier Aper-El's tomb contained remains of cats dating back to 730-160 BC (Zivie & Chapuis, 2008). Remarking on his finds in 1815, Giovanni Belzoni wrote, "I must not omit that among these tombs we saw some which contained the mummies of animals intermixed with human bodies….and one tomb was filled with nothing but cats, carefully folded in red and white linen, the head covered by a mask representing the cat, and made of the same linen" (Belzoni, 1890, p. 168) *(figure 2.8).*

Figure 2.8. Giovanni Belzoni, From Narrative of the Operations and Recent Discoveries Within the Pyramids, Temples, Tombs and Excavations in Egypt and Nubia by Giovanni Battista Belzoni, London, 1820

Most of the cats at Saqqara were young, about 4 months old, and were killed by head trauma which was sometimes so violent that the skull split in two. Other cats, based on evidence of dislocated vertebrae, were killed by strangulation. The bodies of the cat mummies were in differing stages of decay and in one of two positions. In the first form of mummification, the front legs are placed downward in front of the body and the back legs, often purposely broken, are folded up in front of the stomach with the tail placed through them, thus making the cat a tubular shape *(figure 2.9).*

Figure 2.9. Cat Mummy, Rosecrucian Egyptian Museum, San Jose, California

The second type of mummy has the head, legs and body individually wrapped *(figure 2.10).* Some, but not all of these cat mummies, have painted faces that show the facial features such as the ears, nose and eyes. Some cats, depending upon the wealth of their owners, have their own mummy cases. The bodies of the cases were usually made of wood and the heads either bronze or gilded. Others, especially those during the late period, had quite opulent sarcophagi. We know from Diodorus Siculus, a Greek historian, that "When one of these animals dies they wrap it in fine linen and then, wailing and beating their breasts, carry it off to be embalmed; and after it has been treated with cedar oil and such spices as have the quality of imparting a pleasant odour and of preserving the body for a long time, they lay it away in a consecrated tomb" (Siculus, trans., 1933, p. 285). He continues by adding, "When any animal dies they mourn for it as deeply as do those who have lost a beloved child, and bury it in a manner not in keeping with their ability but going far beyond the value of their estates"(Siculus, trans., 1933, p. 291).

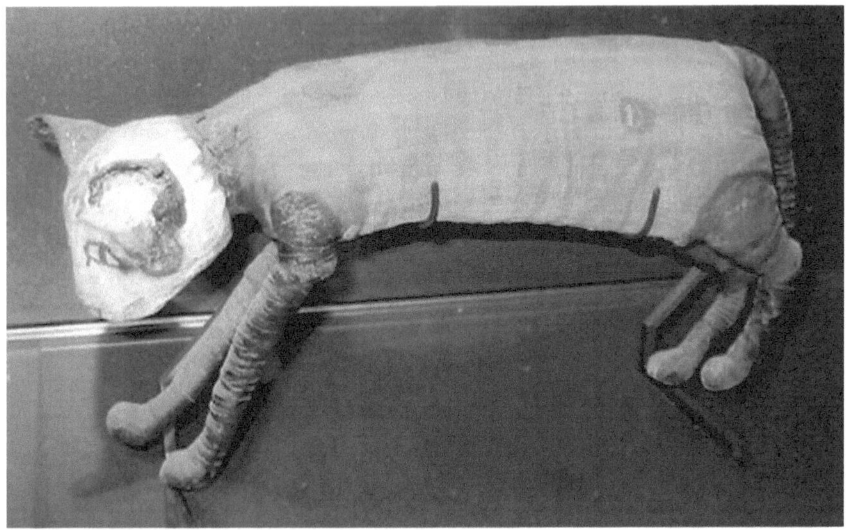

Figure 2.10. Cat Mummy, 332 BC, Antiquité égyptienne, Musée du Louvre, Paris

Most of the mummified cats were raised in the sacred temples to be sold to pilgrims as votive offerings to Bast. Thus, this reinforces the fact that they were domesticated. According to Dr. Ikram, the founder and co-director of the animal mummy project at the Egyptian museum, "....the existence of vast quantities of cats fed in the precinct of the temple (before being ritually killed and eventually buried in dedicated catacombs) tends to prove that the majority of these cats were domestic animals, with the wild cats being an anomaly" (Ikram, 2005, p. 118).

Mummification of a variety of animals, not just cats, was widespread from the earliest dynasties and was carried out for three reasons. Firstly, owners wanted to assure their beloved pets' immortality. Secondly, animals were mummified as a source of food for a deceased human of high status during his or her journey into the afterlife. And finally, the most important reason was simply that of religious belief. Offering a votive mummy to the goddess Bast, for example, was done to receive blessings for fertility, safe childbirth, and healthy children. Because of the importance of garnering favors with the goddess Bast, a whole industry sprung up around the cult. Cats were raised at the temples for the specific purpose of being sold to pilgrims for mummification (Dodson, 2009). Thus, there had to be animal keepers, embalmers and most importantly priests. Here Herodotus writes in his *History*, "...persons have been appointed of the Egyptians, both men and women, to provide the food for each kind of beast separately, and their office goes down from father to son; and those who dwell in the various cities perform vows to them thus, that is, when they make a vow to the god to whom the animal belongs, they shave the head of their children either the whole or the half or the third part of it, and then set the hair in the balance against silver, and whatever it weighs, this the man gives to the person who provides for the animals, and she cuts up fish of equal value and gives it for food to the animals. Thus food for their support has been appointed" (Herodotus, trans., 1890, 2, 65). The pharaohs, ever ready to fill their coffers, encouraged the activity to increase tax revenues, and offered incentives to those who wanted to avoid serving as common laborers or in other less noble endeavors.

The Process of Mummification

The process of mummifying a cat started with first removing all its internal organs and then stuffing the empty body cavity with sand or straw. Once this was accomplished, the body was arranged into a sitting or tubular position. The cat's body was then anointed with fats/oils as well as beeswax, sugar gum and various spices such as cinnamon and marjoram. Afterwards the body would then be wrapped tightly in white or other colored linen. In the Roman period, cat mummies were wrapped in linen with various geometrical designs and colors. Their faces were then modeled in linen and plaster. Sometimes small gold amulets were placed in between the wrapping layers (Malek, 1993). Once completely wrapped and sealed with various resins and bitumen, the cat would be ready to have its facial features drawn and painted in black ink.

Pyramid Texts

Saqqara has not only offered archeologists a treasure trove of tombs and mummies, but also the pyramid texts: texts written in limestone which contain thousands of lines of hieroglyphs describing myths and religious rituals. Gaston Maspero, in 1894, was the first to discover and then translate these texts in which we find a reference to the cat goddess Bast.

"28. Litany of Ascension, Utterances 539
When he ascends and lifts himself to the sky,
The heart of Nefekare is like that of Bastet"
(Mercer, 1952).

Bast is again mentioned on *The Metternich Stele* found at Heliopolis, not far from Saqqara. *The Metternich Stele* or *Magical Stele (figure 2.11),* dates to the 30th dynasty around 380-342 BC during the reign of Nectunebo II and was later taken to Alexandria by Alexander the Great. In 1828, Mohammed Ali Pasha, ruler of Egypt, gave it to Prince Metternich, a well-known German-Austrian diplomatic strategist. The main purpose of the stele is to give magical remedies for healing poisoning, mostly caused by scorpions. Below is an example of one of the spells used to cure Bast of the sting of a scorpion by invoking Ra.

O Re! Come to thy daughter (Bast), whom a scorpion has bitten on a lonely Road!
Her cry reaches even to heaven…..poison oppresses her limbs, and
Flows in her flesh, and she turns her mouth to it, (i.e. She attempts to suck the injured part)
Re answers her: Do not fear, do not fear, my splendid daughter;
Behold, I stand behind thee. It is I who destroy the poison, that is in all the
Limbs of this cat (Erman, 1907, p. 150).

Even though much of the necropolis of cats at Saqqara has been desecrated throughout the ages, and the sanctity of the spot has long

Figure 2.11. The Metternich Stele, From The Gods of The Egyptians, E. A. Budge, 1904

been lost, the memory of the power of the cat in ancient Egypt cannot help but live on there and in Thebes to which we now turn.

THEBES

Thebes was known in the ancient Egyptian language as Waset, and also as "No Amun." The Bible refers to it as the City of Amun, and to the Greeks, it was *Diospolis* meaning "Heavenly City". The Theban tombs are located in the mountains on the western side of the Nile. A short boat ride across from the city of Luxor, the temple of Luxor and the temple of Karnak border the eastern side of the great river. Tombs with depictions of cats are centered in four major burial sites: Deir el Medina, Sheikh Abd el Qurna, Dra Abu el Naga, and El Khokha.†

Theban mostaba tombs date back as far as the 3rd and 4th dynasties, but nothing remains of the Old Kingdom settlement today. During that time, the main area for burials of nobles and royalty was Saqqara. However, there is a tomb dating to the 11th dynasty in which a statue of a person named King of Hana, a Babylonian title, was found. Imperiously sitting at the king's feet is a cat named *Bouhaki* (Simpson, 1903, p. 5). The name roughly translated means the house of the divine healer. *"Bou"* meaning house and *"hak"* the symbol of the divine healer, form the first cat name to appear in history.

The Goddess Bast in Art

It was only during the Middle Kingdom 18th Dynasty through the late period that Thebes became an important site for nobles' tombs where depictions of scenes from everyday life decorate their walls. In contrast, the wall paintings in the tombs of the pharaohs tend to concentrate more on religious scenes. Consequently, it is from these nobles' tombs that we are able to understand more about ancient Egyptians' every day activities such as hunting and fishing, as well as their pastimes of dancing and attending banquets. Of significance, however, is the fact that on these tomb walls are various depictions of cats that obviously played an integral role in everyday life.

Of all the depictions of the ancient Egyptian cat, those found on the walls of the tombs at Thebes are among the most fantastic and illuminating. These tombs contain the greatest number of cats in hunting and domestic scenes. Cats are hunting birds and fish, as well as posed in domestic scenes where they are sitting under or tied to chairs usually occupied by women or the mother goddess Mut. They also appear gnawing on bones or sitting with other animals such as geese and monkeys.

Found in the tomb of Puimre dating to about 1450 BC is another cat named, *Nedjem* or translated the *Pleasant One*. From this date, wall paintings became even more prevalent amongst the tombs' of the nobles. One of the most famous wall paintings comes from the tomb of Nebamun, now in the British Museum, and shows a cat helping a young noble catch wild fowl *(figure 2.12)*.

---

† *See Appendices for a list of tombs where cats are pictured.*

Figure 2.12. Tomb of Nebamun, 18th Dynasty, 1350 BC, British Museum, Photograph by Marcus Cryon

Additionally, on a wall painting in the tomb of Pharaoh Siptah (19th Dynasty) the cat is so revered that it is included among the 75 manifestations of Ra.

In addition to the tomb paintings, many small pieces of limestone, called ostraca, have been found with comic portrayals of cats serving mice. In one, a spotted cat, tail wrapped to the right, holding a fan and a dead goose, makes an offering to a seated rat. The rat looks like he is holding a cocktail in his right hand and a fish bone in his left *(figure 2.13).*

Another shows a sword-bearing cat holding a criminal to face a rat judge leaning on a staff. In the figure on the next page, a spotted cat holding a stick is herding six geese *(figure 2.14).*

One rather comical papyrus shows cats guarding a fortress against rats. The rats are propping ladders against the ramparts and are preparing to climb them. A more senior rat, riding in a chariot drawn by dogs, shoots arrows at the cats in a Ramses-like fashion. Such a scene easily brings to mind a 4,000 year old rendition of the cartoon *Tom and Jerry.* The ancient Egyptians clearly had senses of humor and adeptly used anthropomorphism.

Surprisingly, there were no sanctuaries or temples built to Bast at Thebes. Instead, Thebes was built in honor of Amun, Mut and

Figure 2.13. Painted Ostracon of Cat and Mouse, Deir El Medina, 1150 BC, Brooklyn Museum

Figure 2.14. Drawing on limestone of a scene from a fable, 19th Dynasty, 1120 BC, Cairo Museum

Khonsu. Amun, the Father of all, Mut the Mother of all and Khonsu their son, were a trinity so to speak. This is the reason that fewer cat mummies have been found at Thebes than at other sites. Even so, the son of Pharaoh Amenhotep III (1386-1348), Prince Thutmose, brother to Pharaoh Amenhotep IV (Akhenaton) was so grieved by his cat, *Ta Mit's* death that he had her mummified and commissioned a sarcophagus *(figure 2.15),* now in the Cairo Museum, which was engraved with funerary texts that were meant to protect her in the after-life just like any person (Yurco, 1990).

Figure 2.15. Prince Thutmose's Cat Ta Mit's Sarcophagus, Photograph by Larazoni

Ironically, however, during the Armana period (1353-1335) reign of Akhenaton, representations of cats do not appear in the royal tombs, most probably due to the monotheism that he promoted.

The Goddess Bast Mentioned on Stele and Papyri

Many more references to the cat goddess Bast are present on steles, papyri and inscriptions from the 18th through the 26th

Dynasties at Thebes. On a stela in Miramar a man says: "I gave bread to the hungry, water to the thirsty, clothing to the naked; I gave food to the ibis, the hawk, the cat, and the jackal"… "And I have buried them according to the ritual, anointing them with oil and wrapping them in cloth" (Breasted, 1906, p. 327). An inscription by Sehetepibre refers to Amenemhet III as "He is Bast protecting the two lands." In a dedication tablet stele found at Elephantine Island, Amenhotep II states: "There is none among them that escapes from the overthrow, like the foes of Bastet on the road of IR-Amon" (Breasted, 1906, Vol. 2, p. 311). A Karnak relief equates Mut, the goddess of all and Bast stating: "Mut, the Great Bast, ruler of Karnak, mistress of amiability and love" (Breasted, 1906, Vol. 3, p. 74). On *The Book of the Dead* papyrus of Ani (18th Dynasty), the longest known papyrus at 78 feet, 1 foot, 3 inches, now located in the British Museum, there is this statement:

> I am the Cat which fought near the Persea tree† in Anu on the night when the foes of Neb-er-Tcher were destroyed. Who is this Cat? This male Cat is Ra himself, and he was called 'Mau' because of the speech of the god Sa, who said concerning him: 'He is like (Mau) unto that which he hath made; therefore, did the name of Ra become 'Mau.' (Budge, 1895, p. 287) *(figure 2.16)*

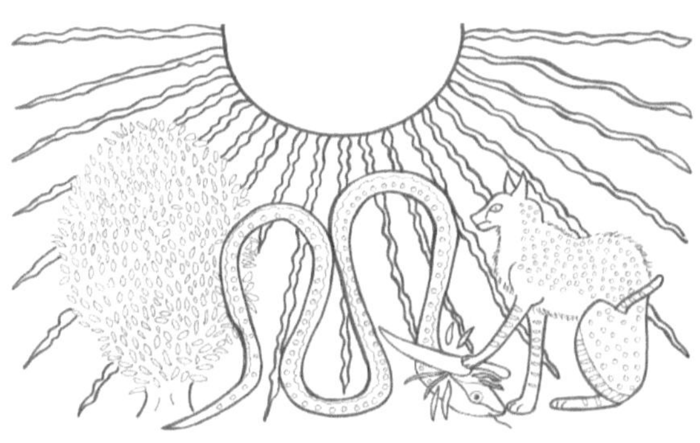

Figure 2.16. Ra as a Cat Slaying Apophis, Author's drawing

† The Persea tree's small yellow fruit is symbolic of Horus's heart, and the Phoenix was thought to come to life again from the tree, as it is evergreen.

Mau or *Miu* was the ancient Egyptian name for cat, obviously named after the meowing sound that they make. Children were even named *Mit* or *Miut.* In Mentuhotep's 11th Dynasty temple at Deir El Bahri there is a mummy of a five year old girl with the name *Miut.*

Besides the various references to cats during the 18th thru 26th dynasties, records indicate that the goddess Bast received many gifts. On the papyrus Harris, it records the gift of a herd of cattle to Bast stating, "The Herd of Ramses Ruler of Heliopolis, L.P.H. Doer of Benefactions for his Mother Bast" (Breasted, 1906, Vol. 4, p. 184). A list of gifts given to Bast during the 22nd Dynasty includes a "gold and silver vessel presented before Bast, mistress of Bubastis" (Breasted, 1906, Vol. 4, p. 364). Another inscription of Mentemhet states, "I fashioned the august image of Bast residing in Thebes; with staves of electrum and every ….costly stone" (Breasted, 1906, Vol. 4, p. 463). And finally, in the 26th Dynasty Psamtik I records that "I brought out Bast in procession to her barge, at her beautiful feast of the fourth month of the second season (eighth month), the fifth day …" (Breasted, 1906, Vol. 4, p. 496). Finally, in a letter regarding Nubian tribute, cats from *Miw* (a district of Nubia) were listed as gifts (1295-1069 BC) (Petrie & Currelly, 1906). Could a whole district in Nubia have possibly been named after the cat since *Miw* was the name for cat in ancient Egyptian?

Bast was deeply ingrained in the ancient Egyptian culture and religion at Thebes. The cat was loved, cherished and respected as reflected in the art-work on the tombs, ostraca, steles, papyri, and inscriptions commissioned by both nobles and pharaohs. Reverence for Bast, however, was not just apparent at Thebes, as her worship had spread throughout both Upper and Lower Egypt.

BENI HASAN

Large numbers of cat mummies and tomb paintings have been found near a small village called Beni Hasan, located 23 kilometers south of Minya, between Asyut and Memphis. With its necropolis located high in the limestone cliffs on the eastern side of the Nile, it was here that the famous archeologist, Flinders Petrie, found a small tomb dating to 1950 BC that contained 17 cats with little bowls that presumably held milk to sustain them on their journey to the afterlife. One of the earliest paintings of a cat is also found at Beni Hasan, on the north wall of the tomb of Bakhet III, a governor of the Oryx Nome (province) during the early Middle Kingdom, 11th Dynasty. In the painting, a cat facing right confronts a rat of equal size. In another tomb, that of Khnumhotep, a governor of the Oryx Nome during the reign of Amenemhat III (12th Dynasty), cats are also present *(figure 2.17)*.

The most surprising and notable find at this site was the discovery in 1888 of 80,000 mummified cats and kittens dating back to 1,000-2,000 BC. An eyewitness account by William Martin Conway, the Baron of Allington (1856-1937) states, "The plundering of the

Figure 2.17. Cat in the Marshes, Howard Carter, 1891-1893
Detail from scene on tomb of Khnumhotep II, Beni Hasan, 1900 BC

cemetery was a sight to see, but one had to stand well windward. The village children came…and provided themselves with the most attractive mummies they could find. These they took down the river bank to sell for the smallest coin to passing travelers. The path became strewn with mummy cloth and bits of cats' skulls and bones and fur in horrid positions, and the wind blew the fragments about and carried the stink afar" (Tabor, 1991, p. 26). Egyptian fellahin had un-wrapped a great majority of the mummies looking for gold amulets. The cat mummies' linen wrappings were then sold and exported to the United States and turned into linen-based paper during the American Civil War (1861-1865) (Yurco, 1990). The remains of the 20 tons of unwrapped cat mummies were then sold by Egyptian farmers to a British entrepreneur who had them shipped to

Liverpool where he then sold them for fertilizer for four pounds a ton, a sad end to a once revered goddess (Mery, 2006).

Not far from Beni Hasan is Speos Artemidos, as named by the Greeks, or cave of Artemis. Artemis was the equivalent Greek goddess to Bastet. The cave is located near the small village, which is today called Istabl Antar. Here, during the Middle Kingdom, Hatshepsut built two temples dedicated to Pakhet *(figure 2.18)*, a cat goddess who had the combined attributes of both Bast and Sekhmet.

Figure 2.18. Temple of Pakhet, Speos Artemidos, 18th Dynasty, Photograph by Einsamer Schütze

Near the temples, large numbers of mummified cats filled the vast catacombs. Those Egyptians dedicated to the goddess Pakhet traveled great distances to bury their cats in devotional ceremonies there. However, it was at Bubastis that the true importance of the cat was to reach its peak.

BUBASTIS

Bubastis, a city that had flourished for more than 4,000 years, is today nothing more than piles of scattered red granite blocks and a few empty graves and tombs overgrown by grass. Bubastis now lies within a fenced area near the modern day city of Zagazig, where 20th century apartments look down in sharp contrast to man's unsuccessful attempts to challenge time and decay *(figure 2.19)*. With its grandeur almost nonexistent and forgotten, we can only imagine the great city as it once was. Located in Lower Egypt in the eastern Delta, southwest of Tanis, its placement was strategic. Throughout history, Syrian and Persian invaders, with dreams of conquest, made their way through the Delta area, and Bubastis, to enter the heart of Egypt.

Bubastis, Tell Basta (house of Bastet) or Per-Bastet (the domain of Bastet), located in the ancient Egyptian nome of Am-Khent (Petrie, 1906), was known as a thriving city dedicated to the cat goddess Bast from at least the 4th dynasty (2613 BC), if not earlier, until the Roman period (AD 395). In fact, Manetho (305-285 BC), a priest and the earliest Egyptian historian to document the pharaohs of Egypt, noted that there had been civil unrest in Bubastis during the 2nd Dynasty rule of King Boethos, but no artifacts dating to that time have been found. However, the names of the 4th dynasty

Figure 2.19. Bubastis Today, Photograph by Einsamer Schütze

pharaohs Cheops and Chefren, who built the great pyramids at Giza, are clearly written on several of the blocks, proving that the city at least dates back to that time.

Bubastis reached its zenith during the 22nd dynasty of Osorkon I (924-889 BC) Sheshonk I's eldest son. But it was his father, Sheshonk, a mercenary commander of Libyan Berber decent who proclaimed himself pharaoh in 945 BC and went on to rule Egypt from Bubastis for 21 years, bringing the city to the forefront of the ancient Egyptian empire. Even though his son, Osorkon I, was to initiate many building projects in the city during his own reign, Sheshonk too "....beautified Bubastis, his Delta residence and at

Thebes undertook a vast enlargement of the Karnak Temple" (Breasted, 1909, p. 531).

During the late period, Bubastis was visited by several important Greeks such as Herodotus, Diodorus Siculus, and Strabo. The writings of these men offer the best descriptions of Bubastis and the cult of the cat. Herodotus (484-425 BC) gives us a wonderful eyewitness description of the Temple of Bubastis. He writes, "In this city there is a temple very well worthy of mention, for though there are other temples which are larger and built with more cost, none more than this is a pleasure to the eyes" (Herodotus, trans., 1890, 2, 137). "Except the entrance it is completely surrounded by water; for channels come in from the Nile, not joining one another, but each extending as far as the entrance of the temple, one flowing round on the one side and the other on the other side, each a hundred feet broad and shaded over with trees; and the gateway has a height of ten fathoms, and it is adorned with figures six cubits high, very noteworthy. This temple is in the middle of the city and is looked down upon from all sides as one goes round, for since the city has been banked up to a height, while the temple has not been moved from the place where it was at the first built, it is possible to look down into it; and round it runs a stone wall with figures carved upon it, while within it there is a grove of very large trees planted round a large temple-house, with which is the image of the goddess; and the breadth and length of the temple is a furlong every way. Opposite the entrance there is a road paved with stone for about three furlongs, which leads through the market-place towards the East, with a breadth of about four hundred feet; and on this side and on that grow trees of height reaching to heaven: and the road leads to the temple of Hermes" (Herodotus, trans., 1890, 2, 138).

When Gaston Maspero visited Bubastis in the early 19th century, he noted that the city had been destroyed and rebuilt many times, thus making the debris of the previous cities compound and rise up higher than the site of the temple just as Herodotus had noted (Maspero, 1914). A Frenchman who was part of Napoleon's research campaign in the late 1700's wrote, "This city, like all others, was raised on great masses of bricks. The extent of Bubastis in all directions is from twelve to fourteen hundred meters. In the interior is a great depression, in the middle of which are the monuments…" (as cited in Naville, 1891, p. 2). "According to Aristotle, Strabo and

Pliny, Sesostris was the first to conceive and carry out the idea of a water connection between the two seas, by means of the Pelusiac branch of the Nile from Avaris to Bubastis, and by rendering navigable the irrigation canal which already existed between Bubastis and Herolopolis" (Maspero, Rappoport, King, & Hall, 1903, p. 250). Thus the temple to Bast stood on high ground surrounded on all sides with canals filled with water.

Annual Festival to Bast

Within the temple, priests cared for cats with donations from pilgrims, and eventually killed and mummified them to be sold as votive offerings to Bast. Cat amulets and statues made of bronze and gold were also sold to enthusiastic pilgrims especially during the annual festival of Bast. *The Decree of Canopus*, a stele written during the Ptolemaic era in two languages and three scripts, provides us with information regarding the festival of Bast. "All Egypt on the day on which the star (the Dog Star) riseth, which is called the beginning of the year in the writings of the House of Life, which shall be celebrated in the 9th year of the 1st day of the second month of the season of Shemu (summer)…on which are celebrated the festival of the goddess Bast and the great festival procession of Bast, which is the period when the crops are gathered in, and the inundation of the Nile taketh place…And the festival shall be celebrated for a period of 5 days, during which the people shall wear garlands and libations shall be made, and burnt offerings shall be offered up" (Budge, 1929, p. 272). Herodotus gives us a first-hand account of the festival: "Now, when they are coming to the city of Bubastis they do as follows: they sail men and women together, and a great multitude of each sex in every boat; and some of the women have rattles (sistrums) and rattle them, while some of the men play the flute during the whole time of the voyage, and the rest, both women and men, sing and clap their hands; and when as they sail they come opposite to any city on the way they bring the boat to land, and some of the women continue to do as I have said, others cry aloud and jeer at the women in that city, some dance, and some stand up and pull up their garments. This they do by every city along the river-bank; and when they come to Bubastis they hold a festival celebrating great sacrifices, and more wine of grapes is consumed upon that festival than during the whole of the rest of the year. To this place (so say the natives) they come together year by year even to the number of seventy myriads (700,000) of men and women, besides children" (Herodotus, trans., 1890, 2, 60). As described by Herodotus, the festival devoted to the cat goddess Bast was one of the largest celebrations held in all of ancient Egypt.

Killing a Cat is a Crime

During the years 1887-1889, Edouard Naville excavated Bubastis and found huge pits filled with the remains of cremated cats near brick ovens that were blackened from use. In one pit he found 720 cubic feet of bones, but he noted that in many cases ichneumons (mongoose) were buried along with the cats. Naville's find is troubling since Herodotus recounts an instance whereby cats are swallowed up by fire. "...when a fire occurs, the cats seem to be divinely possessed; for while the Egyptians stand at intervals and look after the cats, not taking any care to extinguish the fire, the cats slipping through or leaping over the men, jump into the fire; and when this happens, great mourning comes upon the Egyptians" (Herodotus, trans., 1890, 2, 66). This is a very strange observation that contradicts the very essence of the ancient Egyptian religion according to which the Ka (soul) should never be destroyed. How is it that the same Egyptians that forbid the killing of a cat could systematically incinerate hundreds? Killing a cat was a crime punishable by death as Diodorus Siculus states, "And whoever intentionally kills one of these animals is put to death, unless it be a cat or an ibis that he kills; but if he kills one of these, whether intentionally or unintentionally, he is certainly put to death, for the common people gather in crowds and deal with the perpetrator most cruelly, sometimes doing this without waiting for a trial. And because of their fear of such a punishment any who have caught sight of one of these animals lying dead withdraw to a great distance and shout with lamentations and protestations that they found the animal already dead. So deeply implanted also in the hearts of the common people is their superstitious regard for these animals and so unalterable are the emotions cherished by every man regarding the honour due to them that once, at the time when Ptolemy their king had not as yet been given by the Romans the appellation of "friend" and the people were exercising all zeal in courting the favour of the embassy from Italy which was then visiting Egypt and, in their fear, were intent upon given no cause for complaint or war, when one of the Romans killed a cat and the multitude rushed in a crowd to his house, neither the officials sent by the king to beg the man off nor the fear of Rome which all the people felt were enough to save the man from punishment, even though his act had been an accident. And this incident we relate, not from hearsay, but we saw it with our own eyes on the occasion of the visit we made to Egypt" (Siculus, trans., 1933, 83). In addition, Herodotus noted that if a cat dies in a house all the people living in that house must shave off their eyebrows in a show of mourning.

Excavation at Bubastis

Naville never did find any evidence of cats having been embalmed at Bubastis (Naville, 1891) even though Herodotus' wrote that cats were brought from miles around to be mummified there. Later excavations in the area, however, revealed hundreds of mummified cats and rats buried in holes in the walls overlooking the human tombs. Naville instead was only able to find many bronze cat statuettes, "We discovered a few of them sitting cats, heads, the inner part of which is empty; a good specimen representing Bast standing under the form of a woman with a slender body and a cat's head, wearing a long dress and holding in her hands a sistrum and a basket, and having at her feet four crouching kittens" (Naville, 1891, p. 53).

Perhaps it was here too that the now famous Gayer Anderson cat *(figure 2.20)* was found for its exact origin is unknown. Revealing every nuance of the cat's body, the bronze statue of the cat goddess Bastet displays exquisite workmanship. Given as a gift by Gayer Anderson to the British Museum, the cat now regally sits in a prominent display.

The Decline of Bubastis and the Cult of the Cat

Since Bubastis was at the edge of the Egyptian empire, invasions were commonplace and, as Egypt began to weaken and fragment in the later dynasties, both Greek and Persian invaders tried their luck at conquest. Since his father Cyrus had conquered the

Figure 2.20. Gayer Anderson Cat, The British Museum, London, Author's Photograph

Middle East, it was left for his son Cambyses II, the new king of the Persian Empire, to conquer Egypt. Thus, in 525 BC he set off toward his prize, aided by Arab Bedouin who supplied the army with water along the way. They reached the city of Pelusium located at the very tip of the Delta region not far from modern day Port Said. There the cunning Cambyses II thought of an ingenious battle strategy. Being familiar with the Egyptians' religious practices, he had the image of Bast painted on his soldiers' shields and drove hundreds of the sacred cats in front of his army, thus putting them between his army and the Egyptians. Naturally, the Egyptians would not fight, but turned and fled, for they would not kill a cat or any other sacred animal. Cambyses forced the ill prepared, newly appointed Pharaoh Psamtik III to retreat to Memphis, where he defeated him, and sacrilegiously killed the Apis bull. He proclaimed himself the next pharaoh of Egypt, and thus ushered in the Persian period of rulers that would last to approximately 425 BC.

During these periods of foreign domination, the Egyptians continually fought for the return of their throne and finally in 404 BC

Amyrteos regained control of the empire after the death of Darius II, beginning what is now known as the Late Period. The next to last ruler of the Late Period, Dynasty 30, was Nectunebo I, who rebuilt the temple sanctuary at Bubastis adding a peri-style court with columns on the eastern, southern and northern sides. His successor, Nectunebo II, the last native Egyptian to rule Egypt, was defeated by the Persian Artaxeres III. A cruel vicious man, he ransacked temples and seized treasures carrying them back to Persia. Sacred animals were killed, and their temples and cities completely destroyed. As a result of the Persian invasion, Bubastis in 350 BC entered a period of slow decline. The last dynasties 31 and 32 of the ancient Egyptian empire were ruled by invading Persians and Greeks.

Despite foreign rule and the destruction of her temples, the cat goddess Bast remained in the hearts of the Egyptians. Bast continued to be worshipped by the Greeks and Egyptians alike, evidenced by a recent discovery in the city of Alexandria of a temple dedicated to Bast and belonging to Queen Berenice, wife of Pharaoh Ptolemy III, which dates to the 3rd century BC.

With the slow demise of the empire, however, so too came the demise of the cult of the cat. When Rome annexed Egypt in AD 30 for its abundant grain supply, it was just three years later that Mark the Evangelist brought Christianity to Alexandria. There was not much resistance to the new religion, as various aspects of the old were incorporated, thus making the transition more palatable for the pagan Egyptians. In AD 380 Theodosius I, the last emperor of both the eastern and western Roman Empire, proclaimed Christianity the official religion. Approximately ten years later, in AD 394, Theodosius I secured the importance of this new religion by banning pagan worship of any kind throughout the empire. Now with the last vestiges of the ancient Egyptian religion crumbling under threat of lawful punishment, temples were destroyed or left to become derelict. Animal cults vanished, and along with them the cult of Bast. The cat would never again be worshipped on such a grand scale, and Egypt would not be able to secure its independence from foreign rule for almost 2,000 years.

Chapter Three

THE CAT IN EARLY AEGEAN AND MEDITERRANEAN CIVILIZATIONS

Although the ancient Egyptians forbade the export of their beloved cats, determined smugglers stole the prized and worshipped animals to trade or sell. In an effort to reclaim the kidnapped beasts, whole armies were dispatched to repatriate them, and in some cases emissaries were even given the duty to buy them back (Jennison, 1937). Unfortunately, these efforts were not enough to keep the rare and worshipped cat confined to Egypt.

Taken aboard trader ships and sailed across the Mediterranean to Greece and Italy, whether by accident or as prized cargo, the first evidence of domestic cats in the Minoan civilization has been dated to around 1800-1700 BC. Minoans had a healthy trade relationship with the ancient Egyptians. Evidence of Minoan ceramics at Egyptian archeological sites confirms this. Additionally, Egyptian scarabs and amulets have been found on Crete at Knossos, and there is evidence that Minoans imported papyrus and fine linen from Egypt.

The Cat in Minoan and Mycenaean Art

The Minoans were the first in the Mediterranean to portray the cat in lovely relief on a pitcher and two cups found at the palace of Malia on the island of Crete, while a fresco dating to 1628 BC, on the island of Santorini, also includes a representation of a cat. On a Knossos fresco a cat hunts birds, and at the palace of Agia Triada yet another stealthily stalks a pheasant. A figurine of a snake goddess found at Knossos, dating to 1600 BC, has a cat perched atop her head indicating some religious significance, most probably associated with fertility *(figure 3.1)*. And found at Palaikastro, Crete, a terracotta head of a cat dates to the 1400's BC (Engels, 2001). In addition to these immortalizations of the cat, Minoan seal stones, dating from 1800-1700 BC engraved with cats chasing a group of water fowl, are reminiscent of the bird hunting scene in the tomb of the Theban noble Nebamun. Scholars suggest that cats trained to hunt water fowl were introduced to Crete from Egypt (Castleden, 1993).

Figure 3.1. Minoan Snake Goddess, Photograph by C. Messier

Unlike the art work of the ancient Egyptians, Minoan frescos adorning palace walls did not have religious or political agendas; instead, historians believe the Minoans were the first people to pursue art for art's sake. The beautiful compositions of bulls, octopi, plants, fish, women, men and cats were done seemingly for pleasure and decoration. They had even developed a writing system called Linear A script which includes a letter '*ma*' represented by a cat's head (Engels, 2001). Unfortunately, the script has yet to be completely deciphered, but archeologists think that most writings would reflect the Minoan's mercantile endeavors, focusing on facts and figures as in most early civilizations, instead of any true literature. Plagued by natural disasters, notably the eruption of Mt. Thera in 1627-1600 BC, it was not long before the Minoans, a peaceful people weakened by this traumatic event, were soon dominated by the conquest driven Mycenaeans in about 1600 BC. Even so, the Minoan style continued to influence Mycenaean art.

The Mycenaean civilization lasted a mere 500 years, ending abruptly due to infighting, the invasion of the Dorians and/or an invasion of the "Sea People". Primarily warriors, the Mycenaeans enlarged their empire by conquest rather than by trade, as the Minoans had, and inhabited what is today the whole of the Peloponnesus and Crete. However, Mycenaean artifacts have been found as far away as Russia, Germany and Ireland. Whether through the influence of the Minoans or from their own respect for the cat's symbolic strength and cunning, feline representations adorn various Mycenaean artifacts. For example, an inlaid dagger dating to 1600 BC depicts a gold cat hunting water fowl surrounded by lotus plants. "The familiarity with Egypt is further proved by the lotus pattern on the dagger blade, by the cat on the dagger, and the cats on the gold furl ornaments, since the cat was then unknown in Greece" (Mahaffy, 2007 p. 393). In addition, found in a shaft grave in Mycenae, two gold images of cats pose strangely like they could have been used on a coat of arms (Engels, 2001). Although the Mycenaeans represented the cat in various attitudes and on various works of art and even on daily utensils, no mention or reference is made to the cat in Mycenaean Linear B script.

The Cat and the Phoenicians

To date there is very little archeological evidence of our ubiquitous *Felis sylvestris libyca* during this time period in Canaan or Phoenicia, what is now modern day Israel, Lebanon and Syria. Even so, the Phoenicians are important because they were the greatest seafaring traders of their time, and they were partly responsible for the spread of the cat throughout the Mediterranean basin. Following the lead of their predecessors, the Minoans, the Phoenicians took cats aboard their ships to fight the rats that plagued their grain shipments, and ended up transporting them to all the localities on their trade routes (American Genetic Association, 1917). From the few artifacts found, we can see that the Phoenicians themselves borrowed the idea of the creation of amulets from the Egyptians, modifying them into anthropomorphic and zoomorphic figures of their own. An example is a Phoenician amulet from Tharros dating from the 7th-4th century BC, depicting a cat with a collar.

The Cat and the Etruscans

The Phoenicians most probably introduced the Egyptian domestic cat to the Etruscans, as there is evidence of Phoenician trade in Etruscan tombs located in the area of Civeta Castellani (Hamilton, 1896). Pictured on many of these tombs walls, the vermin-killing domestic cat was familiar to early Etruscans. On one of the stone pillars, in the Grotto Dei Rilievi at Cervetri in Etruria, dating to 350-200 BC, a sculpted cat and mouse play together (Hamilton, 1896). On a wall painting in the Tomb of Golini, near the modern day Italian city of Porano, a cat named *Krankru* dismembers its kill under a couch (Dennis, 1878). In Corneto, in the Grotto del Triclinio, an expectant cat crouches under a banquet table overflowing with food, again reminding us of the cats painted on the walls of the tombs of ancient Egyptian nobles. And in yet another banquet scene, in the Tomb of Triclinium in Tarquinia dating to 470 BC, we find the cat conspicuously apparent. Moreover, in the tombs of Scrofa Nera, Francesca, Querciolu and others, cats as well as other animals appear either above or below banquet table scenes (Cameron, 2009). Did the Etruscans understand the character of the cat as being that of a scavenger, beggar? Why are these tomb paintings so reminiscent of ancient Egyptian banquet scenes? The only answer has to be that trade relations were firmly in place between the Aegean civilizations and Egypt, and that the cat was obviously a part of Etruscan domestic life.

Strikingly painted with detailed spotted grey and black or brown or even orange coats, the cats painted in these Etruscan tomb frescos are realistic representations of domestic cats. When not under tables begging for food or killing mice, the cat was depicted as a natural predator of birds (Depuma & Small, 1994). In one bas-relief a lady is playing a pipe for a cat which is standing up on its back legs begging for the two ducks hanging from a tree in the background (Hamilton, 1896).

The cat also appears on Etruscan vases and Bucchero ware on which the common motifs are those of a woman walking a cat, a cat being held up by its back leg upside down, and a cat standing up on its back legs. Cat heads also decorate the edge of a Bucchero ware bowl from Chuisi dating to the 6th century BC (Engels, 2001). Etruscan cats represented on vases are seen primarily with humans and birds, and are never depicted with women and children alone as they would be on later Greek vases (Depuma & Small, 1994, p. 162).

The Cat in the Southern Greek Islands

With the help of opportunistic merchants, domestic cats made their way to the port city of Taranto, a center for trade in the south of Italy, inhabited by Greeks from the 8th century BC. The Greek Spartans called the city Taras, as legend states that Taras was the son of Poseidon, who was saved from a shipwreck by dolphins. Later the dolphin as well as the cat became important symbols on Taras coins. With the coming of the Romans, Taras would eventually be renamed Tarentum, and reach its zenith between 500-400 BC. During this period, representations of cats appear on vases and coins. On one vase a girl lovingly snuggles up to a cat, and on another a girl holding a cat looks at herself and her pet's reflection in a mirror. On a Tarentine coin, the founder of the city, Phalanthos, teasingly plays with a cat that jumps up to grab something from his hand. On another coin, dating between the 5-4th centuries BC, a Taras is riding a dolphin, and on the reverse side a seated boy holds a bird in his right hand, while a cat is trying to scramble up and snatch it (Hamilton, 1896; Ross, 1889, p. 137).

In the modern day port city of Reggio di Calabria, located near Sicily, known as Rhegium under the Romans, coins portray King Iokastos in much the same pose as Phalanthos with a cat playing near his chair (Engels, 2001 p. 89). On a vase from Sicily dating to 330 BC, now in the British Museum, we see two women, one standing and holding what looks like a ball, while the other is sitting with a ball and thread attached to her wrist while holding up a bird. In between the two women, a small spotted cat stands on its back legs and reaches for the bird. The women are obviously happily playing with the cat and have brought various toys to do so.

A group of tiny bronze cats found on the island of Samos dating to the 8th century BC indicates that the cat spread to other islands off Asia Minor (Engels, 2001). And finally, from the Greek prefecture of Laconia, located in the southeast Peloponnese, a vase with a cat in a sphinx-like repose lies under the chair of the King of Arkesilas of Cyrene, ancient Libya, dating to 550 BC. Not unlike the depictions of cats under chairs in Egypt, obviously a quite common motif throughout the region.

The Cat in Greece

Unfortunately, compared to its prominence as a worshipped goddess in ancient Egypt, the domestic cat played a rather small role in the history of Hellenistic Greece. As Repplier writes of the Greeks in *The Fireside Sphinx*, "This race (the Greeks) so admirably endowed, with ambitious ever unsatisfied, modeling, in insatiable pride, its gods after its own likeness, and forcing Olympos to bear a part in its quarrels; this superb race was far too arrogant to permit the cat to participate in its apotheosis" (Repplier, 1901, p. 15). Instead, grander cats such as the cheetah, lion and panther played a more prominent role in early Greek art and mythology. This is partially attributed to the fact that in early times, the domestic cat was not yet the important rodent killer in Greece that it had been in Egypt. Greeks, too, for religious and cultural reasons did not hold the natural affinity toward animals that the Egyptians did. Prior to the importation of the cat from Egypt, Greeks used weasels, ferrets, martens and pole cats to reduce the damage done by invading vermin. These animals, however, did not take to any sort of domestication and preferred to roam wild, and wandered away from the granaries, eventually leaving them unprotected. They were also quite vicious to humans. In fact, some states in America ban the ownership of ferrets to protect people against possible attacks. So when the cat entered the scene, the Greeks immediately realized that it was a much better protector of granaries, as the cat could be domesticated and would stay near its food source, the ravaging rodents. After recognizing the utility of the cat and its endearing nature, the Greeks allowed themselves to be seduced by its crafty wiles, but never to the extent that the ancient Egyptians had.

The cat made its way to the shores of mainland Greece in several ways. First, the Greeks and Phoenicians traded scarabs and amulets with the ancient Egyptians, particularly in Egypt's Delta region near the ancient Hyksos capital of Avaris or modern day Tell el Daba (Turcan, 1996). And it stands to reason that cats were most probably included in this trade, albeit illegally. Often-times the pharaohs enlisted the aid of Greek mercenaries, and they too could have helped in the spread of the cat to Greece. Known to have sailed the Mediterranean, especially during the New Kingdom, ancient Egyptians even settled in small Greek communities, no doubt in some cases bringing along their beloved cats. Furthermore, Diodorus writes of a country called Numidia, modern day Algeria, where he says that Agathocles in around 307 BC, after conquering Pkillena, Mishcela Hippaci and Miltene, led his army over a mountainous area so crowded with cats that no birds could be found for miles. He adds that the soldiers captured some of the cats and took them to Greece (Repplier, 1901). It is also claimed that Mount Hermon, in modern day Israel, "….was named Suner…Sunar or Sinnaur … the Chaldean (Babylonian) name for cat. It was named this by the Amorrheans, or the Mountain of Cats" (Dureau de la Malle, 1829 p. 309). These cats could have made their way with Phoenicians to the shores of Greece as well. We cannot of course forget the fact that the Minoans, Mycenaeans, Etruscans and Tarentines had already obtained the domestic cat from the Egyptians through their trade, giving the animal, even though still rare, a foothold in Greece, its surrounding islands and Italy.

The Merging of Bast with Greek and Roman Gods

Owing to their geographical proximity, the relationship between Greece and Egypt was a close one. Around 450 BC Herodotus writes of the ancient Egyptians' treatment of the cat at great length in his *Histories.* With the ongoing trade and merging of cultures, Egyptian gods and goddesses were assimilated and renamed to fit into the Greek pantheon. For example, the Egyptian gods Osiris and Isis became the Greeks gods Dionysos and Demeter; Isis' son Horus became Harpokrates; Set was to be Typhon; Neith of Sais- Athena, Min- Pan, Amun- Zeus and Bast- Artemis (Erman, 1907).

Both Isis and Artemis/Bast merged and were familiar goddesses in the Greek Isles and Asia Minor. Artemis, daughter of Zeus and twin of Apollo, was the Greek goddess of childbirth, virginity, fertility, forests, hills and the hunt. "…it was exactly in the city of Bubastis, where the cat was the sacred animal, that the Greeks could find the Egyptians worshipping 'Artemis.' The assimilation and subsequent identification of Isis with Artemis could not have taken place without the goddess of Bubastis" (Witt, 1971 p. 147). Later, under Greek influence, Bast, too, came to be identified with the Greek goddess Artemis, as they shared the nurturing qualities of motherhood. At Bubastis, "Ostia, a priestess of Bubastis, dedicated an altar to 'Isis Bubastis.' By traditional 'Greek interpretation' the

Egyptian Bast of Bubastis had been labeled Artemis in the Graeco-Roman world. The dedication therefore is one more sign of the syncretism which leads to the fully blended Isis-Artemis" (Witt, 1971 p. 81).

Artemis, Isis and Bast, linked through their association with the mystical powers of the moon, directed the moon's light to serve as a protector of mothers and their children and to also be a symbol of love. "The statues of Isis which wear horns are representations of the crescent moon, and her black raiment is a sign that she can be over shadowed and obscured as in her yearning she seeks the sun. This is the reason for invoking the moon in the love affairs, over which [1]according to Eudoxus, Isis presides" (Witt, 1971 p. 147). Furthermore, a well-known statue of Artemis has multiple breasts with a lunar disc positioned between her shoulders, combining motherhood with the moon (Schoors & Willems, 1998 p. 546). Sometimes called the Madonna of the Silver Bow, Artemis' arrows symbolized moonbeams lighting up the darkness. However, the Greeks soon identified both Isis and Artemis with magic and the dead, and even the underworld, because of their association with the moon (Forrest, 2001). Artemis', and hence Bast's association to the moon, through Isis, caused Bast by default to also become linked with magic, death and the underworld.

The Greeks believed that either the sun or the moon[†] created all animals. The lion or Leo, a symbol of the sun, represented Apollo, while the cat, a symbol of the moon, represented Artemis. As Manly Hall writes in *The Secret Teachings of All Ages*, "For ages the feline family has been regarded with peculiar veneration. In several of the Mysteries—most notably the Egyptian…the priests wore the skins of lions, tigers, panthers, pumas or leopards. Hercules and Samson (both solar symbols) slew the lion of the constellation Leo, and robed themselves in his skin thus signifying that they represented the sun itself when at the summit of the celestial arch" (Hall, 2003 p. 284). Heracles killed the lion that Hera had sent to terrorize the city of Argos and thereafter wore its pelt as a symbol of his victory.

Ovid, in his epic poem *Metamorphoses,* recounts the story of Galinthias, a servant to the Princess Alcmene, the wife of

---

[†] As an added note it is interesting that in the Arabic alphabet consonants are referred to as sun and moon letters.

Amphitryon. In the poem, the sly Zeus changes himself into Amphitryon and impregnates Alcmene. Furious, Hera, Zeus' wife, naturally resolves to prevent the birth. However, Galinthias, in order to help her mistress, deceives Hera and enables Alcmene to give birth to Heracles[†]. Hera then turns Galinthias into a cat[††] and sends her to the underworld as a priestess of Hecate. Here we have the cat associated with the underworld and the evil of Hecate, and one of the first instances of a person being transformed into a cat (Ovid, trans. 1955).

Hecate, often described as an evil female vampire[†††] and serpent beast, was yet another goddess associated with the moon. The Greeks believed that Artemis and Hecate represented the two phases of the moon. While the lunar goddesses Artemis, Isis and Hecate were associated with magic and the dead, the cat was identified with the moon through its sexual and nocturnal behavior. Aristotle wrote of the cat in his *History of Animals* that "the females are very lascivious, and invite the male, and make a noise during intercourse" (Aristotle, trans. 1897). The theme of the moon and its powers over sexuality, darkness and magic converge.

It was Hecate who was the guardian of the gate of death, the goddess of the crossroads. And even though she was most often associated with dogs, as dogs are the guardians of crossroads and doorways, and it is Cerberus who guards the gates of hell, she was bound to the cat through her association with Artemis. The assimilation of Hecate/Artemis and the cat becomes apparent while fighting Typhon, the god of wind. Hecate/Artemis, according to the myth retold by Antoninus Liberalis in *Metamorphosis,* escaped Egypt and the wrath of the god Typhon with the other Olympians by taking on the features of the cat, Bast, and seducing Typhon so that Zeus could destroy him with a thunderbolt. Here we see the ongoing association of the cat with devious sexuality. After all why did Hecate/Artemis have to turn herself into a cat; why couldn't she seduce Typhon as she was?

Through the influence of immigrants from Egypt, the cult of Isis began to take hold in Greece from the 4th century BC. Worship of

---

[†] Hercules

[††] In the original version she is turned into a cat.

[†††] The worshippers often offered her garlic and the cat, too, would later be associated with vampires especially in Japan.

Isis in the Greek port of Piraeus is evident as early as 333 BC with the cult constructing a sanctuary prominently upon a slope of the Acropolis in Athens. By the 2nd century BC, even local Greeks were worshipping the goddess. In Rome, and most probably as a response to Tiberius' banning of the cult, the Roman emperor Gauis Caligula (AD 12-41) rebuilt The Temple of Isis, *Iseum Campense*. Thereafter, Isis festivals were even noted in the Roman calendar. However, Caligula was not the first Roman emperor to become a patron of the Egyptian goddess Isis. Hadrian and Domitian[†] as well as others also practiced the faith.

In her own native land, Egypt, Isis was also the goddess of the lighthouse of Alexandria, protecting sailors as Isis Pharia *(figure 3.2)*.

Because of the cat's association with Isis, it became good luck for sailors to keep a cat on board a ship, and according to the Roman writer Martianus Capella, an image of a cat was often seen on a ship's bow (Engels, 2001). So pervasive was/is this belief that up until 1975 British ships were required to have a black cat onboard as a good luck charm.

To adorn the temples of Isis, the Greeks even imported Egyptian sculptures and statues. Black granite statues were the most sought after, as they confirmed the mysteriousness of Egypt, and black was the color of Isis. Priests of Isis, who remained under the control of Egyptian immigrants, wore black, and Artemis of Ephesus was a black virgin (Beard, North, & Price, 1998; Turcan, 1996). The ancient Egyptians saw the color black as a positive, magical healing force; conversely, the Greeks associated it with evil, death and the underworld. *Kem* was the ancient Egyptian word for black, and Egypt was often referred to as the black land. *Khemia* meant black art and would later be used in Arabic to mean alchemy (Forrest, 2001). The cat's association with the moon, darkness, the color black and magic originated in Egyptian and Greek myths and history, and have followed it throughout time and are still apparent today.

The Romans, just as the Greeks had, worshipped the goddesses Isis and Artemis. Artemis became the Roman goddess, Diana, cat huntress of the night, and was considered the mother of the world (Hall, 2003, p. 153). Diana, a mirror of Artemis/Hecate/Isis, was the 9th deity in the Roman pantheon. However, even before the Romans,

† Domitian was well known for his persecution of Christians.

Figure 3.2. Hadrian and Isis Pharia Coin, AD 133-134, Isis Pharia standing right, holding sistrum and billowing sail; to right, Pharus of Alexandria.

the Egyptians had nine gods in their pantheon, and most probably the Romans, because of the assimilation of so many gods from Egypt, also borrowed this. An inscription from Bubastis states, "I am the one that becomes two, I am two who becomes four, I am four who becomes eight, and I am one more besides" (Engels, 2001, p. 41). Nine, the sum of three, is referred to in various mythologies as a mystical number and because the number 9 is an inverted 6, it was later considered evil (Hall, 2003, p. 220). The number nine was thus associated with Diana and the cat's being evil and also having nine lives.

Roman mythology asserted that the world was made up of two halves: light and darkness. Diana's brother Lucifer, was the giver of light, while she, Diana, was the darkness. Lucifer had a beautiful cat that he loved more than anyone or anything, and it slept in his bed every night. Diana, wanting the attention of Lucifer, begged the cat to change forms with her so that she could sleep with Lucifer. The cat obliged, and once in bed with Lucifer, Diana changed back into her real self and became pregnant with a daughter, Aradia. After Lucifer realized that he had lain with his own sister, and that Diana's darkness had conquered his light, he was outraged. However Diana, being adept at magic and sorcery sang a hypnotic song and charmed him so that he forgot this abomination (Leland, 1899, p. 19). Here we see the cat being coerced into deceiving its master and siding with the magic and witchcraft of Diana. In Medieval times witches were often accused of changing shapes with cats which can be traced back to their relationship with the Roman goddesses Diana and Hecate.

The Cat in Greek Art

Well-known for their grandiose sculptures and artwork, it stands to reason that the Greeks should also depict the cat. One of the earliest Greek representations of a cat, located in the National Archeological Museum in Athens, is a marble funeral relief dating to around 500 BC, showing two men holding a dog and a cat on leashes trying to make them fight. A 4th century vase shows two women playing with a cat which is attempting to attack a pigeon held in one of the women's hands. On another vase, a cat perches on the back of a young boy, hungrily eyeing a small bird that the boy holds in his hand (Rogers, 2001). From Athens, a red figured askos[†] 470-400 BC, shaped like a lobster claw, depicts a cat, dog and cock. On a grave stele, dating 430-420 BC, a young boy standing in profile holds a bird in his left hand, and reaches for a cage with his right, while a now headless cat sits in a sphinx-like position atop a pillar next to him *(figure 3.3)*.

Another funerary stele dedicated to a young girl, Salamine, dating to 420 BC shows her with her pet cat (Engels, 2001). Most of the representations of cats on vases and sculptures carry the same themes of the cat hunting birds or as being a simple pet. But could there be a deeper symbolism to these depictions, especially those on funerary stele? Because of the cat's affiliation with Hecate, it very well could have been symbolic of the crossroads between life and death.

The Cat in Early Greek Literature

The Greeks named the cat *ailouros,* meaning wavy or plumed tail, and the terms ailourophile and ailourophobe are still commonly used today. There were early mentions of the cat in the writings of Theocritus, a Greek, who lived in the 3rd century BC, and who spent a good part of his time in Alexandria, Egypt, during the Ptolemaic period. He refers to a cat in his dialogues of the *Syracusans* in *The*

---

† An oil or wine jar.

Figure 3.3. Grave Stele Pentelic Marble 430-420 BC, Photograph by Tilemahos Efthimiadis

Women at the Adonis Festival. In those dialogues he has the mistress Prassinoé call to her slave, Ennoa, "Bring water!" and then complain, "How slow she is! The cat wants to lie down and rest softly. Bestir thyself. Quick with the water, here!" (Champfleury, 2005, p. 16).

Amusingly, even in the 3rd century BC cats were demanding comfortable places to sit and sleep.

Anaxandrides, an Athenian comic poet, writing in 376 BC mentioned the cat when a Greek character remarks to an Egyptian in his play *Poleis, (The Cities).* He says, "If poor puss appears in pain you weep, I kill and skin her," (Anaxandrides, trans., 1961). Egyptians truly loved their animals unlike the Greeks and Romans who first considered what use they could provide.

The great comic playwright, Aristophanes, also mentioned the cat in some of his plays. In the *Wasps* he draws the attention of one of his characters to the fact that the cat is a flesh stealer, and when the character Philocleon tries to start a story with, "Once upon a time there was a rat and a cat," Bdelycleon snaps, "Are you going to talk of cats and rats among high-class people?" (Aristophanes, trans., 1822). Finally, in his play, *The Ecclesiazusae,* a black cat is referred to as a bad omen (Aristophanes, trans., 2004). So, by at least the 5th century BC, the Greeks clearly viewed the black cat as an omen of evil, and cats in general as determined scavengers.

Aesop (620-546 BC) used the cat[†] as a prominent character in approximately 15 fables. Based on Greek myths, some of the fables such as *The Cat and Venus,* and others are in fact borrowed from stories originating in India. The fables have been added to and changed throughout the centuries, and it is certain Aesop did not write all the fables that we have today. The cat's character in these stories is predominately one of an intelligent, sly, conniving trickster bent on self-preservation.

For example, in the fable *The Fox and Cat* the cat outsmarts the Fox. Even though the Fox boasts of having many tricks, ferocious hounds devour him in front of the wily cold-hearted cat who humbly proclaimed that he had but only one trick, that of climbing trees *(figure 3.4).*

The slyness of the cat while trying to catch mice is highlighted in the fable *The Cat and the Old Rat (figure 3.5).* Here the cat hangs himself upside down so that the mice think he is being punished, but when the mice appear, he loosens himself from the rope and drops down for the inevitable kill.

[†] The cat has now replaced the ferret and weasel in the earlier Latin versions of the fables.

The Fox and the Cat. 41

A Ranting Fox boasts to ye Catt, how hee
Himselfe wth numerous wily shifts could free
The ingenious Catt reply'd she had but one,
And if yt [illegible] was then she had none.
A noyse of full Mouth'd Hounds did straight possess
Theyr frighted eares which made ye Fox address
Himselfe to Flight, whilst ye more active Catt
Scaling a tree, declines an angry fate.
Whilst by ye sent the Doggs ye Fox persue
And force him from each winding avenue
His stratagems not shrouding him at all
Now he's thus hunted to his funerall

FAB. XX.

De Cato & Vulpe.

Contrahebant inter ſe amicitias Catus, et Vulpes, cui Vulpes aſtutiarum ſuarum grandem recenſebat numerum, Catus replicuit; Aſt ego uno tantum conſilio, & quod Natura ad meipſum preſervandum ſuggeſſit, contentus ſum. Inter hæc, odoram Canum vim appropinquantium audiunt, Catus confeſtìm altiſſimos Arboris ſcandebat ramos & ſecurè deſpectans ſedebat; Vulpes autem & hic, & illic trepidè currebat, & nullâ aufugiendi ſpe relictâ, nullâ uſpiam latebrâ inventa, à canibus apprehenſus laceratur.

MORALE.

Genuina & Naturalis Prudentia omnia figmenta fraudeſque ſuperat; Qui aliis inſidias molitur, ſibimet ipſi plerunque imponit, & eſt indeploratus artifex ſuæ ipſius Mortis.

R FAB.

Figure 3.4. The Fox and Cat,
From Aesop's Fables by Frances Barlow, 1687

In two other fables the only animal characters that manage to trick the cat are the stork and the monkey. In *The Stork and the Cat,* the stork refuses to relinquish its eel to the hungry cat and surprisingly lives. And in *The Monkey and the Cat (figure 3.6),* the monkey somehow manages to persuade the cat to get chestnuts from the fire which the monkey greedily devours before the cat has a chance to eat any herself. Instead, with an empty stomach, she limps away with burned paws.

Later, around AD 550 we have the Greek poet and historian, Agathias, mentioning a ravenous cat attacking one of his beloved partridges.

Figure 3.5 The Cat and the Old Rat, Illustration by Milo Winter, 1919

Figure 3.6. Cat and Monkey, Illustration from Jan Griffier, 1680-1717

O CAT in semblance, but in heart akin
To canine raveners, whose ways are sin;
Still at my hearth a guest thou dar'st to be?
Unwhipt of Justice, hast no dread of me?
Or deem'st the sly allurements shall avail
Of purring throat and undulating tail?
No! as to pacify Patroclus dead
Twelve Trojans by Pelides' sentence bled,
So shall thy blood appease the feathery shade,
And for one guiltless life shall nine be paid (Agathias, trans., 1889).

Agathias now in what can only be thought of as a highly exaggerated grief goes on to write another poem dedicated to his dead partridge.

My partridge, wand'rer from the hills forlorn,
Thy house, light-woven of the willow-bough
No more, thou patient one, shall know thee now;
And in the radiance of the bright-eyed morn
Shalt stretch and stir thy sun-kissed wings no more.
A cat struck off thy head--but all the rest
From out the glutton's envious grasp I tore!
Now may the earth lie heavy--so 'twere best--
Upon thee, and not lightly, so that she
May ne'er drag forth these poor remains of thee
(Agathias, trans., 1889).

In reference to the above incident, Damocharis, a friend of Agathias sympathetically writes, “Detestable cat, rival of homicidal dogs, thou art one of Actæon’s hounds. In eating the pet partridge of thy master, Agathias, it was thy master himself thou wast devouring. And thou, base cat thinkest only of partridges, while mice play regaling themselves upon the dainty food that thou disdainest!” (Champfleury, 2005 p. 18). Agathias’ grief seems real since he has taken the time to compose two poems about his poor partridge. Obviously, the nuisance of bird killing was taken quite seriously, and it is amusing that the cat’s persnickety eating habits were even noticed and written about in AD 550.

The Cat in Rome

The Roman character was even less inclined than the Greek to truly appreciate the cat's positive attributes. The very traits of duty, obedience and loyalty that the Romans highly prized were quite obviously non-existent in the domestic cat. In contrast, though, by its very nature, "the cat represented freedom, independence, and autonomy" (Engels, 2001), characteristics the Romans clearly admired.

In a temple dedicated to Libertas, the goddess of freedom and independence, erected on Mount Aventine, it was the Roman Tiberius Gracchus who placed a cat at the feet of the goddess who was adorned in a white robe, holding a scepter in one hand and a Phrygian cap in the other (Repplier, 1901, p. 17). The velvet Phrygian cap worn by freed Roman slaves signified liberty and the cat of course symbolized independence, for who can deny the cat's basic nature of abhorring confinement? Rome honored the cat with the saying, "*Libertas sine Labore,*" liberty without labor *(figure 3.7),* an apt association to our independent *Felis sylvestris.*

Figure 3.7. Libertas-Sine-Labore, From Harper's Monthly, 1869

One of the first mentions of the cat in Rome is in the 4th century BC when Palladius recommends using cats, referred to officially for the first time as *cattus,* instead of ferrets to stop moles from eating up the artichoke beds (Turner, Bateson, & Bateson, 2000). Pliny the Elder in his book, *Natural History* (1st century AD), instructs those that want to guard their bread from the voracious appetites of mice by writing, "Mice are kept away by the ashes of the weasel or a cat being steeped in water and then thrown upon the seed, or else by using the water in which one body of a weasel or cat has been boiled. The odour, however, of these animals makes itself perceived in the bread" (Pliny, trans., 1890, 8.155). Pliny also suggested that a fever could be avoided if "the salted liver of a cat killed when the moon is wane" is then mixed in wine and drunk (Pliny, trans., 1890, 8.155). As disgusting as it might seem, cat dung was even a remedy for removing a thorn from the throat (Turcan, 1996). We can only imagine that having to endure cat dung in the mouth would surely bring up anything and everything. Of course the Greeks and Romans were not the first to use cats for medicinal purposes. The ancient Egyptians used the fat from tomcats to scare mice away, the placenta in a tonic to keep hair from going gray, and female cat hair was mixed with milk to soothe burns (Malek, 1993, p. 70). Some odd medicinal cures still persisted up until about 100 years ago, with one stating a cure for shingles as laying the skin of a freshly killed cat over the infected area (Bergen, 1890).

The Cat in Roman Art

From what we can tell from the artifacts left to us, the Romans were not keen on capturing the cat in statuary or in bombastic attitudes as they did, for example, horses. However, there are mosaic representations of cats in Roman Pompeii, where the remains of domesticated cats have recently been excavated. The Pompeiians had cats, although probably few, but detailed mosaics catch the cat's innate character. Two mosaics from the *House of the Faun* show spotted cats, often assumed to be Persians or Angoras because of their long hair. One mosaic depicts the cat grasping a rooster or chicken by the neck, while underneath him are two ducks, four other birds, some sea shells and some fish quietly awaiting their inevitable fate *(figure 3.8)*. In the other, an expectant cat looks up at the birds perched around a bird bath, its teeth bared and its paw ready to strike at an opportune moment *(figure 3.9)*.

Van Vechten (2004), in a footnote in *Tiger in the House* states, "But there is proof enough that classical antiquity loved the cat. Among the objects unearthed at Pompeii was the skeleton of a woman bearing in her arms the skeleton of a cat, whom perhaps she gave her life to save" (p. 214).

Figure 3.8. Central emblem of a floor mosaic with a cat and two ducks, first quarter of the 1st century. National Archeological Museum, Naples, Photograph by Marie-Lan Ng

Figure 3.9. Birds Drinking from Bird Bath, National Archeological Museum, Naples, Photograph by Marie-Lan Ng

The Cat in War

In war the cat accompanied Roman legions emblazoned upon their shields and flags. "The company of soldiers, *Ordines Augustei,* who marched under the command of the Colonel of Infantry, *sub Magistro peditum,* bore on their 'white' or 'silver' shield, with a light green cat the colour of the mineral prase, or sea-green"(Simpson, 1903). The cat is seen running while turning its head over its back *(figure 3.10).* Another company of the same regiment, called 'the happy old men' (*Felices Seniores*) carried a demi-cat, red, on a buckler, (a small shield hung from the belt) with its paws up, as if trying to catch something. Under the same chief, a third red cat with one paw raised and with one eye and one ear, was carried by the soldiers *qui Alpini Vocabantur.*

Finally, in the 6th century AD, we find a cohort of the Praetorian guards named *Cattiar* or the Cats, and according to inscriptions found, soldiers even had the name *Cattius* included in their names (Engels, 2001). Both the Romans and warrior tribes clearly esteemed the cat for its courage and cunning.

Figure 3.10. Felices Seniores, Notitia Dignitatum - Magister Peditum

Cats on Roman Burial Steles

The cat accompanied the conquering Roman legions not only on banners and in name, but also physically. With the spread of the Roman Empire, the cat too enlarged its world, evidenced by the fact that Gallo-Roman burials included images of cats on funerary steles and sarcophagi. The Tombstone of Laetus's daughter[†], now in the Museum of Bordeux, stands as a fine representation of the spread of Roman culture and that young children along with their pets and toys were often forever memorialized on funeral steles and tombstones. On the tombstone stands a young girl, some think a boy, with her pet rooster and cat in her arms *(figure 3.11)*.

Figure 3.11. Laetus' Daughter's Grave, From Les Chats, Champfleury, 1869

On five additional funeral steles from Roman Gaul (southern France), young children are either holding cats or the cats are seated next to them. In east central France, carved in relief upon part of a table pedestal, a boy holds a cat facing forward wearing a red collar

[†] The child could be a boy, as the name has been eroded over time.

and a bell (Engels, 2001). Furthermore, mosaics of cats can be found from Jordan to Morocco. On a Roman mosaic found in the Church the Apostles in Madaba, Jordan, and now housed in the Bardo Museum, Tunis, a brown cat stands erectly facing forward haughtily posing for the artist, while on a mosaic from Volubilis, Morocco, a cat, Vincentius (conqueror), kills a mouse named Luxurius.

Evidence from archaeological digs proves that the cat accompanied the Romans to the far reaches of their empire. Roman era cat remains, many near ancient military encampments, have been found in North Africa (Libya, Tunisia, and Algeria), and Europe (France, England, Italy, Belgium, The Netherlands, Austria, Germany and Hungary, and Turkey) (Engels, 2001). The cat even hitched a ride on Roman ships that sailed to meet Chinese merchants in Ceylon where they exchanged goods as early as AD 166, just around the time that the cat was first documented in China (Gibbons, 1900, Vol.7 p. 392).

Popularity and Origin of the Cat's Name

With the coming of the Roman imperial age, the cat grew more popular especially among young women. The name "Little Cat or Kitten" *Felicula, Felicla* was a common nickname given to women as evidenced by the fact that there are over 250 references to this name in various inscriptions. A tombstone dedicated to Calpurnia Felicla (*kitten),* and her husband includes a small bas-relief of a cat. The name *cattus,* first used by Palladius, even came to be used as an adjective for someone who was sharp witted.

Some historians believe that the name *cattus* originated from the North African Berbers' name for the cat, *kaddiska,* or from the Nubian name, *qadis.* It is interesting to note that many terms for the cat in differing languages begin with a *k* or *g* sounds, derived from the Roman name *cattus*[†] (Rogers, 2001). The Latin name for cat, *felis,* preceded that of *cattus* and was the universal name for cats, martens, ferrets, polecats, and tomcats, so actually there was no differentiation between the various animals in early Roman writing. Today, the domestic cat is referred to as *Felis cattus.* However, many other names

---

[†] Gato-Spanish, Katze-German, Katt-Swedish, Kot-Polish, Koshka-Russian, Kedi-Turkish, Qotta-Arabic

for cat begin with '*p*' or *puss*. Some argue that the origin of the names for cat starting with a '*p*' sound derive from the name of the ancient Egyptian cat goddess Pasht.[†] Others believe that the origin of these names for cats came from the *psst* sound that one uses when calling them, or possibly from the Sanskrit, *putchha*. And there is of course the Chinese who refer to the cat as *mao* which must be a derivation of the ancient Egyptian name for cat, *miu*, again originating most likely from the "meow" sound they make.

Historical Basis for the Cat Being Reviled

The foundation for our fair feline being reviled throughout most of the rest of history lies in the final years of the Roman Empire and the rise of Christianity. The last 200 years of the Western Roman Empire were marked with constant attacks and instability of rule. Before Diocletian became emperor, from the years AD 235-285, there had been on average a new emperor every two years. So, when he decreed a tetrarchy, a rule of 4, Diocletian, with this provision for a smooth succession, brought some semblance of stability to an otherwise chaotic government. However, most important of all, in AD 285, he divided the rule of the empire between east and west preparing the way, years later, for a Christian Byzantine Empire.

In AD 324, by moving Rome's capital to Constantinople in the East, and by declaring that Christianity officially be tolerated, Constantine I perhaps made some of the most important changes to the Eastern Empire. Up until the time that Constantine I converted to Christianity, there were various Roman emperors who did not tolerate the Christian threat to paganism, such as Diocletian who tried to unsuccessfully purge it from the Empire. But in AD 312, just before a battle with Maxentius, known as the enemy of the Christians, Constantine is said to have had a dream[†] wherein Jesus told him that if he put the letters XP ☧ on his standards, he would be victorious. ☧ represents the first two letters of the name *Christos* in Greek and still appears on Greek orthodox churches even today. Constantine won the battle and is said to have converted to

[†] Pusag-Erse, Pus-Saxon, Puis-Gaelic, Pus-Irish, Pusei-Tamil, Pasha-Afghan, Pushak-Persian, Pus-Danish, Poes-Dutch, Piso-Albanian, and Pisica-Romanian just to name a few.

[†] Some sources say that he had a vision on the day of the battle.

Christianity immediately thereafter. In AD 313, he instituted the Edict of Milan, whereby Christians were to be tolerated, and their property was to be returned to them. Canonized even though he murdered his first son Crispus and his wife Faustus, he is known as the first Roman emperor to totally embrace Christianity.

With Theodosius I's rule from AD 379-395, Christians gained even more rights, and paganism was declared illegal throughout the Roman Empire. The fate of the cat was forever changed when in AD 380, Theodosius proclaimed Catholic Christianity the official religion of the Roman Empire. According to Gibbons, in *The Decline and Fall of the Roman Empire*, Theodosius says, "It is our will and pleasure….that none of our subjects, whether magistrates or private citizens, however exalted or however humble maybe their rank and condition, shall presume, in any city or in any place to worship an inanimate idol by the sacrificing of a guiltless victim. The rites of pagan superstition, which might seem less bloody and atrocious are abolished, as highly injurious to the truth and honor of religion; luminaries, garlands, frankincense and libation of wine are especially enumerated and condemned; and the harmless claims of the domestic genius of the household gods, are included in the rigorous proscription. The use of any of these profane and illegal ceremonies subjects the offender to the forfeiture of the house or estate where they have been performed; and if he has artfully chosen to the property of another for the scene of his impiety, he is compelled to discharge, without delay a heavy fine of twenty-five pounds gold----" (Gibbons, 1900, Vol. 1. p. 91-92). Just one year before Theodosius' death in 395, Nicomachus Flavianus held the last festival in honor of the goddess Isis in Rome.

Even though paganism was forbidden under the new decree, pagans continued to worship their gods in secret. To meet this new threat, Theodosius established two principles that would become important later on in history when persecuting pagans, heretics and even cats. The first was if a judge did not prosecute a religious crime, he would be guilty of that crime himself, and the second, idolatry,[†] which was to be considered the most heinous crime against God (Gibbons, 1900).

This new law ushered in a period of pagan persecution. The tide had turned, and now it was the victims' turn to terrorize, plunder and

[†] Paganism and later witchcraft

murder. The Christians, armed theologically with Theodosius' idea that there could be nothing more of an effrontery to God than a pagan, and with St. Augustine's belief that whosoever is not baptized is of the devil, started their devastating destruction. Monks proceeded to destroy the library at Alexandria and to forbid women from holding any church offices of responsibility as they had done from Christianity's very inception. In Gaul, the Bishop of Tours led his monks in the destruction of all pagan idols and temples. In Syria, the Bishop Marcellus condoned the killing of pagans, and immediately destroyed the temple of Jupiter. Other temples and edifices were simply turned into Christian churches. Gibbon offers an apt description, "…in almost every province of the Roman world, an army of fanatics, without authority and without discipline, invaded the peaceful inhabitants; and the ruin of the fairest structures of antiquity still displays the ravages of those Barbarians (Christians), who alone had time and inclination to execute such laborious destruction" (Gibbons, 1900, Vol. 5. p. 84).

By the year AD 476, unrelenting Barbarian hordes were attacking the Western Roman Empire. Quickly disintegrating under the strain, and with Romulus Augustus' abdication to Odoacer, a Germanic King of Italy, Rome ultimately saw its death. The Western Empire had lasted approximately 500 years. In most of those 500 years, before the onslaught of Christianity, the Romans managed to include the cat in their daily lives, worship her in the form of Isis and Diana, and carry her to the far reaches of the empire. Even though sometimes aligned with the evil and darkness of Hecate and Diana, the Romans never thought to torture and kill our beloved cat. Both Greeks and Romans simply accepted it, as they did all of nature. Moreover, all the ancient Aegean civilizations as well as both Greek and Roman found the cat important enough to capture in their art. Some postulate that it was the coming of Christianity that brought the Roman Empire to its inevitable doom, as it surely did the cat. The Dark Ages and fanatical Christianity would consume paganism and the cat together, and the cat once adored, then tolerated, would soon become demonized.

Chapter Four

THE DARK AGES

Christianity and Paganism

The Dark Ages were a time of great turmoil and instability. Hegemony over territory and religion were the driving factors in the ongoing conflicts of the age, and amidst this upheaval, the plague of Justinian claimed all those it could. Tribal kingdoms remained in continuous conflict over territory, and with the beginning of the Islamic era, Islam and Christianity competed for power and influence in both Europe and Asia. In the years AD 500-1000, barbarian tribes in Europe and the British Isles gradually shifted their pagan beliefs to Christianity, which led to the slow and continual demonization of female goddesses and their companion cats.

The struggle for religious domination between Christianity and paganism, which had begun in the 4th century, continued on throughout the Dark and Middle Ages. Ruthless Christian fanatics in their quest for pagan conversion began to systematically discredit their beliefs. As St. Patrick headed to Ireland to convert the Irish in the 5th century[†], St. Cyril, the Patriarch of Alexandria, had a vision of the goddess Isis as a devil (Engels, 2001). Goddesses and, by association, the cat came under constant attack.

Pagans believed that all creatures had spirits, and Christians believed all those spirits were evil (Russell, 1972). Paganism and Christianity represented opposing ideologies which led to diametrically opposed faiths: polytheism versus monotheism, man versus woman, nature versus man, freedom versus control. During the Plague of Justinian AD 541-547, Christians surrounded by

---

[†] Prior to St. Patrick's arrival in Ireland, cats were worshipped in a cave in Clough and Knowth (Graves, 1966, p. 221).

nothing but death, knew that they, and especially the non-believers, had angered their God. And while the plague that killed over 5,000 people a day in Constantinople, and ultimately over 50-60% of the total European population was ravaging his own empire, Justinian sent his emissaries to spitefully mutilate the Isis Temple on the Island of Philae (Engels, 2001; Thompson, 1908, 2003). According to Procopius, a Byzantine historian, the 6th century plague started in Pelusium, Egypt (Zahler, 2009). Ironically, this was the site of Cambyses' wily defeat of the Egyptians by driving cats and other holy animals in front of his army.

The Roman Christians knew that a fragmented empire meant eventual destruction, so Christianity became a vehicle for conquest and unification. Using the Christian religion as their ideological sword, they set out to convert and thus control their two most powerful adversaries, the Vendels (AD 550-793) and the Franks. From the north, with their Norse Gods Odin, the god of war; Thor, the god of thunder; and Freya, the goddess of love, the Vendels threatened the weakened Roman Empire and hindered the spread of Christianity. But as the Vendels, and later the Vikings, came into contact with Christians through their attacks, especially on the British Isles, they started to convert due to intermarriage and the fact that only Christians were allowed to trade goods. Clovis[†], (AD 466-511) the king of the Franks, converted to Roman Catholicism in the early 6th century, and he encouraged his Germanic tribal leaders to embrace Christianity too. In AD 530-35, the Byzantines took control of Italy and spread Christianity through the building of churches. St. Benedict of Nursia founded the Abbey of Monte Cassino on the site of the former temple to the Greco-Roman god Apollo.

In AD 596, Pope Gregory, who was said to have always had a cat on his lap, (Winslow, 1900) sent a group of forty Benedictine monks called the Gregorian mission to convert the Saxons in Britain. A year later, the kingdom of Kent converted. The mission was successful, and missionaries based in Britain headed for Europe to convert the pagans of the Netherlands and Germany. Paganism was to be eradicated.

With the demise of paganism the nature goddesses slowly lost

[†] The emblem of the Burgundians was the wildcat and Clothilde of Burgundy, Clovis' wife, used an emblem that pictured a sable cat killing a rat on a gold background (Oldfield, 2003, p. 231).

their power and importance. Threatened by female cults, the patriarchal Christian church wished to totally crush them. The cat, inextricably linked to the female goddesses Isis, Artemis, Diana and Freya, also became demonized. The goddesses of the moon became goddesses of the devil. Luna became lunatic. Pushed out of their roles of authority, women had to submit to the patriarchy of the church. The Canon of Eposcopi (AD 892), a list of regulations for bishops, stated, "It is also not omitted that some wicked women perverted by the devil, seduced by illusions and phantasms of demons, believe and profess themselves, in hours of the night to ride upon certain beasts with Diana, the goddess of pagans, and an innumerable multitude of women, and in the silence of the dead of night to traverse great spaces of earth, and to obey her commands as of their mistress and to be summoned to her service on certain nights" (Waddell, 2003, p. 84).

But not all tribal leaders accepted the new faith. They simply pretended to convert for their own advantage while continuing to worship their forest gods and goddesses. Christianity's stronghold was in the cities, while the pagans[†] kept to the countryside where deep in the forests their rituals continued. And so, Christians considered the old faiths that the pagans continued to adhere to as forms of magic (Erman, 1907 p. 237).

The Cat and Early Saints

During this time the cat, not yet completely reviled, still had its admirers even amongst those closest to the church. As the contest between Christianity and paganism raged, St. Gertrude of Nivelles in AD 640 became known for her benevolence towards cats. Most often pictured with rats and mice at her feet, she was known for her vigilance against vermin, and so it makes sense that she welcomed the help of the cat. Prior to St. Gertrude, St. Agatha (d. AD 251) known as a frequent visitor to cemeteries, became the patron saint of death and cats in some parts of southwestern France. Some believe that she appears on her feast day, February 5th, in the form of a cat to punish those who have angered her. Moreover, the ascetic, St. Jerome[†] (AD

[†] Pagan originally meant country dweller.

[†] A supporter of asceticism, St. Jerome did not think highly of women. (Grössinger, 1997, p. 1).

340 - 420), owned a cat as seen on the left hand side of da Messina's painting *(figure 4.1)*. Finally, the patron saint of lawyers, St. Ives (1253-1303), has a cat as his emblem, a symbol of constant vigilance (Spence, 1917).

Figure 4.1. St. Jerome in his Study, Antonello da Messina, National Gallery, London

Charlemagne's Purge of Paganism

By no means a saint, Charlemagne (AD 768-814), the first Holy Roman Emperor, led an assault against paganism by publishing a code of laws for Saxony, which included the death penalty for those still clinging to the old faiths. Not willing to convert, over 4,500 Saxons were beheaded in the massacre of Verden in AD 782. In addition, with the Council of Salzburg making torture lawful in AD 799, Charlemagne was the first ruler to condone torture in cases of witchcraft (Gage, 1893). These were troubling times for cats as well. Ample evidence from recent excavations proves that the Saxons kept cats as pets, and they must have served as evidence of witchcraft e.g. paganism to the intransigent Charlemagne.

Continuing his purge, Charlemagne demolished numerous pagan temples throughout Europe including a temple in Mageleburg, Germany, erected in honor of Freya *(figure 4.2),* the Norse goddess of love and fertility, who rode in a cat drawn carriage. Freya was also known as the beloved goddess of the good harvest, and many followers put dishes of milk out for her cats in their corn fields to secure an abundant harvest. Christianity, however, deemed this benevolent goddess to whom Odin had bestowed such power as dominion over the ninth world, a malefic and demonic priestess of the devil (Oldfield, 2003, p. 59-60).

Figure 4.2 Freyja, Cats and Angels, Nils Blommer, 1852, National Museum of Stockholm

Pagan Rituals are Incorporated into Christianity

To make the transition from paganism to Christianity easier and more appealing to the recalcitrant heathens, Christians incorporated pagan festivals and holidays into their religious calendar. The Christians "persuaded themselves that the ignorant rustics would more cheerfully renounce the superstitions of paganism, if they found some resemblance, some compensation in the bosom of Christianity" (Gibbons, 1900, Vol. 5, p. 106).

The assimilation of pagan and Christian rites would come in the form of Samhain, an ancient Celtic festival and precursor of today's Halloween, where black cats still play an integral part because of their pagan ties which originated in Ancient Egypt as discussed earlier. Samhain celebrated the end of summer harvest, marking the beginning of the Celtic New Year. Celts thought that the change of seasons brought about a time when the line between life and death was easily crossed. So as not to attract the wrath of the roaming spirits which Saman, the Celtic God of Death, gathered together, people impersonated the dead by wearing masks and costumes. Along with offerings of food, a cat or horse might also be sacrificed to appease unruly spirits. The Romans, after conquering the Celts in AD 43, adapted Samhain into a festival celebrated in late October in honor of Feralia and the goddess Pomona, who was associated with fruit and especially apples. Later, pagan rituals merged into Christian ones, so Feralia became All Saints Day and All Souls Day and eventually Halloween. The Christians believed that souls wandered the earth for 48 hours from October 31 thru November 2. Carrying a turnip lantern, symbolizing the soul in purgatory, devotees went from door to door asking for soul cakes in exchange for prayers for the dead. Celtic Druids, who held fast to their beliefs, were accused of witchcraft and persecuted as witches that led to the murder of many men, women and cats. Thus the festival Samhain, with some Roman influences, is the basis of today's Halloween, which is associated with witches, cats, bobbing for apples and going from door to door asking for offerings. Other pagan festivals such as Mayday became the Virgin Mary's day; Midsummer's Eve became associated with the Christian St. John's Eve; and festivals for the Roman gods Saturnalia and Bacchanalia became the celebration, Carnival.

In addition to Ash Wednesday, Shrove Tuesday and Easter, all these occasions were celebrated with cat massacres (Engels, 2001). In 1575, a receipt signed by Lucas Pommoreux states, "…for having supplied for three years all the cats required for the fire on St. John's Day, as usual" (Champfleury, 2005, p. 34). The barbaric activities were not ended until 1604 when the young Louis XIII forbade their continuance through an edict issued by Henry IV. In Picardy, on the first Sunday of Lent, festival goers celebrated while viewing live cats being dropped from long poles into burning bonfires, their tortured howls louder than the festival goers screams of delight (Reppelier, 1901). On the second Wednesday of Lent, in Ypres, Belgium, the villagers simply dropped the ill-fated animals from a tower *(figure 4.3)* located in the center of town until 1817 when it was finally officially forbidden.

Figure 4.3. Ypres Tower-Cloth Hall, Ypres, Belgium, Author's Photograph

The Cat in Early Christian Books

Even though, on the one hand, Christianity sought the total destruction of the old ways and temples, on the other, in their place, it began to erect a handful of churches and monasteries that blossomed into isolated centers of art, writing and education. Art especially benefitted from Christianity, and it was in these first monasteries that monks forever immortalized the cat in illustrations adorning their gospels and psalters. The cat made its first appearance in the margins of the *Lindisfarne Gospels* and the *Book of Kells* in the 7th and 8th centuries. The Irish illuminated manuscript of the *Lindisfarne Gospels*, crafted at the monastery of Lindisfarne in Northumbria, is a mixture of Saxon, Celtic, Roman and Coptic traditions. The gospels, created as a tribute to St. Cuthbert in about AD 710, are intricately decorated pages that reveal the gospels of Matthew, Mark, Luke and John interspersed with stylized animals, in particular cats. In one lovely illustration, the long, almost snake-like body of a cat bordering a page from the gospel of Luke has just eaten some cormorants, which are visible within his stomach; seemingly unsatisfied, he greedily eyes more in the bottom border of the manuscript page *(figures 4.4, 4.5))*.

Figure 4.4. Lindisfarne Gospel, British Library, London

Figure 4.5. Lindesfarne Gospel, Detail of Cat, British Library, London

In addition to the *Lindisfarne Gospels*, the *Book of Kells* (AD 800), offers an exquisite example of insular art based on Celtic Christianity from the post-Roman era on the British Isles. Monks began its creation on the Island of Iona between Scotland and Ireland, but because of Viking raids, fled to Kells forty miles from Dublin where it was unfortunately never completed. Like the *Lindisfarne Gospels*, the illuminated pages of the *Book of Kells* contain the first four gospels of the New Testament. With all but two of its 680 pages illustrated, vibrantly colored cats and other zoomorphic designs are woven carefully within and around the intricate manuscript *(figure 4.6).*

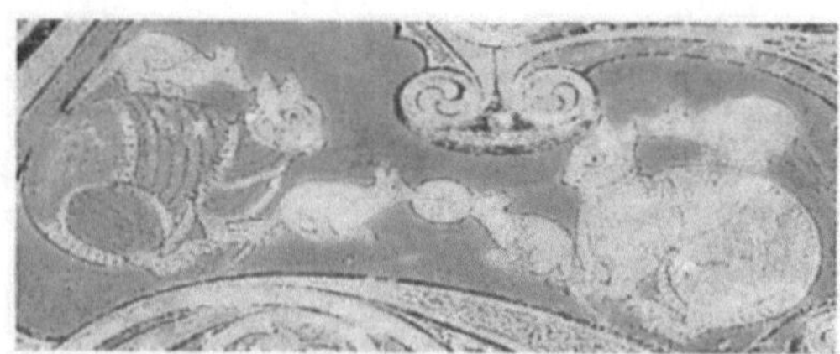

Figure 4.6. Cat Fighting a Mouse for a Wafer, Book of Kells, AD 800, Trinity College Library, Dublin

Because Viking raids continued into the 9th century, Irish monks fled the on-going invasions by travelling to far off havens.

One such monk exiled in Reichenau on Lake Constance is immortalized for writing a now famous poem in honor of his cat, Pangur Ban†. The cat, not yet completely identified with the devil and demonized, found its way into the heart of this lonely exiled monk *(figure 4.7).*

I and Pangur Ban my cat,
'Tis a like task we are at,
Hunting mice is his delight,
Hunting words I sit all night
'Tis a merry thing to see,
At our task how glad are we
When at home we sit and find,
Entertainment to our mind.
'Gainst the wall he sets his eye,
Full and fierce and sharp and sly,
'Gainst the wall of knowledge I,
All my little wisdom try.
So in peace our task we ply:
Pangur Ban my cat and I
In our arts and in our bliss,
I have mine and he has his (Rowling, 1979).

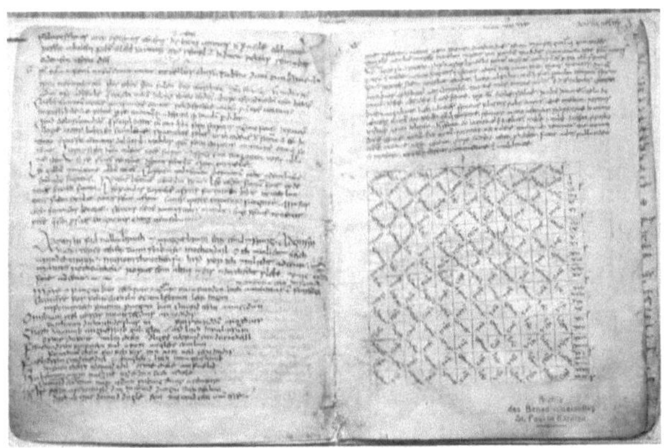

Figure 4.7. Pangur Ban, Reichenauer Schulheft, 1v, 2r., St. Paul's Abbey, Lavanttal

† Pangur is a traditional Irish name, while Ban means white.

Laws to Protect Cats

Cats were also a valued commodity in the Welsh kingdom of Hywel Dda or Howell the Good (AD 880-950). After a trip to Rome in AD 928, Hywel became interested in establishing a legal system and decided that Wales needed a set of codified laws. These detailed laws address how animals should be treated as well as the prices that should be asked for them. For example, the king forbid the killing of cats, and anyone caught killing a cat that guarded the royal granary had to pay with the fine of a ewe, its fleece, and a lamb, or a pile of wheat that was as high as the cat's length from head to tip of tail with the body of the cat suspended with its head touching the floor. According to the laws of Hywel, a kitten before it could see was worth one penny; up to the time it killed a mouse, 2 pence; and if it had proven itself an excellent mouse catcher, 4 pence (Simpson, 1903). The Law states, "Her qualities are to see, to hear, to kill mice, to have her claws whole, and to nurse and not devour her kittens. If she be deficient in any one of these qualities, one third of her price must be returned" (Probert, 1823, p. 228). The Gwentian Code, another part of the law, also states, "Whoever shall catch a cat mousing in his flax garden, let its owner pay for its damage" (Clutton-Brock, 1994, p. 42-43). Cats, obviously highly prized for their utility, were less important than flax, as it was used to make linen that was very rare during this time.

The Cat in the Bible

No doubt due to the cat's association with the devil, evil and paganism, only one obscure reference to the cat appears in the Bible. The Letter from Jeremiah contains one mention of the cat when referring to pagans in the *Book of Baruch*[†]. There are yet other references to cats in *The Gospel of the Holy Twelve* published in 1924 by Reverend G.J. Ouseley. Even though condemned by the church, this gospel, which Ouseley claimed had come to him in dreams, closely

---

† [20]Their faces are blacked through the smoke that cometh out of the temple.[21] Upon their bodies and heads sit bats, swallows, and birds, and the ***cats*** also.[22] By this ye may know that they are no gods: therefore fear them not. Letter from Jeremiah, Book of Baruch, Chapter 6.

coincides with the *Essene Gospel of Peace* only released from the Vatican in 1940. Both depict a much more compassionate, vegetarian Christ. *The Gospel of the Holy Twelve* includes an account of the birth of Jesus somewhat different from the one recorded in the Bible. In addition to the other animals in the stable, the gospel adds that a cat with her kittens lay beneath the manger (Ouseley & Udny, 1924, 2004, p. 7). The mention of the cat and her kittens was perhaps deleted because of the cat's association with paganism, but makes perfect sense to be included in the scene since the cat has always been a symbol of fertility and motherhood. Another section of the gospel proves Christ's compassion for the cat. While he was walking through a village, he noticed a group of boys tormenting a cat. Jesus asked them to stop, but they did not listen. After unsuccessfully trying to persuade them to stop, he drove them away with a whip, saying: "This earth, which my Father-Mother made for joy and gladness, ye have made into the lowest hell with your deeds of violence; and cruelty…" (Ouseley & Udny, 1924, 2004, p. 38-39). Yet another incidence of Jesus's kindness to cats is recorded, "And as Jesus entered into a certain village he saw a young cat which had none to care for her, and she was hungry and cried unto him; and he took her up, and put her inside his garment and she lay in his bosom. And when he came into a village he set food and drink before the cat, and she ate and drank and showed thanks to him" (Ibid, p. 56-57).

The Cat in the Talmud and Hebrew Folklore

The Talmud, the Jewish book of law, refers to the cat as having magical powers because it is able to see demons. The Talmud goes on to detail how this ability is gotten from the cat by taking the placenta of a first born black female cat and roasting it in a fire and grinding it to powder. Once a tiny bit of powder is put in the eye, it causes demons to become visible.

Hebrew legends also mention the cat. When God was deciding how each animal would make its living, he asked the cat, "From where do you wish to receive your daily bread; the shopkeeper, the peasant or the pedlar?" The cat replied, "Give me my daily bread from an absent-minded woman who leaves her kitchen door open!" In another reference to the cat in Hebrew folklore, Lilith, Adam's first wife, was unruly and refused to obey him. After being expelled from Eden as a punishment, Lilith haunted the night. In Spain, Jews believed that she became a vampire cat called *La Broosha* who victimized babies by sucking their blood. According to custom, for a period of nine days after a birth, a mother and her new born child should never be left alone. In one story, a nurse unwittingly leaves the mother and baby by themselves. When the nurse returns, the mother tells her she had had a dream of a huge black cat that had come into the room and changed into a jar. Just then the mother could hear a meowing from the street, and the cat who had become a jar returned to being a cat again. At that point, the cat went to the bed and took the baby, and threw it out of the window to another cat. Horrified, the nurse realized that it had not been a dream because she could see from the window the cat carrying the baby in its mouth as it crossed a nearby field.

The Cat in Islam

The story of Noah and the creation of the cat comes to us from the Egyptian naturalist and scholar Ad-Damiri, who began *Hayāt al Hayawān*, *The Life of Animals* in the 9th century AD. "When Noah made a couple of each kind of animal enter the Ark, his companions, as well as the members of his family, said to him, 'What security can there be for us and for the animals so long as the lion shall dwell with us in the same vessel?' The patriarch betook himself to prayer and entreated the Lord God. Immediately fever came down from heaven and seized upon the King of the beasts, so that tranquility of mind was restored to the inhabitants of the Ark. But there was in the vessel an enemy no less harmful---this was the mouse. The companions of Noah called his attention to the fact that it would be impossible for them to preserve their provisions and their clothes intact. After the patriarch had addressed renewed supplications to the most High, the lion sneezed, and a cat ran out of his nostrils. From that time forth the mouse became timid so that it contracted the habit of hiding itself in holes" (Simpson, 1903, p. 1) *(figure 4.8)*.

Unlike Christianity, Islam took a much kinder view of the cat primarily due to the Prophet Mohammed's (PBUH) (AD 570-632) compassion for the enigmatic beast. There are several stories of Mohammed interacting with cats. The first is that his favorite cat, Muezza, fell asleep on his sleeve and rather than awakening her to go to pray, he cut off the sleeve of his robe. Another is again of Muezza, who supposedly bowed to him to thank him for some kindness, and Mohammed by passing his hand over her back three times, gave all Tabby cats stripes on their backs and the ability to always land on their feet (Geyer, 2004, p. 28). Another common legend states that the '*M*' on a tabby's forehead stands for the '*M*' in Mohammed. Even one of Mohammed's closest friends, Abu Horeirah, "the father of the cat," was so nicknamed by Mohammed because of his fondness for a particular cat that he always carried around with him. Consequently, after being constantly called by this name, his real name has disappeared from history (Ockley, 1847, p. 376).

Figure 4.8. Noah and the Flood, 16th Century, Mogul

There are several *Hadith*[†] referring to the cat. And according to Hadith - Bukhari 3:553, narrated by 'Abdullah bin 'Umar, "A woman entered the fire (Hell) because of a cat which she kept and did not give it food or water, nor did she set it free to eat of the vermin of the earth." Two later translations have it that the woman "was punished because she imprisoned a cat until it died," or "entered Hell because of a cat she tied up and did not feed." And in several other Hadith it is expressly stated that Mohammed had a firm respect for all animals. Hadith - Muwatta 2.13 states, "Yahya related to me from Malik from Ishaq ibn Abdullah ibn Abi Talha from Humayda bint Abi Ubayda ibn Farwa that her maternal aunt Kabsha bint Kab ibn Malik, who was the wife of the son of Abu Qatada al-Ansari, told her that once Abu Qatada was visiting her and she poured out some water for him to do *wudu* [††]with. Just then a cat came to drink from it, so he tilted the vessel towards it to let it drink. Kabsha continued, "He saw me looking at him and said, 'Are you surprised, daughter of my brother?' I said, 'Yes.' He replied that the Messenger of Allah, may Allah bless him and grant him peace, said, cats are not impure. They intermingle with you.' " In yet another Hadith narrated by Aisha, Ummul Mu'minin Dawud ibn Salih ibn Dinar at-Tammar quoted his mother as saying that her mistress sent her with some pudding (*harisah*) to Aisha (the wife of Mohammed) who was offering prayer. Aisha made a sign for me to place it down. A cat came and ate some of it, but when Aisha finished her prayer, she ate from the place where the cat had eaten. She stated, The Messenger of Allah said, It is not unclean; it is one of those who go round among you. She added, I saw the Messenger of Allah performing ablution from the water left over by the cat (Omisdsalar, 1990).

In stark contrast, Christians believed that the cat licked the back of toads and drank from where the Christians drank and defiled their water causing long illnesses. If a cat even sneezed or a drop from its eye went into the water, it would cause sickness and death. For Christians, the cat was dirty (Williams, 1967).

Through a story passed down orally to Ad-Damiri, Muslims' acceptance and respect for the cat is quite clear. "The grammarian

---

[†] In Islam, a traditional account of things said or done by the Prophet Mohammed or his companions.

[††] The ritual of washing before prayers in Islam.

Ibn Babshad was sitting with his friends on the roof of a mosque in Cairo eating some food. When a cat passed by, they gave her some morsels; she took them and ran away, only to come back time and time again. The scholars followed her and saw her running to an adjacent house on whose roof a blind cat was sitting. The cat carefully placed the morsels in front of her. Babshad was so moved by God's caring for the blind creature that he gave up all his belongings and lived in poverty, completely trusting in God until he died in 1067" (related orally to 14th century Theologian and zoologist Damiri) (Chittock & Schimmel, 2001, p. 40).

Ibn Alalaf Al Naharwany, a poet of Bagdad who died around AD 930, wrote about the mischievous adventures of his ill-fated cat. Al Naharwany metes out a much harsher solution to the problem than Agathias did when faced with the death of his own partridge that his cat killed in AD 550. When Al Naharwany's cat simply tried to kill one of his doves, he coldly shot it dead, and then wrote this poem lamenting her death.

To A Cat

Poor puss is gone! Tis fate's decree----
Yet I must still her loss deplore,
For dearer than a child was she,
And ne'er shall I behold her more.

With many a sad presaging tear
This morn I saw her steal away,
While she went on without a fear
Except that she should miss her prey.

I saw her to the dove house climb,
With cautious feet and slow she stept,
Resolved to balance loss of time
By eating faster than she crept.

Her subtle foes were on the watch
And mark'd her course, with fury fraught,
And while she hoped the birds to catch,
An arrow's point the huntress caught.

In fancy she had got them all
And drunk their blood, and suck'd their breath;
Alas! She only got a fall,
And only drank the draught of death.

Why, why was pigeon's flesh so nice,
That thoughtless cats should love it thus?
Hadst thou but lived on rats and mice,
Thou hadst been living still, poor Puss.

Curst be the taste, howe'er refined,
That prompts us for such joys to wish,
And curst the dainty where we find
Destruction lurking in the dish
(Gooden, 1946, p. 25; Repplier, 1901, p. 24).

In another poem, Abbasid Prince Ibn Al MuTazz, who was assassinated one day after becoming king, mourns the loss of his cat. "Cat you went and you didn't come back. You were like a son to me! Loving you so, how could we forget you?"

Moreover, during the Middle Ages Sultan Baybars (1260-1277), the first ruler of the Turkish Mameluk dynasty, so loved cats that within the mosque that he built in a northern district of Cairo there was a garden where stray cats were fed every day between noon and sunset.

The Cat in Persia

Before reaching the Far East, cats travelled through Persia and India via the Silk Routes where Persian Zoroastrians, in sharp contrast to the Arab Muslims, considered the cat evil and treacherous. During the Sassanian Empire (AD 224-651), the cat in Zoroastrian mythology was said to have been created by an evil spirit based on a myth in the *Dadestān ī dēnīg*[†],where Jamak mated with a demon and thus gave birth to a cat (West, 2009, p. 419). Moreover, if a cat urinated in water, all the fishes in the sea would die (Omisdsalar, 1990). In contrast to the Muslim beliefs mentioned in the *Hadith*, Zoroastrians, much like Christians of the time, believed that even if a

[†] 9th century Persian Zoroastrian religious judgments.

bowl from which a cat had eaten were washed seven times, it would still be unclean. Finally, eating food that had even touched a cat's whiskers caused one to waste away (Boyce, 1977, p. 163).

Even though demonized, Zoroastrians still kept cats as pets and mousers. In the 7th century, the king of the Sassinands, Khosrow Parvez (AD 590-628), wanting to destroy the city of Ray because it was his enemy's home town, sent a newly appointed governor there who ordered all the cats to be killed. With the merciless murder of all the cats, the mouse population went unchecked, forcing the people to abandon their homes. And as the wicked King had wanted, this ultimately threatened the collapse of the city. However, by persuading the king to remove the governor with the playful antics of a kitten, the queen saved the city and the cats again took up their vigilant guard against the mice (Omisdsalar, 1990).

Eating Cat Meat

Both Arabs and Berbers often ate cat meat even though laws forbade it. According to both Persian and Arabic sources, eating the meat of a black cat offered protection from magic. Furthermore, a consistent diet of cat's meat inspired amazing feats of courage because cats habitually attacked prey much larger than themselves. For this reason, Isma'ili assassins regularly ate cat meat (Omisdsalar, 1990).

Not everyone was a connoisseur of cat meat, however, and several stories survive of Persians and Sufis fondly keeping cats as pets. Kittens were more valuable than adults, and women often fawned over them so exceedingly that they even dressed them up in earrings and necklaces, dyed their fur, and would allow them to sleep with them.

In addition, the Deylamite prince Rokn-al-Dawla (AD 947-77), became so attached to his cat that petitioners tied their written requests to the neck of his favorite pet in order to make sure that the prince would notice them. Even a Sufi sheikh had tiny shoes made for his cat that slept on his prayer carpet in order to protect it against the pampered feline's sharp claws. When one of the Sheikh's servants found cause to beat the cat, the sheikh demanded that he apologize to the discontented animal (Omisdsalar, 1990).

In Persian folklore black cats and even white were often seen as manifestations of Jinn or even the devil himself. Because of this, Persians believed the cat was an ill omen especially if seen first thing in the morning. And if a cat appeared in a dream, it was considered a symbol of thievery.

Persians used cats in many medicinal concoctions just as the ancient Egyptians and Greeks had. A cure for a fever was to use cat's dung mixed with oil, and cat's blood was said to cure leprosy. A Persian proverb states that because the cat realized that its dung was useful as medicine, our recalcitrant feline decided to bury it. Because of the cat's close association with fertility and child birth, stories of its ability to cure infertility were well known. To cure infertility, a woman held the placenta of a cat over her head while pouring water on it. The water running over the woman's head cured her. Another cure for infertility was to take cat hair, game meat and a string of seven colors to the bathhouse and then put them into an oven (Omisdsalar, 1990).

The Cat in India

In India the cat, known in Sanskrit as *Acoubouk*[†] or *Margara*, was frequently mentioned in the original fables of *Bidpay*, also known as the *Panchatantra*. The original of the *Panchatantra*, or the *Five Discourses*, is credited to a king who feared that his sons would not be able to wisely rule his kingdom. Duly concerned, he asked his *wazir*[†] to help him solve this problem. The *wazir* decided to write the easily understood fables that contained lessons the king's sons needed in order to rule their kingdom successfully. The original fable *The Belling of the Cat,* which is often accredited to Aesop, appears in this collection. Another fable, *The Devout Cat,* is a short tale wherein a partridge and a hare go to a wise, ascetic cat to seek a resolution to their dispute. Both the partridge and hare are wary of the cat and stand a safe distance from him. After some time, however, the two start to trust the cat and move closer to him as the cat feigns not to be able to hear them. Once they approach near enough, the cat grabs and kills them both. Thus, the cat is proved to be both treacherous and evil *(figure 4.9)*.

A cat is also carved in a huge stone created in the 7-8th centuries

---

[†] Meaning eater of mice.

[†] Wazir or vizier is a high ranking minister or advisor.

in Mahabalipuram. Called Arjun's penance, some scholars believe that the carving depicts Arjun's quest to find a weapon to vanquish his enemies; others believe it is the legend of the River Ganges arrival on earth.

Figure 4.9. Cat with a Fish, Calcutta, 19th Century, Victoria and Albert Museum, London

Even more disastrous to the cat's reputation, was that it was blamed for the death of the Buddha. Legend states that a mouse was sent to fetch the dying Buddha some medicine but was attacked and devoured by a hungry cat. Not receiving the medicine, the Buddha died, and the unrepentant cat did not even shed a tear nor mourn the Buddha's death.

As if this were not enough to demonize the cat completely, in Bengal, located in the northeast region of India, a black vampire cat was thought to be the vessel of a witch called a Chordewa. Visiting the houses of the sick and dying, she ate their food and then summoned the soul of the helpless one to depart the body through lips that she licked (Summers, 1926).

The Cat in China

By some Western accounts the domestic cat arrived in China around 200 BC (Turner, Bateson, & Bateson, 2000) having been most probably acquired from Roman merchants. However, much earlier Chinese mythology mentions the cat goddess Yifan Zhang, who was known to have led a legion of cats to uphold righteousness and to found the Chinese nation before the Shang Era. This might support new found proof of the cat's domestication in China as early as 3000 BC. In addition, the *Chinese Book of Rites*, compiled during Confucius' time (1050-256 BC), describes an annual sacrificial offering in honor of cats made by the Emperor. "They met (and gave sacrifice to) the representatives of the cats, because they devoured the rats and mice which injured the fruits of the field." (Legge, 1885, rite 25).

Above all, the Chinese believed the cat to be a mystical creature that had unfathomable spiritual powers (Werness, 2006). The Emperor Wen, during the Sui Dynasty in AD 598, believed that his brother-in-law and his mother had used cat spirits to cause his Empress to fall ill. At the trial, a female servant testified that the brother-in-law's mother had regularly made sacrifices to cat spirits encouraging them to murder the rich Empress. If killed by a cat spirit, all the possessions of the victim were inherited by those who lived in the same house as the spirit. The brother-in-law's mother had wanted the riches and jewels of the Empress, and had hoped by persuading the cat spirit to haunt her, she could cause the Empress to die. The Empress took pity upon them and spared their lives, but consequently, the Emperor exiled all those who summoned cat spirits (Van Vechten, 1921).

The Empress Wu Zetian (AD 624-705) established the short lived Zhou Dynasty and was the only woman to rule China as an Emperor rather than an Empress. By ruthlessly manipulating the Emperor Gaozong into believing that his wife, the Empress Wang, had killed his only daughter, Wu, who was only a lowly consort at the time, began her plot to cast suspicion on the Empress in order to take her place. In fact, historians today believe that she herself had cold-heartedly killed the daughter. However, the Emperor believed the story and replaced the Empress Wang with Wu. It was not enough to have the Empress's throne, and Wu tortured the Empress

Wang and her consort Xiao, causing them to suffer slowly in wine jars before they were taken out and beheaded. The consort Xiao cursed Wu as a monster and said that she hoped to be reincarnated as a cat and Wu as a rat so that she could chase her into eternity. The Chinese believed that after death a person became a cat, and the Empress Wu took the curse seriously, thereafter forbidding anyone in the palace to keep one.

Other fearful beliefs concerning the cat took the form of eerie tales, myths and legends. In one such story an old woman was accused of keeping a baby up at night by riding around on her cat and terrifying the poor child. To solve the problem, the woman was starved to death and the cat beaten to death; the child was said to have slept peacefully afterwards. Additionally, if a cat jumped over a coffin, the deceased would rise and live again. The zombie only succumbed to complete death if beaten with a broom. If a cat jumped over a corpse, the person's soul entered the cat. If a cat jumped over a girl's coffin, she would become a vampire if the cat was not found and killed (Van Vechten, 1921).

Strict measures ensured that a cat never entered a room with a corpse, as it was feared that the cat, while leaping over the dead body, would impart an evil force causing the person to turn into a vampire.

Although seen as a magical animal with supernatural powers over life and death, in many instances the cat was a loved and devoted pet. The poet scholar Chang Tuan in around AD 1,000 had seven cats with names such as, Phoenix and Drive-Away-Vexation, Guardian of the East, White Phoenix, Purple Blossom, Brocade Sash, Cloud Pattern and Ten Thousand Strings of Cash (Bast, 1995, p. 21, 87).

In fact, during the latter part of the Chinese T'ang and Sung Dynasties (AD 618-1279) cats were pampered and often interesting subjects of poems and paintings. Here Mei Yao Ch'en (1002-1060) writes a heartfelt poem to his dead cat.

Sacrifice to the Cat that Scared all the Rats

When I had my Five White cat,
The rats did not invade my books.
This morning Five White died,
I sacrifice with rice and fish.
I see you off in the middle of the river,

I chant for you: I won't neglect you.
Once when you'd bitten a rat,
You took it crying around the yard.
You wanted to scare all the rats,
So as to make my cottage clean.
Since we come and board this boat,
On the boat we've shared a room.
Although the grain is dry and scarce,
I eat not fearing piss or theft.
That's because of your hard work,
Harder working than chickens or pigs.
People stress their mighty steeds,
Saying nothing's like a horse or ass.
Enough—I'm not going to argue,
But cry for you a little.

Cats in Chinese Art

Cats also became the main subjects of many Chinese paintings. The Chinese word for cat is a homonym for the word octogenarian, and so from this association, the cat symbolized long life. The calico cat, for some unknown reason, has been blessed as the symbol of wealth (Lang, 2004). And so, when pictured in paintings or scrolls, cats denote the meaning of longevity and wealth. In the early 10th century painting *Wasps and Cat* from Tiao Kuang-Yin's album *Flowers and Sketches from Life* a white cat intently watches a wasp flying in front of it. Another early painting called *Lady* by Chou Wen-Chu of the Five Dynasties, portrays a lady sitting peacefully reading a book in her garden as a black and white cat sits at her feet *(figure 4.10)*.

Sung Dynasty (AD 960-1279) representations are so detailed that each hair has been drawn in separately while capturing the feline emotions of fear, surprise, and joy. Many depictions show cats as prized pets with some wearing red ribbons around their necks, and later, in the Ming Dynasty, they are adorned with red tassels and gold bell collars. In the painting *Calico Cat Under Noble Peonies* a black and white cat is even tied up, implying that it must be someone's pet *(figure 4.11)*.

A calico cat bristles and hisses at an intruding dog in a hibiscus garden in the painting *Hibiscus and Rocks* by LiTi *(figure 4.12)*.

Figure 4.10. Lady, Chou Wen-Chu, Five Dynasties, 10th Century, National Palace Museum, Taipei

Figure 4.11. Calico Cat Under Noble Peonies, 12th Century, Sung Dynasty, National Palace Museum, Taipei

Figure 4.12. Hibiscus and Rocks, Detail, 12th Century, Sung Dynasty, National Palace Museum, Taipei

In yet another painting by LiTi entitled *Portrait of a Cat,* an orange and white cat holds its paw up expectantly waiting for something interesting *(figure 4.13).*

Figure 4.13. Portrait of a Cat, Sung Dynasty, National Palace Museum, Taipei

I Yuan-chi, another Sung Dynasty artist, captures a monkey clutching one of two kittens. The kitten's features clearly express fear as the second kitten looks on worriedly. The monkey's expression is one of unconcern. Both kittens have red ribbons around their necks *(figure 4.14)*.

Figure 4.14. Monkey and Cat, I Yuan-chi, Sung Dynasty National Palace Museum, Taipei

In the painting *Children Playing on a Winter Day,* two children, most probably a sister and a brother, holding cat toys, are ready to play with their black and white cat that is again wearing a red ribbon collar *(figure 4.15)*.

Figure 4.15. Children Playing on a Winter Day, Su Hanchen, 1130-1160, National Palace Museum, Taipei

In an anonymous painting of the same period called *Cats Playing,* eight cats are in various positions of play in a garden *(figure 4.16).*

Figure 4.16. Cats Playing, Anonymous, Sung Dynasty, AD 960-1279, National Palace Museum, Taipei

The Cat in Japan

The cat reached Japan from China in the late 900's during the Edo period reign of Emperor Ichigo (AD 986-1011). At first only the rich could afford such a rare pet, and so the cat became popular amongst royalty. The young Emperor loved his cats, and when on the 19th day of the 9th month of the year 999[†] a cat in the palace gave birth to kittens, he gave orders that a wet nurse take care of them as if they were the Emperor's own new born children. The Emperor even went so far as to order tailors to make tiny suits of clothing for them. Giving the mother cat the name *Myobu No Omoto,* the Emperor granted her a rank equal to that of a lady in waiting (Van Vechten, 1921).

Lady Sarashina, in her diary that covered the years AD 1009-1059, lovingly describes the relationship that she had with her pet cat. "Once in the Rice-Sprout month, when I was up late reading a romance, I heard a cat mewing with a long-drawn-out cry. I turned, wondering, and saw a very lovely cat. 'Whence does it come?' I asked. 'Sh,' said my sister, 'do not tell anybody. It is a darling cat and we will keep it.' The cat was very sociable and lay beside us. Someone might be looking for her [we thought], so we kept her secretly. She kept herself aloof from the vulgar servants, always sitting quietly before us. She turned her face away from unclean food, never eating it. She was tenderly cared for and caressed by us. Once sister was ill, and the family was rather upset. The cat was kept in a room facing the north [i.e. a servant's room], and never was called. She cried loudly and scoldingly, yet I thought it better to keep her away and did so. Sister, suddenly awakening, said to me, 'Where is the cat kept? Bring her here.' I asked why, and sister said: 'In my dream the cat came to my side and said, I am the altered form of the late Honoured Daughter of the First Adviser to the King. There was a slight cause [for this]. Your sister has been thinking of me affectionately, so I am here for a while, but now I am among the servants. 'O how dreary I am!' So saying she wept bitterly. She appeared to be a noble and beautiful person and then I awoke to hear the cat crying! 'How pitiful!' The story moved me deeply and after this I never sent the cat away to the north-facing room, but waited on her lovingly. Once, when I was sitting alone, she came and sat before me, and, stroking her head, I addressed her: 'You are the first daughter of the Noble Adviser? I wish to let your father know of it.' The cat watched my face and mewed, *lengthening her voice.* It may be my fancy, but as I was watching her she seemed no common cat. She seemed to understand my words, and I pity her. At midnight of the Deutzia month [April, 1024] a fire broke out, and the cat which had been waited on as a

[†] Again the cat is associated with the number 9.

daughter of the First Adviser was burned to death. She had been used to come mewing whenever I called her by the name of that lady, as if she had understood me. My father said that he would tell the matter to the First Adviser, for it is a strange and heartfelt story. I was very, very sorry for her" (Omori & Doi, 1920, pp. 23-26).

The poet and writer Lady Murasaki Shikibu in *The Tale of Genji* (11th century) also noted cats' behavior at court. "The most unsociable cat, when it finds itself wrapped up in someone's coat and put to sleep upon his bed—stroked, fed, and tended with every imaginable care—soon ceases to stand upon its dignity" (Rogers, 2006, p. 24).

Unfortunately, not all of Japanese society shared this good will towards cats. Superstitious Japanese believed the cat's tail to be the source of its magic, so it became a custom to cut it off. Thus, by doing so, the cat was unable to become a demon. One folktale describes the demise of a whole city owing to a cat's tail. The cat's tail catches on fire, and the cat runs through the town setting it all ablaze ultimately destroying the city. As a result, the Emperor decrees that all cats must have their tails cut off. Today the most popular cat in Japan is the bobtail.

A *Bakeneko*, or spirit cat, by its very nature eventually became a cat with a forked tail called a *Nekomata (figure 4.17)*. The transformation of the *Bakeneko* to a *Nekomata* was sometimes dependent upon the cat's age or its weight. Spiritual strength increased with age and weight, and so a cat could speak at 10 years old and, some years later, could even transform itself into a human being.

Killing a cat was not advisable, as a curse would doom the killer and his family to continuous haunting for seven generations. The Ainu, who primarily inhabit the northern island of Hokkaido, believe that if a person kills a cat, the spirit of the cat will take revenge by enchanting his murderer and causing him to die. The only way to prevent this is if the cat killer eats a part of the same cat. If this is not done, the spirit of the cat possesses him, and causes him to act like a cat as he gradually dies. However, the cat's killer, while he is still able, can cure himself by killing another cat and eating part of it. Otherwise, he finally dies a painful death while meowing like a cat. The name of this affliction in the Ainu language is *meko pagoat* or "cat punishment" (Refsing, 2002, p. 36). In contrast, in other Ainu villages, killing a cat causes a deadly disease (Etter, 1949, 2004, p.138).

Figure 4.17. Nekomata, Toriyama Sekien, 1712-88

The Japanese, not unlike the Chinese and Indians, believed in vampire cats, and plenty of stories and myths are deeply rooted in the culture. One such story is *The Vampire Cat of Nabéshima.* One day while Prince Hizen and his favorite concubine, O'Toyo, were walking through the palace gardens, an enormous black cat followed them. The day passed, and O'Toyo retired early only to be awoken at midnight by the same black cat sitting right next to her on her bed. She screamed and the cat attacked, biting her neck so fiercely and sucking her blood so greedily that she quickly died. The cat dug a grave and buried her and assumed her form with a plan to enchant the Prince. As time passed, the Prince grew weaker and paler. No medicine could cure him. Even though servants guarded his door at night, they suddenly fell asleep at ten o'clock. This was the time when the demon cat in O'Toyo's body would come and suck the prince's blood *(figure 4.18).* His odd sickness was soon suspected as witchcraft, and a young dedicated soldier, Ito Soda, offered to try and save the

Prince by remaining awake all night. By deeply cutting his leg, Ito managed to stay awake all night and confronted the demon. The demon was no longer able to suck the Prince's blood, and as time passed the Prince started to get better. Ito unsuccessfully tried to kill the cat, as it escaped by running across the roofs to the mountains afar. There the healthy Prince was able to hunt it down and eventually kill it, but only after it had terrorized many villages (Mitford, 1871/2010).

Figure 4.18. Vampire Cat Attacking O-Toin, Prince of Hizen, Algernon Bertram Freeman, Mitford Tales of Old Japan, 1871

In contrast, another Japanese story relates the love of a family for its deceased cat. In *The Faithful Cat,* a family in Osaka celebrates the 100th anniversary of the death of their ancestor's cat. The family reminisced that the cherished cat would follow the great grandfather's daughter around everywhere so that the great grandfather feared that the cat had fallen in love with her and wanted to cast a spell on her. Fearing the worst, he threatened to kill the cat, but the cat hearing the plan that night, whispered in his ear that he was in fact protecting his daughter from a large rat that lived in the granary. The cat instructed the great grandfather to go the next day and find another cat well known for its excellent hunting abilities and bring him back to the house. The great grandfather did as he was asked and brought the cat back. The two cats then went together into the granary to fight the rat. Even though the two cats managed to trap the ferocious rat so that the man could cut its throat, the two cats were so severely injured that they would not heal and eventually died. Thus, because of the bravery and devotion of their cat, the family devotedly celebrated its birthday each year (Mitford, 1871, 2010).

In addition, another positive legend is of the *Maneki-neko* based on a story of a temple cat that beckoned to a Samurai to move away from a tree right before it was struck by lightning, thus saving the Samurai's life. Today's Hello Kitty is loosely based upon this legend.

All in all throughout the Dark Ages, the cat served as both pariah and inspiration. Christians who had demonized the cat would ironically glorify it by adding its images to their holiest books, psalters, and bestiaries. While the cat would be associated with magic and vampires in the Talmud, in Islam it was highly respected and protected by the Hadith. As the cat spread east to China and Japan, stories and myths grew up around it that magnified the cat's imagined magical powers. Deeply rooted beliefs, based on the ancient goddess Bast's powers, mingled with fear and loathing, brought about the beginning of the cat's long period of persecution.

Chapter Five

THE MIDDLE AGES

The Middle Ages were plagued by continued social and religious strife. Commencing in 1096, the world would suffer through nine crusades finally ending in 1272. Muslims, Jews and non-believers alike would be the victims of the wrath of the Christian church in its goal to secure its pervasive control over all. "The powerful Christian authority structures of Medieval Europe were only interested in one kind of relationship with other forms of religion: the total destruction of these religions and the Christianization of all peoples; by force if necessary" (Waddell, 2003 p. 63). No matter what the segment of society, non-Christians were persecuted and burned especially in Italy and France for refusing to take the sacrament. During this time the church controlled both civil and criminal courts, book production and education (Bishop, 2001). Amidst this power struggle, the curse of the Black Death would kill millions of people between the years 1347 and 1352, while the unrelenting church would proclaim any divergence from the main Catholic faith as heretical. Accusations of witchcraft would slowly rise, and these years would see the steady demise of the cat culminating in its increased vilification as the familiar of witches and its embodiment of the devil.

However, in the early Middle Ages the cat was not treated as harshly as it would later be, as the benefits of keeping this helpful unassuming creature were still widely appreciated. Henry I of England (1068-1135) referred to as 'Beauclerc,' was not unlike Hywel Dda in that he instituted laws that protected the cat. Realizing its importance in protecting grain stores, he declared that anyone caught killing a cat would be subject to a fine of 60 bushels of corn (Choron, Choron, & Moore, 2007). Not just fond of writing laws, Henry I founded a Benedictine Abbey at Reading as a testament to his faith. Beak-head ornaments of cats' heads decorate the abbey *(figure 5.1).*

Figure 5.1. Cat Beak-head Ornament, Reading Abby, 1121

The Use of Cat Fur

Unfortunately for the cat and other small animals, during the Middle Ages it was not uncommon for those from the lower social strata to use cat, rabbit, and even badger furs as trim and linings for blankets, gloves and mittens. Some even wore complete cat coats made of up to 24 skins (Newman, 2001, p. 126; Simpson, 1903). Furthermore, in 1127, shortly after Henry I's death, the Canons of Archbishop Corbeuil mention that nuns were forbidden to wear any fur more expensive than a cat's (Clutton-Brock, 1994). According to Sumptuary Laws only royalty could wear ermine, whereas the under-classes could only wear fox, cat or rabbit (Sider, 2005).

Bartholomew Anglicus, not to be confused with Bartholomew de Glanville, was a member of the order of St. Francis and is famous for writing a popular encyclopedia of science in 1240, *De proprietatibus rerum*. Making sure to include a reference to the use of cats' fur, he has described the cat as "...a beast of uncertain hair and color. For some cat is white, some red, and some black, some calico and speckled in the feet and in the ears...And hath a great mouth and saw teeth and sharp and long tongue and pliant, thin, and subtle. And lappet therewith when he drinketh...And he is full lecherous in youth, swift, pliant and merry, and leapeth and rusheth on everything that is before him and is led by a straw, and playeth therewith; and is a right heavy beast in age and full sleepy, and lieth slyly in wait for mice and is aware where they be more by smell than by sight, and hunteth and rusheth on them in privy places. And when he taketh a mouse, he playeth therewith, and eateth him after the play. In time of love is hard fighting for wives and one scratcheth and rendeth the other grieviously with biting and with claws. And he maketh a ruthful noise and ghastful, when one proffereth to fight with one another, and unneth is hurt when he is thrown from a high place. And when he hath a fair skin, he is as it were proud thereof, and goeth fast about. And when his skin is burnt, then he bideth at home. And is oft for his fair skin taken of the skinner, and slain and flayed" (Harteley, 1979, p. 124).

The most famous hunting book of the Middle Ages, *Livre de la Chasse,* written by Gaston Phoebus, the Comte de Foix, between 1387-89, includes many brightly detailed drawings of hunting scenes and serves as proof that wildcats were hunted for their fur. Edward the second Duke of York, who added descriptions of the pictures when he translated it into English between 1403 and 1413, wrote, "Of common wild cats I need not speak much, for every hunter in England knoweth them, and their falseness and malice are well known. But one thing I dare well say that if any beast hath the devil's spirit in him, without doubt it is the cat, both the wild and the tame" (Baillie-Grohman & Baillie-Grohman, 1909, p. 71).

The Cat's Significance in Religious Sects

Many different Christian sects began to flourish during this time. One of the first was the Waldenses, founded in 1170 by Peter Waldo. The Waldenses believed that the individual could communicate directly with God. This of course threatened the church, as the pope and the rest of the church hierarchy would no longer be able to sustain power, nor collect fees for indulgences that absolved sinners of their earthly misdeeds. Hence, the church promptly excommunicated Waldo and declared the Waldenses heretical (Bishop, 2001). To further malign the sect, William of Paris accused the Waldenses of worshipping the Devil in the form of a black cat, an accusation that would later be used against the Cathars and even the Knights Templar. As devil worshippers the church easily condemned the sect for witchcraft and thus heresy *(figure 5.2).* The church accused the Cathars of refusing the sacraments of the Church. "Pope Gregory IV said that they carried the sacrament of Christ's body in their mouths to their homes where they spit it out into their toilets" (Von Nettesheim, 1913 p. 116). In roughly the same year, 1182, that St. Francis was born, Alain de Lille (1128-1202) a French

Figure 5.2. Waldensians as Witches in Le Championdes Dames
Martin Le France, 1451

theologian, proclaimed that the Cathars name meant 'cat' and was derived from the Latin, *cattus* when in actuality the name came from the Greek *Katharoi*, meaning pious ones (Turner, Bateson, & Bateson, 2000). Sealing the Cathars' fate, the medieval writer Walter Map described a ceremony where they worshipped a cat. "About the first watch of the night, when gates, doors, and windows have been closed, the groups sit waiting in silence in their respective synagogues†, and a black cat of marvelous size climbs down a rope which hangs in their midst *(figure 5.3)*. On seeing it, they put out the lights. They do not sing hymns or repeat them distinctly, but hum through clenched teeth and pantingly feel their way toward the place where they saw their lord. When they have found him they kiss him, each the more humbly as he is the more inflamed with frenzy—same the feet, more under the tail, most the private parts" (Russell, 1984 p. 130). The church linked heresy with witchcraft and deemed the Cathars' heretical behavior so dangerous that Pope Innocent II launched the Albigensian Crusade against them in Southern France. The crusade and the inquisition which followed completely wiped out

† Up until the 15th century the word synagogue was used to describe a meeting of witches.

the Cathars in the 13th century. The Church also tried to eradicate other major sects such as the Manichaens, Lollards and Templars in the same way by declaring their adherents heretics while also accusing them of worshipping the Devil in the form of a black cat. St. Augustine would even go so far as to accuse the Manichaens of eating their own babies in *The Nature of Good* (Russell, 1984 p. 124).

One of the five accusations against the Templars was that they worshipped a black cat, which appeared during their ceremonies (Lea, 2005). Consequently, St. Dominic and the Dominicans would declare the black cat the embodiment of Satan, and they would be at the forefront of the Inquisition. From now on the church would use any association with cats as a tool to discredit those who threatened the power and control of the papacy by labeling them witches and/or heretics.

Figure 5.3. The Devil Appears to St. Dominico of Caleruega, Folio 313, Le Miroir Historical, 1400-1410, National Library of the Netherlands

The Cat and the *Vox in Rama*

Pope Gregory IX (1227-1241) was the first to appoint inquisitors to seek out and prosecute heretics. Previously, bishops had been appointed this duty, but because they did not bring cases unless someone complained the church viewed them as ineffectual. The inquisitors were mostly Dominican and Franciscan friars vested with the power to charge anyone and anything with heresy and/or witchcraft as they saw fit (Kieckhefer, 2000). Due to the claims made by the inquisitor Conrad of Marburg that satanic sects existed in Mainz, Pope Gregory IX on June 13th, 1233, issued a papal bull, *Vox in Rama,* wherein the church proclaimed the cat a vessel of the devil. The bull states in reference to the sect, "The following rites of this pestilence are carried out: When any novice is to be received among them and enters the sect of the damned for the first time, the shape of a certain frog [or toad] appears to him. Some kiss this creature on the hind quarters and some on the mouth, they receive the tongue and saliva of the beast inside their mouths. Sometimes it appears unduly large, and sometimes equivalent to a goose or a duck, and sometimes it even assumes the size of an oven. At length, when the novice has come forward, [he] is met by a man of wondrous pallor, who has black eyes and is so emaciated [and] thin that since his flesh has been wasted, seems to have remaining only skin drawn over [his] bone. The novice kisses him and feels cold, [like] ice, and after the kiss the memory of the [C]atholic faith totally disappears from his heart. Afterwards, they sit down to a meal and when they have arisen from it, the certain statue, which is usual in a sect of this kind, a black cat descends backwards, with its tail erect. First the novice, next the master, then each one of the order who are worthy and perfect, kiss the cat on its buttocks. Then each [returns] to his place and, speaking certain responses, they incline their heads toward the cat. 'Forgive us!' says the master, and the one next to him repeats this, a third responding [says], 'We know, master!' A fourth says: 'And we must obey.' When this has been done, they [put] out the candles, and turn to the practice of the most disgusting lechery. [They] make no distinction between strangers and family. Moreover, if by chance those of the male [sex] exceed the number of women, surrendering to their passions, [...] men engage with depravity with men. Women change their natural function making this itself worthy of blame among themselves. [When] these most abnormal sins have been completed, and the candles have been lit again and each has resumed his [place], from a dark corner of the assembly a certain man come[s], from the loins upward, shining like the sun. His lower part is shaggy like a cat" (Rodenberg, 1883, pp. 423-425, 537).

Heretics were to become known as *ketzer* from the German name for cat, *katze*. The heretic, like the cat, defied Christian beliefs and appropriated souls (Williams, 1967). Jews often depicted with the heretical symbol of the cat in the *Bible Moralisée,* were considered heretics as well. In one illustration there are two clerics devoted to the church. One reads a book and the other prays, while two bearded men who are obviously Jews shun the church. One of whom holds out a money bag to a seated idol in a temple, while the other kneels holding a striped cat that looks away from him. The cat's tail is up and the man seems to be kissing him underneath it. Another illumination shows a cat sitting on a table of gold coins, a symbol of idol worship, the gold coins a symbol of money lending (Lipton, 1999).

The 13th Century

The 13th century did not begin well for the cat. Henry III (1207-1272), unlike Henry I, detested cats and would faint at the mere sight of one (Karras, 2005). Even so, records indicate that Henry's sister purchased a cat upon arriving at Oldham and another when she moved to Dover in 1265; however, the purpose is unclear. St. Thomas Aquinas (1225-74) wrote *Of God and His Creatures* in 1264 and in a section entitled, *That the Souls of Dumb Animals are not Immortal* he posited that animals do not have a consciousness or a soul and are unable to reason or understand. Instead, they live by their basic natural instincts (Engels, 2001). According to this treatise, the brutal handling and killing of animals was condoned, and the soulless cat's basic instinct was judged evil.

Although condemned by the church, cats continued to be prized as excellent household companions because of their mousing abilities. Ancrene Riwle, most probably a Dominican friar, wrote in the years 1225-40 in *The Rule of Anchoresses* that "You shall not possess any beast, my dear sisters, except only a cat" (Morton, 1853, p. 228). However, true to this dualistic idea of the cat as good and evil in the Middle Ages, Riwle also wrote of the cat as the devil intent upon sexual seduction. "Has the cat of hell ever clutched at her, caught with his claws her heart head? Yes, truly; and drew out afterwards her whole body, with hooks of crooked and keen temptations; made her to lose both God and Men, with open shame and sin" (Morton, 1853, p. 66).

The Plague

Living conditions in the Middle Ages were by no means sanitary. Houses made from waddle and daub accommodated 90 percent of the population, who were primarily living in the countryside working on feudal estates. These thatched roofed shacks shared by both animals and people attracted all sorts of vermin, especially rats. Researchers today believe that an average of 9.6 rats infested each house (Zahler, 2009). In addition, people rarely washed themselves or their clothes because they could not afford to heat water. Prior to the Black Death, the population had been severely weakened by the great famine of 1314-1317, which had killed more than 10 percent of the inhabitants of Europe. So dire were the living conditions during the famine that the fairy tale *Hansel and Gretel* was based upon the fact that many families left their children in the forest to die because they could not afford to feed them (Bishop, 2001). So when the Black Death[†] appeared in 1347, weakened with malnutrition, living in an unsanitary environment and also burdened with the Hundred Years War that had begun in 1337, the population easily succumbed. In addition, to the lack of sanitation, there were few hospitals[††] available for the victims *(figure 5.4)*. Perhaps most ironically a lack of cats, due to their vicious killings for being associated with the devil, caused the black rat population to explode. With their numbers unchecked, rats invaded cities spreading the deadly disease through the fleas they carried. Even after a third of Europe's population had been decimated between the years 1347-1352, scientists of the day remained ignorant of the plague's cause; consequently, the importance of the cat remained unknown.

Cats in Architecture

Throughout the Middle Ages, primarily because of the cat's vermin-killing skills, it continued to be regarded with some semblance of importance in art related to the church. In the Spanish

---

[†]The plague originated in Asia where the Mongols purposely infected the Genoese by throwing diseased bodies over the ramparts during a siege at Caffa on the Black Sea (Bishop, 2001).

[††] There were only 400 hospitals in all of England during the Middle Ages (Bishop, 2001).

Figure 5.4. A Plague Victim at Home, Ketham Woodcut from The Book of Venice, 1493-94

cathedral of Tarragona built in 1154 there is a sculpture on a column that looks like a burial of a cat or the carrying of a cat to be executed. The cat lies on a litter which is supported by rats and mice carrying banners. The executioner, a rat, is holding an ax in anticipation of performing his duty. However, in the next scene the cat jumps up and catches a rat while all the rest run for cover in a chaotic bid for survival. Obviously, the rat did not manage to execute the wily cat. This scene cannot help but revive memories of the ancient Egyptian ostraca representations of cat and rat dramas discussed in Chapter Two.

In addition to the Benedictine Abbey at Reading founded by Henry I and Tarragon Cathedral, which were built in the 12th century, various other churches built from the 13th through 16th centuries contain evidence of the cat in either their architecture or in their interior decorations. In the nave of The Cathedral at Rouen, later made famous for having been painted by Monet, a hungry cat chases a mouse around a column. In the onetime Benedictine monastery of San Giorgio Maggiore in Venice, cats surround St. Benedict (Van Vechten, 1921), while a stately and rather fearsome cat sits in the capital of the church of St. Pelagius in Denkendorf, Germany. Moreover, at Exeter Cathedral in a door located in the north transept wall, an apparent cat hole allowed the official rat catcher to come and go as it pleased. The Exeter cat, which controlled the mouse population at the Cathedral, had a penny a week salary to supplement its diet. In the obituaries documented at the Cathedral from 1305-1467 there is even mention of a *custoribus et cato* or a cat custodian (Reeves, 1998).

Misericords[†] on many churches' wooden seats often include cats. For example, at St. Botolph's in Lincolnshire, England, two 14th century jesters hold two cats tightly while biting their tails. At the Wells Cathedral, Somerset, three separate 14th century misericords depict a puppy biting a cat, a cat playing the violin[††], and a cat attacking a rat, while a witch and cat decorate another in the Great Malvern Priory, Worcestershire.

Cats Depicted in Psalters, Bestiaries and other Books

Psalters and bestiaries, second in popularity only to the Bible, as well as books of hours and even books of poetry, were widely read by the nobility and those well-to-do enough to purchase them. They contained many illustrations of cats, some with double meanings. In one illustration in *The Psalter of Louis Le Hutin* (1314), a grotesque with a lion's hindquarters brandishes a huge sword in order to stab a large cat *(figure 5.5)*. Swords often symbolize penises and their sheaths vaginas. Cats of course have always been equated with women from the earliest times, beginning with the cat goddess Bast, hence the sexual overtones of this illustration.

In contrast, *The Luttrell Psalter* (1320-1340) contains marvelous depictions of every day medieval life in addition to its psalms and

---

[†] Small ledges on the back of the fold up chairs that afforded those who had to stand some comfort.

[††] The cat's association with the violin or fiddle goes back to the ancient statues of Bastet who was often depicted holding a sistrum, which resembled a violin or fiddle (Engels, 2001, p. 42).

Figure 5.5. Detail of Swordsman with a Cat, Psalter of Louis Xl Hutin and his first wife Tournai, 1315, Archives de l'Eveche, no number, Folio 114

Figure 5.6. Cat and Mouse, Luttrell Psalter, 1330, British Library, London

calendar. On one page a striped grey cat with exceedingly long whiskers holds a mouse between his front paws *(figure 5.6)*.

In *Queen Mary's Psalter* (1553) a wildcat is jumping at a dragon, and in another illustration a cat is beating a tabor *(figure 5.7)*. There is also an illustration of "… the fall of men, in which there is a modification of the idea which gained wide currency during the Middle Ages that it was the serpent woman Lilith who had tempted Adam to eat the forbidden fruit. In this picture, while the beautiful grace and ample hair of Lilith are shown, instead of the usual female breast she has the body of a cat" (Conway, 1879, 2003 Vol. 2, p. 301).

Figure 5.7. Donkey and Cat, Queen Mary's Psalter, British Library, London

While psalters contained psalms, bestiaries were illuminated manuscripts that used animals and mythical beasts to teach theological principles and moral lessons. In one of the earliest bestiaries from England, *The Workshop Bestiary* (1185), three very colorful cats sit side by side; the one in front holds a very large mouse or rat, while the fourth cat slinks towards another smaller mouse. *The Bodley Bestiary* (1225-50) contains a vivid illustration of three cats highlighted by a deep blue background pierced by yellow stars and crescent moons. One cat is trying to catch a bird in a cage suspended over another sleeping cat, while a third cat stands prominently in the foreground clutching a large black rat *(figure 5.8)*. Bestiaries were popular all through Europe, and perhaps one of the most illustrious of the Bestiaries, *The Aberdeen Bestiary* found in Westminster Palace Library in 1542, contains several images of cats. At the beginning of the book, there is an illustration of Adam naming the animals. The order of the animals in the illustration is symbolic. Wild animals, classified as uncontrollable by man, are the great cats and deer; on the other hand, animals considered beasts of burden are the horse and ox, while goats and sheep are simply food. A hare accompanies two cats in the left hand bottom corner margin and are classified simply, as "beasts". Another illustration *(figure 5.9)* shows three cats sitting together with this accompanying text, most probably borrowed and reworded from Isidore of Seville[†], "Of the cat....The cat is called *musio*, mouse-catcher, because it is the enemy of mice. It is commonly called *catus*, cat, from *captura*, the act of catching. Others say it gets the name from *capto*, because it catches mice with its sharp eyes. For it has such piercing sight that it overcomes the dark of night with the gleam of light from its eyes. As a result, the Greek word *catus* means sharp, or cunning" (Arnott, 1995).

Figure 5.8. Bodley Bestiary, 1225-50, Bodleian Library, MS764, Folio51r, England

The books of hours were another source of devotional literature, which included the psalms, a calendar of the church feasts as well as other religious writings. In the 14th century these reached their height of popularity becoming even more common than psalters. Usually written in Latin, cats and mice, amongst a myriad of other subjects and themes, elaborately decorated their pages. In an *English Book of Hours* dating from 1320-1330, a cat stands at the top of a tower, while

[†]Isidore of Seville wrote an encyclopedia of the Dark Ages wherein he describes the cat, "Musio is so called because it is a foe of mice (muribus)...common people call it (catus) because it catches mice. Others say, because it sees (catat). For it has such sharp sight that it overcomes the darkness of the night by the brightness of its eyes" (Brehaut, 1912, p. 148).

Figure 5.9. Three Cats Gambol and Hunt,
Aberdeen Bestiary, Folio 23v, Aberdeen University Library

two rats try to climb up its sides. In another drawing in the same book a cat plays a rebec†. In the German *Maastricht Book of Hours* dating from around 1400 a cat is pictured in a snail shell. *The Book of Hours of Charlotte of Savoy,* queen consort of Louis XI 1420-1425, contains many illustrations of cats. A dog chases a cat in the margin on one page, on another, a white cat holds a grey mouse, while yet another cat is cleaning itself with a strikingly red tongue *(figure 5.10).*

In the *Book of Hours of Rome,* a cat plays a bagpipe *(figure 5.11).* In another from Rouen, France, (1470) a jester rides a bridled cat. In the *De Costa Book of Hours* (1515), a cat sits as a member of the family in the midst of a peaceful home where a fire roars and a table is laden with food. In a *Book of Hours* (1531) from Belgium we see a cat set

† A Medieval stringed instrument with a pear shaped body resembling a violin.

Figure 5.10. A Cat Licks Itself, Hours of Charlotte of Savoy , Paris, 1420-1425, MSM.1004, Folio 172r, J.P. Morgan Library, New York

back in the center of the illustration underneath a light streaming from a dove positioned directly above it. The dove, a symbol of peace and love, shines its light down upon the potentially evil cat. The idea of above and below, heaven and earth, pervades the picture, while the angel Gabriel and the Virgin Mary are highlighted in the foreground. In a French book of hours from the 15th century, two pages have depictions of a cat in the company of a monkey. On the first, a monkey holds a cat on its lap while feeding it milk through a horn. On the second, a monkey churns butter, while a cat drinks milk from a bowl. According to a fable, the Sun and Moon took turns creating all life. The Sun created the Lion, and the Moon created the cat. When the Moon created the Monkey, all the stars laughed at such a strange animal. The insulted Moon thus cast a spell to cause eternal hatred between the monkey and the cat and the cat and mouse (Van Vechten, 1921). Even so, here the monkey appears benevolent as it nurtures the cat.

Figure 5.11. Cat Playing a Bagpipe, Book of Hours for use of Rome (Hours of the Virgin Office of the Dead) Paris, 1460, MSM. 0282, Folio 133v., J.P. Morgan Library, New York

Other miscellaneous religious books such as the *Moralia in Job* written in the latter half of the 12th century also include portrayals of the cat. In an initial letter of the manuscript a spotted cat claws a mouse and holds one in its mouth, while a dog bites the cat's back. In a theological miscellany by William Peraldus there are contributions from our infamous cat hater Alain de Lille[†], who probably didn't know that cats would decorate its pages. In the middle of one of the pages a striped cat sits and looks at a mouse in front of it. On the next line down a larger mouse, perhaps a rat, sits underneath the cat. A page from *The Pontifical of Guillaume Durand,* created before 1390, shows a rather pleased rat with a bird perching on its paw sitting astride a leashed cat *(figure 5.12).*

In the bottom margin of a page in the *Missale Romanum* (1420-1499) a cat follows a large mouse. In another text of a prayer book, a brown monkey wearing a red hat holds a white cat in the left margin of a richly illuminated page. And finally, in the *Breviary of Eleanor of*

[†] Alain de Lille associated the cat with the Cathars and claimed they were heretics.

Figure 5.12. Rat Riding a Cat, Before 1390, MS 0143, Folio 076v, Pontifical of Guillaume Durand, La bibliothèque Sainte-Geneviève, Paris

Portugal (1500), a cat sits atop a tree looking down at a man praying.

In addition to religious works, many other books of the Middle Ages in both Europe and Asia include illustrations of cats. In a medieval medicine and herb book dating to 1195 a cat crouches in a small square inserted between the lines of a page. In the Persian book, *The Benefits of Animals* (1297-1298), a female cat carries one live kitten toward three dead kittens lying in front of her, while a woman holds out her hands sympathetically *(figure 5.13)*. And in a leaf from an Arabic book dating to 1350 a cat and dog fight. In the *Tacninum Sanitatas* (1370-1400), a medieval medical book based on an earlier Arab text dating to the 11th century, a cat sits contentedly guarding a cheese shop from rats.

Even in one French poetry book written in 1350 entitled *Les Voeux de Paon* a large fanciful flower peacefully separates a cat and a dog on one page; whereas, on another, a woman threateningly chases a cat with a spindle. In this same book a cat is also pictured listening intently to a jester playing a rebec. In a later medical book from Italy dating to around 1440, a cat and mouse appear at the bottom of the page. All over the world during this time the cat was a subject of

Figure 5.13. Female Cat Carries One Kitten to Three Dead Ones, The Benefits of Animals, Persian 1297-1298, MSM 500, Folio 49v, J.P. Morgan Library, New York

interest and had already cleverly managed to insinuate itself into domestic life. The cat's prominent presence in these illustrations as a dog hating, rat catching predator proved that it served the interests of its keepers.

The Cat in Medieval Literature and Poetry

By the 12th century the cat had transitioned from solely a model for illustrations to a full blown character in medieval literature. The cat's first starring role was as *Tibert* in the story *Reynard the Fox*. Written by Pierre de St. Cloud in 1175, it is an allegory of the struggle amongst peasants, aristocracy and clergy. Reynard is a treacherous villain who in one scene tricks Tibert the cat into going into a priest's barn where Reynard promises there will be plenty of mice on which he can feast. However, Reynard knows full well that there will be a trap set since he had entered the barn the night before and had killed a hen. Poor unsuspecting Tibert enters the barn only to be caught in a trap and then beaten so badly that he loses an eye. In some medieval depictions of this scene Tibert escapes and wreaks revenge upon the priest who owns the barn by attempting to castrate him *(figure 5.14)*.

Figure 5.14. Cat Castrates Priest,
Reynard the Fox, Wilhelm Von Kaulbauch, 1846

The story of *Reynard the Fox* became so famous that Geoffrey Chaucer borrowed parts of it and used them in his *Canterbury Tales.* Later even Shakespeare would borrow the name Tybalt (for the King of Cats), for a character in *Romeo and Juliet:* Although Chaucer only briefly mentions the cat in *The Summoner's Tale* when a friar removes a cat from a bench on which he wants to sit, there are other references to the cat in both *The Manciple's Tale* and *The Wife of Bath's Prologue.* In *The Manciple's Tale*, Chaucer writes,

Lat take a cat, and fostre hym wel with milk
And tender flesh, and make his couche of silk,
And lat hym seen a mous go by the wal,
Anon he weyveth milk and flesh, and al,

And every deyntee that is in that hous,
Swich appétit he hath to ete a mous (Pollard, 1894, pp. 325-326).

In *The Wife of Bath's Prologue* cats are mentioned again.
Thou seydest this, that I was lyk a cat;
For whoso wolde senge a catte's skyn,
Thanne wolde the cat wel dwellen in his in;
And if the catte's skyn be slyk and gay,
She wol not dwelle in house half a day;
But forth she wole, er any day be dawed,
To shewe hir skyn, and go on a caterwawed (Pollard, 1894, p. 15).

The act of singeing a cat's fur or cutting its tail off represented doing almost the same thing to a wife in order to keep her at home and under control. Chaucer highlighted the belief of the time that it was woman's nature to stray just like the cat. Earlier in 1320, a Franciscan friar by the name of Nicholas Bozon stated that, "a cat must stay home by shortening her tail, cutting her ears and singeing her fur, women can be kept at home by shortening their dresses, disarranging their headdresses and staining their clothes" (Rogers, 2006, p. 35). In addition, women were often forced to put their hair up into a bun and have it scorched, and likewise cats had their fur burned (Karras, 2005, p. 90). Another gruesome way to keep a cat home was to cut its ears off. Thank goodness women didn't have to endure this cruelty! "Those which will keepe their cattes within doors, and from hunting Birds abroad, must cut off their eares, for they cannot endure to have drops of raine distil into them, and therefore keep themselves in harbor….They cannot abide the savour of ointments, but fall madde thereby; they are sometimes infected with the falling evill, but are cured with Gobium" (Ashton, 1890, p. 156).

Cutting the ears off a cat was also a punishment for unwanted behavior. The story of Duncan, a Scottish cat who had a taste for cheese and had his ears cut off after being caught stealing the precious commodity, is ultimately a sad one. His owner found him lying almost dead after having been hanged for the theft. Bereft with grief, he took poor little Duncan in his arms and said,

Did I not tell you little Duncan,
You had needs of being wary;
When you went where the cheeses were,

The gallows would teach you how to dance.
Evil is it, earless cat,
They have killed, because of cheese;
Your neck has paid for that refreshment,
At this time, after your death.

After some time the cat began to come to life again, and his loving owner went on to say,

A hundred welcomes wait you, cat,
Since in my lap you've chanced to be;
And, though I do not much liberty allow,
Many have you greatly loved.
Are you the uniformed cat that Fionn had,
That hunted wild from glen to glen?
Had Oscar you at the Battle of Bal-sguinn,
And left your heroes wounded there?
You drank the milk Catherine had,
For entertaining minstrel and meeting;
And why should I praise you?
You migh to be, like my kitten,
On the bill side seeking mice,
'Neath grayish grassy stems and bramble bushes (Campbell, 2003, pp. 40-41).

There is no record of Petrarch (1304-1374) writing about his cat. Even so, this great poet laureate of Rome, and the creator of the term 'Dark Ages', was known to have loved his cat so much that he had it mummified after its death and placed in a glass case in his house in Arqua, Italy *(figure 5.15)*. A travel journal written in 1893 offers a description of his house and the cat. "From this dining-room opens, to the right, the door of the room which they call Petrarch's library; and above the door, set in a marble frame, with a glass before it, is all that is mortal of Petrarch's cat, except the hair. Whether or not the fur was found incompatible with the process of embalming, and therefore removed, or whether it has slowly dropped away with the lapse of centuries, I do not know; but it is certain the cat is now quite hairless, and has the effect of a wash-leather invention in the likeness of a young lamb. On the marble slab below there is a Latin inscription, said to be by the great poet himself, declaring this cat to have been "second only to Laura."[†] We may, therefore, believe its virtues, have been rare enough; and cannot well figure to ourselves Petrarch sitting before that wide-mouthed fireplace, without beholding also the gifted cat that purrs softly at his feet and nestles on his knees, or, with thickened tail and lifted back, parades loftily round his chair in the haughty and disdainful manner of cats" (Howells, 1872, p. 226).

Figure 5.15. Earliest image of Petrarch's Cat Found in Giacomo Filippo Tomasini's, Petrarcha Redivivus, Massimo Ciavolella and Roberto Fedi, eds., Padua, 1635

During the 13th and 14th centuries the cat became an important symbol of the beauty of nature in Persian poems. Julaluddin Rumi

[†] Laura was Petrarch's muse.

(1207-1273) in the *Divan-I Kabir* writes,

Rosebuds
Surrounded by thorns:
Mother cat carrying babies in mouth
(Fragos, 2005, p. 36).

Around the same time as Chaucer and Petrarch, a Persian Sufi Master named Hafiz (1325-1389) also wrote a poem about his cat.

Who Will Feed My Cat
I
Will need
Someone to feed my cat
When I leave this world,
Though my cat is not ordinary.
She only has 3 paws:
Fire, air,
Water
(Ladinsky, 1999, p. 145).

A cat plays a pivotal role in the true story of Sir Richard Whittington, who became the Lord Mayor of London from 1397-1420, and was knighted by Henry V. The story, not written down until 1605, describes the plight of a poor, destitute orphan by the name of Dick Whittington. The boy goes to London in search of a better life and is taken in and given a job by the Fitzwarrens, a merchant family. Given a room that is filled with rats, he buys a cat with his first penny earned. The cat soon kills all the rats and because it is such a good ratter, it is taken aboard the Fitzwarren's ship. While traveling, the captain sells the cat for a handsome treasure to the King of Barbary, who was also plagued by such vermin. When the ship returned, the treasure was shared with the boy who became a wealthy man and the Lord Mayor of London three times *(figure 5.16)*. Even though based on a similar Persian tale written in the 10th century, there is no doubt that Dick Whittington was a real person who became a rich and benevolent man giving generously to many charities. As touching proof that Lord Whittington never forgot to whom he owed his gratitude, there is a bas-relief, which was part of a

15th century chimney piece in Whittington's home, showing a boy with a cat in his arms. Discovered in 1862, it is now housed in the Gloucester Folk Museum.

Figure 5.16. Lord Mayor of London, Dick Whittington, by R. Elstrack, 1618

The Cat in Medieval Art

From literature the cat sprang onto medieval European canvases depicted as a force of evil and chaos, fertility and licentiousness, a mouse catcher, or simply as a disinterested spectator. In the 1475 painting *Pilate Washes his Hands,* a white cat lies at the side of Pilate perhaps an indication of the influence of evil as Pilate sentences Christ to death. In the 1480 painting *Girl Making a Garland* by Hans Suess Von Kulmbach, a girl sits in a window frame making a garland. The sash says "forget me not" while a white cat sits in the opposite blackened window frame disinterestedly watching her. In another work from the same year, anonymously painted in the style of the Venetian school, entitled *Birth of the Virgin,* a tranquil domestic scene reveals a woman just having given birth, sitting up in a bed ready to accept some eggs offered to her by St. Anne. Another woman in the forefront of the painting has just washed and swaddled the new born Mary, while a dark colored cat walks alongside the bed, having just entered the room from the open door on the right of the picture. The cat could be a representation of the usual housecat, but its color makes us think that it may forebode some sort of doom. It could, of course, simply be a reference to fertility. In the 15th century painting by Israhel Van Meckenem, *The Spinner and the Visitor (figure 5.17)*, a male visitor holds his sword in a suggestive manner as a cat, a symbol of temptation, looks at us. The painting is a representation of solicitation, the woman a prostitute.

Figure 5.17. The Spinner and the Visitor, Israhel van Meckenem, 1495/1503, National Gallery of Art, Washington, D.C.

During this period, Chinese Ming Dynasty artists, unlike their European counterparts, focused their paintings on cats in tranquil natural outdoor settings. In *Cats and Bamboo* by Shen Chou (1427-1509)*(figure 5.18)* two white cats with red tassel and gold bell collars are demurely looking toward the artist, while a third brown cat approaches the other two. In *Cats and Grasses,* also from the Ming Dynasty, T'ao C'heng portrays twenty-two cats in various poses enjoying a day out. Moreover, the Emperor Hsuan Tsung (1426-1435) is said to have found great pleasure in painting cats in his garden. Depicted as a seemingly peaceful part of an accepted nature, there is great care taken in these cats' representations, which are permeated with a certain love and respect.

Figure 5.18. Cats and Bamboo, Shen Chen-Lin, Ching Dynasty 1644-1912, National Palace Museum, Taipei

Cat Inventions

Not only were cats inspirations for paintings, but they also became the models for strange tortuous inventions. In 1549, a cat organ was made in honor of Philip II of Brussels. A large bear played the organ that contained up to twenty cats perched in separate compartments. The parts of their tails that extended outside the box were tied to cords attached to the keyboard. When the bear hit a key, it pulled the cat's tail, and the cat would scream, amusing sadistic onlookers (Champfleury, 2005) *(figure 5.19).*

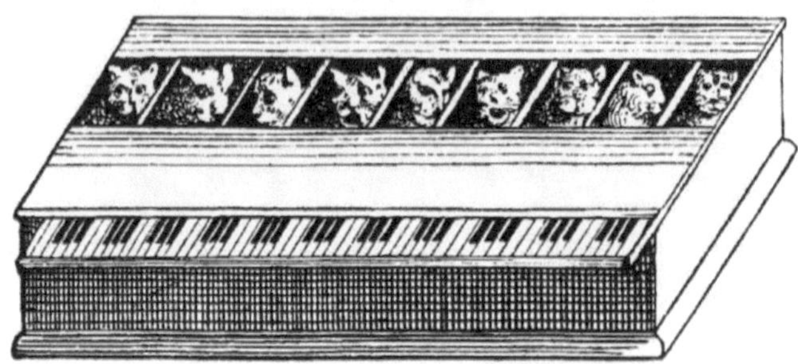

Figure 5.19. Cat Organ, Gaspar Schott, Magia Naturalis, 1657

Cats' tails were also used as an inspiration for an instrument of human punishment. The cat-o-nine-tails consisted of nine round spiked metal balls interspersed down two leather straps which could easily slice into vulnerable flesh *(figure 5.20).*

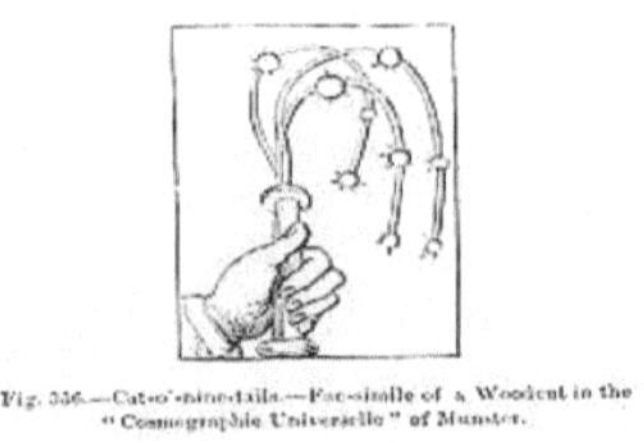

Figure 5.20. Cat o'Nine Tails, Woodcut, 1549,
Cosmographic Universelle of Munster, Basle

Another odd invention, created by Conrad Kyeser (1366-1405), a German engineer, was a battle wagon made in the shape of a cat. Using the cat's fear-inspiring presence to further strike terror into those who would come upon it, Kyeser did not forget to include the cat's sharpened claws (Kieckhefer, 2000). Later, cats would also be expected to participate in warfare. In a 1607 drawing, a German fortress is an object for attack by fire. Attached to the backs of a cat and dove are flammable bombs that they must carry to the fortress in order to destroy it kamikaze style *(figure 5.20).*

Figure 5.21. Ein wahres Probiertes und Pracktisches geschriebenes Feuerbuch, Franz Helm, 1607, Folger Shakespeare Library, Washington, D.C.

Witchcraft and Persecution and the Supernatural Abilities of Cats

During roughly the same time that Emperor Hsuan Tsung was lovingly painting cats in China, in Europe, with the advent of witch and heresy trials ushered in by the Inquisition, the cat was being subjected to the cruelest period of its history. Swept up into the divine plan of the church to undermine the power of women and to eradicate the ancient pagan beliefs, the black cat, in particular, became the symbol of witchcraft and heresy. In part, the cat's own double nature aided its persecution. In many ways, the elusive feline stands between this world and the unknown making it a dualistic, mystical creature. Suddenly appearing in a room and then disappearing, needy yet aloof, lazy yet attentive, loving yet vicious with eyes that seemingly see into one's soul, the cat is unpredictable, and can never be completely tamed. Unlike the subservient, dependent dog, it cannot be controlled and sets the terms of any relationship. Hence, our frowned-upon feline and, to some extent, women were feared and loathed by men in the Middle Ages, who deluded themselves with the idea that they were the masters of this world and should hold dominion over all. Even so, not everyone detested the cat during this time, and society reflected the dichotomy of this love/hate relationship.

The first truly abominable act in the whole repertoire of diabolical plays wherein the cat was the main tortured character had been going on in Scotland since pagan times, and was appallingly last practiced on the Island of Mull in the seventeenth century. Taigheirm, which means to summon evil spirits, required a brutal sacrifice of black cats to the devil in order for the torturers to be granted two wishes. The last two Scots to practice this horrendous rite of continuously roasting live cats on a spit were Lachlan Maclean and Allan Mac Echan. Commencing at midnight between Friday and Saturday, the rite lasted four days and nights. Impaled on a spit, cats were slowly burned alive so that their shrieks of pain would be audible to the dark spirits that the two men wished to summon. Once one cat finally died, another was immediately put upon the spit so that hardly any lapse in the cries of pain occurred. After some time, black cats were said to have started flying around the barn or house where the rite was performed calling out, "Laclain oer," or "Injurer of cats" (Van Vechten, 1921, p. 100), even so, these two cowardly men were able to continue turning the spit. Finally, a huge black demon cat would materialize and threaten the men to make them stop. Once the four days had passed, and dozens upon dozens of cats had been killed, the men, due to their vicious acts, were free to demand their wishes of wealth and prosperity. The devil then, disguised as the demon cat, begrudgingly granted all their wishes.

The ritual of the Taigheirm was perhaps the most shocking evidence of the cat being equated with the devil, but not long after the *Vox in Rama*, as previously discussed, was issued in 1233, accusations of witchcraft involving the cat began to rise amongst common people. Usually these accusations were founded on disputes between neighbors over land or animals or even based on maniacal schemes of stealing a person's cash wealth. One of the first accusations of witchcraft was brought against the Lady Alice Kyteler in Kilkenny, Ireland in 1318. The sinister plot revolved around the fact that she had been married four times, and her step children wanted her fortune. Luckily for the step children, it was just at this time that the inquisition had arrived in Ireland offering them the opportunity to accuse her of sorcery and witchcraft by claiming that she had cast spells that had aided her in the murder of her previous husbands. They also accused her of communicating with Robin Artisson, a demon that appeared before her as a cat. Fortunately, due to her being a woman of wealth and social standing, she managed to escape to England and save her life.

In 1323, a group of monks, of the Cistercian order near Paris, sought to recover some money that had been stolen from their monastery. Desperate to find the culprit, the monks consulted a sorcerer who instructed them to bury a black cat in a box at the middle of four crossroads. The trapped cat was given an air tube by which to breathe as well as food and water. The monks were told to stand in a circle on a cat skin and summon the demon *Bevita,* who would tell them who the thieves were (Kieckhefer, 1998). After some time, a hunter with his dogs passed by. The dogs smelled the cat and began to dig up the box. Once the cat was discovered, the authorities in the city of Chateau Landon found the maker of the box and one of the monks. After confessing to witchcraft, both were burned at the stake with one having the live cat tied around his neck (Williams, 1967).

An accused witch, Riccola di Puccio, was executed in Pisa in 1347 for using magic to cause a husband and wife to split up. The spell called for her to recite charms over an egg from a black hen summoning *Mosectus, Barbectus* and *Belsabact.* She then cut the egg in half and gave one part to a female cat and the other to a male dog while chanting, "In the name of the aforesaid demons may one love between the two be sundered as this egg is divided between dog and cat, and let there be such affection between them as between this dog and cat" (Kieckhefer, 1998, p. 74).

In 1427, St. Bernardo of Siena confessed that he had erroneously indicted a woman, whom he had accused of killing a child and thirty others, by applying an emollient to her skin that supposedly left a mark in the shape of a cat.

Cats, already feared as being vampires in Japan and China and in some Baltic countries, were soon accused of such activity in Europe. Antonio Guaineri, a respected physician, claimed in 1440 that witches could assume the form of cats, and these witches became vampires that drank the blood of infants (Waddell, 2003) *(figure 5.22).* Later on, cats would be known to suck blood from varying places on their mistresses' bodies. Marks of this kind found on the body of an accused witch invariably lead to a trial, torture, confession and perhaps execution. [†]

As early as 1211, Gervase of Tilbury claimed from his own experience that women prowled around at night as cats and, if hurt in any way, showed those wounds on their bodies (Summers, 1926). A German, Johann Hartleib, in 1456 recounted a story of a cat that had attacked a child and escaped even though stabbed by the father. Later, a woman was found to have a wound in the same place as the cat (Trachtenberg, 1939), indicating that the woman was able to shape shift; consequently, she was accused of being a witch.

Another such story is of a haunted mill that had been set on fire threetimes until a travelling tailor offered to keep watch over it. The tailor drew a circle in white chalk inside the mill and wrote the Lord's prayer around the sides of the circle and sat within it for protection. At midnight, cats started to enter the mill carrying pitch, and after heating it, tried to tip the pot over in order to set the mill on fire.

[†] Hans Baldung Gruen's (1484-1545) ink etchings portray women as either a "Madonna or whore" representing either good or evil. Cats are a symbol of the beast within women (Waddell, 2003, pp. 85-88).

Figure 5.22. The Witches Sabbath, Studio of Hans Baldung Grien, 1515, Musée de l'Oeuvre Notre-Dame, Strasbourg

The tailor, still within his circle of safety, somehow managed to scare the cats away. However, one cat tried to attack him, and the tailor, in self-defense, cut off its paw. The next day the mill was still standing, but the miller's wife was in bed with a bleeding stump (Reppelier, 1901).

In a story from Ireland, a fisherman's wife in Connemara always had an abundance of fish. However, every night she noticed that a huge cat would come in and eat all her best catch. So she lay in wait for the cat, and one night it appeared. A huge black cat broke into the house and moved toward the fire where it turned around and growled at the old woman. The cat, annoyed at how she had maligned him, jumped upon her and scratched and bit her. A man confronted the cat in the doorway as it was making its escape and beat it with his stick. As a result, the cat jumped up at him and scratched his face and hands. The cat then said, "It is time for my dinner. Where is my fish?" The woman screamed at the cat to get out and leave, but instead the cat sat and ate to his heart's content. The woman tried to beat him without success, as each time she tried the cat would jump upon her and scratch and bite until blood flowed. Finally, she brought a bottle of holy water and threw it on him, and the cat shriveled up into nothing[†] (Speranza Wilde, 1887).

On the other hand, around the same time there were positive stories about the cat. In another Irish story, an old woman was sitting up late spinning when she heard a knock at the door. She asked who was there three times, but there was no response. The woman grew angry but when she heard a frail voice say, "Judy, let me in I am cold and hungry, let me sit by the fire," she felt sorry for the person begging for kindness behind the door and opened it. To her amazement, a black cat and her two white kittens walked in and went directly to the fireplace where they proceeded to warm and clean themselves while purring with satisfaction. The black cat finally told the old woman that the fairies had wanted to hold a meeting in her house, but because the old woman had stayed up so late, she had prevented them from doing so. In retaliation, they swore to kill her; however, the black cat had saved her life. Do not interfere with the fairy hours, the black cat advised, and asked Judy for a drink of milk. Thanking the woman, the black cat and her kittens ran up and out of

[†] The same fate was experienced by the Wicked Witch of the West in the *Wizard of Oz*.

the chimney leaving a small piece of silver for the woman's kindness (Speranza Wilde, 1887).

In a story from France, a woman went to sleep over-night in a haunted house with her little white cat and a leg of lamb in order to earn 1,000 francs. That night she cooked the lamb and shared it with her cat. The cat, being grateful for her mistress' generosity, advised her on how to avoid the wrath of the ghost. She did as the cat said and the ghost did not bother her, and she received the sum of money. The next night her neighbor decided to try and earn the same reward. She, likewise, took her cat and some lamb into the haunted house. However, she did not share the lamb with her cat. The angered cat then hid and let the ghost eat her mistress, a clear message not to deprive a cat.

Malleus Maleficarum or *The Hammer of Witches*

Unfortunately, in 1484, the fate of women and cats took a dire turn for the worse when the Dominican inquisitors Heinrich Kramer and Jacob Sprenger complained to Pope Innocent VIII that witchcraft and heresy were consuming all of Germany and nothing was being done about it. The Pope thus issued a *Papal Bull Summis Desiderantes Affectibus* stating that all witches and their cats were to be burned at the stake. For the next three hundred years more than nine million people would be executed, the majority marginalized women and children (Gage, 1893).

Three years later, in 1487, the *Malleus Maleficarum*, or *Hammer of Witches*, written by both Kramer and Sprenger was published. Divided into three parts, the first outlines the belief in witches as heresy and explains why women are more apt to be witches than men. The second part explains the investigation of witchcraft and the third describes the legal proceedings that are required for those accused of witchcraft.

Women were more likely than men to be suspected of having relations with the devil because they were considered mentally and physically weak. In fact, through men's interpretation of the Bible, women were defective because they were created from Adam's bent rib. According to *Ecclesiasticus XXV* women were evil. Who could argue with the quote from the Bible, "Thou shalt not suffer a witch to live"? Seen as deceivers and feeble minded, women and their cats were the prime suspects of practicing witchcraft. Even the word *femina* (woman) meant lacking in faith. The *fe* prefix means faith and *minus* means less (Gage, 1893 p. 224). "A witch was held to be a woman who had deliberately sold herself to the evil one; who delighted in injuring others, and who, for the purpose of enhancing the enormity of her evil acts chose the Sabbath day for the performance of her impious rites, and to whom all black animals had special relationship" (Gage, 1893, p. 217). A poem from the Middle Ages states:

Woman is a snake to be venomous.
Woman is a lion for imperiousness.
Woman is a leopard to devour.
Woman is a fox to deceive.
Woman is a bear to be combative.
Woman is a dog to have sharp senses.
Woman is a cat to bite with teeth.
Woman is a rat to destroy.
Woman is a mouse to be sneaky
(Fiero, Pfeffer, & Alain, 1989, p. 124).

Men in the Middle Ages feared women, feared their pagan powers, and feared their ability to create life. So intimidating were women that the *Malleus Maleficarum* even addressed their ability to emasculate a man by removing his "virile member" (Summers, 1926).

In Chapter IX of the *Malleus Maleficarum,* the authors built upon earlier accounts of women changing themselves into cats by citing an account of a man near Strasburg who was attacked by a large cat while chopping wood. When he tried to chase it away, two more cats appeared and scratched and bit him. Looking quite disheveled after these cat attacks, he was arrested and charged with beating three women in the village. The man pleaded that he had not done this crime, as he had never beaten a woman in his life. He thought back to the time of the accused crime, and he told the judge that he had been in the woods and had in fact at the same time beaten three large cats. The judge realizing that the man had been set upon by devils, released him, and the incident was quietly forgotten (Summers, 1486/2009). Accusations of witchcraft became easy excuses for the abuse of women as well as cats.

A similar story about an English hunter originates from Scotland.

The hunter, who had set up camp for the night with his dogs, was confronted by a large cat that moved close to his fire and, as he claimed, grew larger and larger. The hunter, fearing for his life, took the silver buttons off his coat and used them to fire at the cat. The cat ran away, but the next day, since he was a doctor, a farmer sent for him. It seems the farmer's wife had fallen ill, and when the doctor examined her, he found that she had been shot in the right breast from which he extracted a silver button, the same silver button that he had used the night before (Campbell, 2003).

Because of religious unrest, Henry VIII thought it prudent to enact a law against witchcraft in 1542 making the act a felony punishable by death. Ironically, even though most regarded cats as evil, the cunning Cardinal Wolsey seemed to have liked cats very much. So much so that he allowed them to sit next to him in his chair while he gave important audiences.

The first of the famous witch trials held in a secular English court in 1556 involved a cat. The old and frail Elizabeth Francis was accused and confessed to practicing witchcraft in Chelmsford, Essex *(figure 5.23)*. Elizabeth was the descendent of a witch, her grandmother, and had been instructed in the black arts from the age of 12. Her grandmother had also given her a white spotted cat named Satan, who ate bread and milk and occasionally begged for droplets of Elizabeth's blood as a reward for doing her bidding. At first Elizabeth only desired wealth and asked her cat to give her sheep, which he did. Unfortunately for Elizabeth, these ill-gotten sheep soon all died and left her as poor as she had been before. Then she asked her familiar Satan to make Andrew Byles, a rather well-to-do man, marry her. The cat demanded that she let Byles have his way with her first, and after so doing, he refused to marry her. Much angered, she begged the cat to take away all his wealth and kill him, and this Satan did. Again she asked for a husband and the cat granted her a marriage with a not so wealthy man with whom she had a baby girl. Unhappy in her marriage and with her baby daughter, she asked Satan to kill the helpless girl. This was done, and the daughter died at six months of age. Next, according to Elizabeth's wishes, her husband then became lame after the cat was said to have lain in his shoes and turned into a toad. After keeping Satan for nearly 15 years, she gave him to Agnes Waterhouse, also known as Mother Waterhouse, who was 64 years old at the time. Agnes was the first woman to be executed for witchcraft because she had been accused of causing the death of William Fynne and of also causing the deaths of many of her neighbors' livestock through the powers of her familiar, Satan, the cat. Agnes was eventually hanged in 1566, as was Elizabeth in 1579. Elizabeth had been continually in and out of jail for almost ten years until she was finally charged with causing the death of Alice Poole through the use of witchcraft in 1578.

Both executions took place after Queen Elizabeth I implemented a new stricter Witchcraft Act in 1563. The Queen, by no means a cat lover, had great numbers of the abused animals stuffed into an effigy of the pope and burned for entertainment at her coronation ceremony.

In contrast, Elizabeth's adversaries seemed to like cats. The Duke of Norfolk, after having been committed to the Tower by Queen Elizabeth I for plotting to take over her throne, was regularly visited by his favorite cat that entered his cell through a chimney. However, this was not the first story of a cat saving an inmate in the Tower. Sir Henry Wyatt (1460-1537) perhaps had his life saved by a cat too. Imprisoned by Richard III for supporting Henry Tudor, he was sent

Figure 5.23. Hanging of the Chelmsford Witches, Woodcut, 1556, English Pamphlet, 1589

to the Tower of London to starve in a cold bare cell. If not for the kindness of a stray cat that he befriended, he might have died. "A cat came one day down into the dungeon unto him, and as it were, offered herself unto him. He was glad of her, laid her on his bosom to warm him, won her love. After this she would come every day unto him divers times, and when she could get one, bring him a pigeon....Sir Henry Wyatt, in his prosperity, for this would ever make much of cats, as other men will of their spaniels or their hounds" (Bell, 1854, p. 12). A stone memorial to this cat can still be seen in The Church of St. Mary the Virgin and All Saints in Maidstone, Kent. Located near the altar, it states, Sir Henry Wyatt, "...who was imprisoned and tortured in the tower in the reign of Richard the third, kept in the dungeon, where fed and preserved by a cat" (Stall, 2007, p. 45).

Also imprisoned in the Tower of London, it was a cat, too, that saved Henry Wriothesley, the 3rd Earl of South Hampton, by climbing down the chimney with morsels of food. Imprisoned there by Queen Elizabeth for supporting the rebellion against her by the Earl of Essex, Wriothesley's constant companion was his cat, Trixie, who kept him company until he was released by James I in 1603. A portrait of the Earl, with his loyal cat sitting beside him, still proudly hangs in Boughton House, Northamptonshire *(Figure 5.24).*

Figure 5.24. Wriothesley and Cat, Trixie, 1603, Broughton House, Northamptonshire

However, on the other hand, weird stories of cats and witchcraft continued, and in 1569, a servant, Agnes Bowker, claimed in court that she had had sexual relations with a cat six or seven times, and that she had, consequently, given birth to a stillborn cat[†]. The claim was so contentious that it even reached the Privy Council of Queen Elizabeth I. Bowker's midwife even supported her story by swearing that she had received a stillborn skinned cat *(figure 5.25)*. It was not a coincidence that Agnes's neighbors reported days earlier that she had wanted to borrow their cat for some reason. And even though they had refused to give her their cat, it mysteriously vanished and was never seen again. The court also found that the so called still born cat had meat and straw in its gut; thus, proving that it was no monster at all. In reality, Agnes most probably murdered an ill-conceived child and hid it with the aid of her midwife and tried to confuse the authorities with this fantastic story of giving birth to a cat (Cressy, 2000).

Figure 5.25. Agnes Bowker's Cat, 1569, British Library, London

The curse of witchcraft even infiltrated the upper classes, and in

† Stories of women giving birth to monsters were quite common in Europe in the 15th and 16th centuries (Paré & Pallister, 1995).

1590, after accusing Mother Samuel of witchcraft, Lady Cromwell dreamt of a cat that threatened to tear off her skin and flesh. Little over a year later the Lady fell ill and died. Mother Samuel, accused of bewitching the Lady and causing her death, was executed. The poem, *The Old Woman and Her Cats,* written by John Gay, could have been written for poor Mother Samuel.

> A wrinkled hag of wicked fame,
> Beside a little smoky flame
> Sat hovering, pinch'd with age and frost;
> Her shrivell'd hands, with veins emboss'd,
> Upon her knee her weight sustains,
> While palsy shook her crazy brains:
> She mumbles forth her backward prayers,
> An untamed scold of four score years:
> About her swarmed a numerous brood,
> Of cats, who lank with hunger mewed.
> Teased with cries, her choler grew,
> And thus she sputter'd, 'Hence ye crew!'
> Fool that I was, to entertain
> Such imps, such fiends, a hellish train!
> Had ye been never housed and nursed,
> I for a witch had ne'er been cursed.
> To you I owe that crowds of boys
> Wory me with eternal noise;
> Straws laid across my pace retard,
> The horseshoe's nail'd (each threshold's guard)
> The stunted broom the wenches hide,
> For fear that I should up and ride;
> They stick with pins my bleeding seat,
> And bid me show my secret teat.'
> 'To hear you prate would vex a saint;
> Who hath most reason of complaint?
> (Replies a cat) Let's come to proof.
> Had we ne'er starved beneath your roof,
> We had, like others of our race,
> In credit lived as beasts of chase.
> 'Tis infamy to serve a hag;
> Cats are thought imps, her broom a nag!

And boys against our lives combine,
Because, 'tis said, your cats have nine'
(Gay, 1822, pp. 58-59).

The next year, 1591, saw John Fian become Scotland's most famous warlock. He and his coven attempted to sink King James I's ship on its way to Denmark by tying a cat to a dismembered corpse which they then threw into the sea while chanting incantations. Invoked by the spell, a storm arose and forced the ship to return to harbor. As a result, Fian was tried for high treason and witchcraft for the attempted murder of King James I and Queen Anne and was subsequently executed.

For having visited Adam Clark and his wife in the form of a cat, Isobel Grierson was tried for witchcraft on March 10th, 1607. Clark claimed that Grierson, in the company of many cats, had terrorized them throughout the night by making frightening noises in their bedroom. Accused of other such incidents of witchcraft, she was eventually burned at the stake.

Further inflaming the fire of witchcraft accusations that revolved around cats, in the same year, 1607, Edward Topsell (1572-1625) first published his book *The History of Four Footed Beasts*, wherein he stated, "The familiars of witches do most commonly appear in the shape of cats, which is an argument that this beast is dangerous to the soul and body." He also added that cats were able to cause serious illnesses. Their breath could cause consumption, their teeth vicious bites, and swallowing their hair would cause suffocation (Topsell, 1658, pp. 81-83) *(figure 5.26)*.

Ambroise Paré, a famous physician of the age, had earlier claimed that by even looking at a cat a person could come under its spell and lose consciousness and that sleeping with one was highly risky as it would cause tuberculosis (Rogers, 2006). Joannes Jonstonus (1603-1675) wrote a similar book to that of Topsell's and agreed with both Topsell and Paré that cats' "breathe is pestilent, and breeds consumptions, and …, for the brains are poyson, and made an Uratislavian Girl mad..."(Jonstonus, 1678, p. 97). However, Jonstonus does claim that there are several cures to be gotten from cats. He states that, "The ashes of the head burnt in a pot and blown into the eyes, clears them; the flesh sucks weapons out of the body, and eases emrods, and back-ache; the liver burnt to powder eases the

Figure 5.26. Cat, Edward Topsell's Four Footed Beasts, 1658, University of Houston Digital Library

stone, the gall fetches away a dead child, the fat is smeared on gouty parts; the pisse stiled helps the thick of hearing, the dregs of the paunch with rosin, and oyl of roses in a suppository, stops woman's flux of blood. Some mince the flesh, and stuff a fat goose with it, salt, and rost it by a soft fire, and distill it, and annoint gouty joints with successe. The fat keep iron from rusting" (Jonstonus, 1678, p. 97). Ironically, the black cat would later become a cure for a myriad of diseases. Its skin, blood and excrement would be used to cure shingles, hives, ringworm, stys, and fevers (Bergen, 1899).

Some years after Topsell's book was published, the witch trials were still quite common. The trial of Joan Flower and her two daughters Margaret and Phillipa Flower, also known as the witches of Belvoir, took place in 1618. Joan and Margaret worked for the Earl and Countess of Rutland at Belvoir Castle until Margaret was eventually let go for stealing. Seeking revenge, they set about a plan to kill the Earl's son. Rightly suspecting some sort of retribution, the Earl had them all imprisoned. Shortly after their incarceration their mother died, and the two sisters confessed that their mother had taken the glove of Lord Henry Roos, the Earl of Rutland's eldest son, and had rubbed it on the back of Rutterkin, her cat familiar. After that she boiled the glove and stabbed it with a sharp knife and buried it in a dung heap while reciting certain curses over it with the intent to do him harm. Not long afterward, the Lord fell ill and died. The two sisters were convicted and hanged.

The young infamous Puritan Witch Finder General, Matthew Hopkins *(figure 5.27),* and his partner John Stearne found plenty to keep them busy in the districts of Essex, Suffolk and Norfolk. Through torture, the finding of so called witches' marks, and the himself receiving 20 shillings for each conviction (Ross, 1868, p. 169). It is often written that Hopkins was in the end convicted of being a witch just like his victims after having failed the swimming test; dreaded swimming test[†], Hopkins managed to make a fine living for however, this is just a myth, and he died quietly of consumption in 1647 (Hopkins, Stearne, & Davies, 2007).

Anne Randall and Anne Goodfellow, both interrogated by Hopkins, claimed to have had cat familiars. Anne Randall stated that she had two familiars who came to her in the form of a blue cat and kitten. Their names were Hangman and Jacob, and they had regularly sucked her blood for thirty years[†] as evidenced by marks found on her body. Randall, intent upon using the powers of darkness, sought revenge from her neighbor, William Baldwin, by asking her familiars to kill his horse after he had refused to give her wood. She also confessed to asking Hangman to kill a hog of Stephen Humfries' simply because he said something to her she did not like. Goodfellow confessed that after her aunt's death, the aunt's spirit, which had been taken over by the Devil, came to her in the form of a white cat. The cat asked her to deny her faith in the covenant and

[†] A test initially used by James I to discern whether or not a person was a witch. The accused was lowered into a body of water and if she floated that meant she had not been baptized and was a witch. If she sank, she was cleared of witchcraft and of course ironically died from drowning.

[†] Note that the life span of a cat is about 18 years.

Figure 5.27. Frontispiece from Matthew Hopkins' The Discovery of Witches (1647), showing witches identifying their familiar spirits.

even renounce her own baptism. This she did, and the cat bit her on her second finger and sucked her blood to seal the pact.

Even though a law instituted in 1653 in Scotland stated that all those who used witchcraft or even pretended to would be punished by death, the most virulent use of the law came about during the Scottish witch hunts of 1661 and 1662 incited by the influence of John Kincaid and John Dick. Isobel Gowdie, one of 660 accused of witchcraft, (Burton & Grandy, 2004), was tortured and confessed and then convicted for claiming that her sisters regularly turned into cats to run wildly through the night. However, she told the court that she herself preferred to turn into a hare[††]. Having denounced Christianity, she had become one of 13 members of a coven. The court realized that she was mentally infirm and was perhaps lenient in her sentence as there are no records of her execution.

Alice Duke of Somerset in 1664 was convicted of witchcraft for confessing that her cat would regularly suck her right breast at around 7pm every night, and she would thus fall into a trance (Van Vechten, 1921). Likewise, in 1665 Abre Grinset, an old homeless woman, confessed that a grey-black cat came to her at night and sucked blood from a mark on her body.

In Cornwall in 1671 a witch, accused of crimes against the state, was blamed for causing the English fleet some problems during a campaign against the Dutch. She was said to have also caused a bull to kill a member of Parliament, and to top it off, was even accused of causing the barrenness of the queen. Ridiculous as it seems, all these accusations stemmed from the fact that a cat had been seen playing near her house (Notestein, 1911).

The craze of witchcraft affected all of Europe. In a small Swedish village in 1699, over 300 children from the ages of 6-16 were believed to have been taken over by the devil, who gave them each a cat whose job it was to steal cheese, milk and bacon as offerings to their demon king. The children willingly confessed and fifteen of them were executed. Thirty-six were beaten every Sunday in front of the church doors, and the others were given varying punishments (Repplier, 1901 p. 46).

Jane Wenham was convicted and sentenced to death on the testimony of James Burville and Ann Thorn, who both claimed to have seen a cat with Jane's face. However, Jane confessed to having heard cats speaking to her and was also convicted for speaking to the devil. Neighbors noticed that cats surrounded her house, and those inside the house could hear scratching and screaming that resembled children's cries coming from outside (Bragge, 1712).

Incidents of witchcraft not only plagued Europe, but also spread to the New England colonies as well. In 1619, *Dalton's Country Justice* was published and included instructions on how to deal with witchcraft (Taylor, 1908) *(figure 5.28)*. On the morning of

[††] It is interesting to note here that both hares and cats were called 'puss' until the 18th century.

Figure 5.28. Riding a Cat Backwards, German Woodcut, 15th Century

December 8, 1679, a man claimed that while his wife was making their bed, she had been accosted by a flying cat, and that a cane had danced around the room (Burr, 1914). The Salem witch trials took place between 1692 -1693 and more than 20 were executed. In one case, two girls had fits and illnesses believed to have been caused by the devil. Elizabeth, the daughter of Reverend Samuel Parris aged 9, and his niece Abigail aged 11, blamed 3 women, two of whom, Sarah Good and Sarah Osborne, were elderly and lived on charity. The third was Parris's slave, Tituba, who confessed that she had been controlled by the devil and had even seen his familiars, one of which was a red cat. Tituba managed to escape execution, and Sarah Osborne died before her trial. However, Sarah Good was eventually executed by the Reverend Nicholas Noyes. Upon the gallows Sarah continued to proclaim her innocence even though Noyes still insisted that she was a witch. Sarah cursed him, "You are a lyre; I am no more a witch than you are a Wizard, and if you take away my life God will give you Blood to drink" (Calef, 1700, p. 209). Legend has it that Noyes suffered a cerebral hemorrhage and died choking on his own blood.

As late as 1718 a Scottish man, William Montgomerie, claimed that he could no longer live in his house, as it was filled with cats that spoke to each other. Losing his temper one night, he went out and killed two and wounded a third. Days later a witch, Helen Andrew, had died and another had committed suicide and a third woman, Margaret Nin-Gilbert, had lost her leg. She and the others were immediately thought to have taken the form of the cats that had entered Montgomerie's house. Nin-Gilbert was imprisoned and eventually confessed. She died there most probably from complications associated with her leg (Oldfield, 2003).

The stubborn fear of witchcraft hung on, and even though the church had abolished all witchcraft laws in 1736, in 1749 a German nun was beheaded for talking to her three cats that were of course considered demons (Aftandilian & Scofield, 2007) *(figure 5.29).*

Paranoia and injustice continued in the Western world, with sporadic cases of witchcraft still appearing in the 18th, 19th and even into the 20th century. Even though some courts began to refuse to hear witchcraft cases in the 1700's[†], in Britain a woman was accused of witchcraft as late as 1944. In the United States the threat of witches continued, and in an 1867 trial, a woman was accused of practicing witchcraft by using the blood of a black cat to cure a child with the croup. Amazingly, witnesses agreed that the cure had been successful (Gage, 1893). And even in early 20th century Baltimore two women of impeccable behavior were said to have gone out at night and changed into cats. They were cured only by rubbing salt on their skin (Cross, 1919).

MAGIC

No description of the cat and its involvement with witchcraft is complete without the accompanying examples of it as an essential ingredient in magic. It was commonly believed that the blood of a black cat when mixed with certain herbs was extremely powerful for incantations and to also ward off disease. Only three drops of the cat's blood were needed, and these were gotten by making a small cut on its tail. In addition, the ashes of a black cat were very potent to magicians. By killing a very black cat without any white on it, and taking only its heart and mixing it with swallows and burning them together, one could produce a very strong magical brew (Thompson,

[†] Scotland repealed its witchcraft act in 1735.

Figure 5.29. Witches with a Cat, Jacob de Gheyn II, 1600's, State Hermitage Museum, St. Petersburg

1908/2003). Another belief was that if a black cat were killed and a bean placed in its heart before it was buried, beans sprouting from that seed would contain amazing magical powers. If a man placed one in his mouth, he would become invisible and be able to go anywhere without being seen (Speranza Wilde, 1887). Yet another spell for invisibility was made by gathering the following ingredients: a black cat, a new pot, a mirror, a piece of flint, an agate, charcoal, dry wood, and water drawn from a fountain at midnight. After lighting a fire, the cat would be put in the pot making sure that the cover was held down firmly with the left hand without moving or looking behind. After the cat had boiled for 24 hours, the contents were put into another dish. The cat carcass then would be thrown over the left shoulder while repeating these words, *Accipe quod tibi do et nihil amplius.* Then by chewing the bones of the cat while looking into a mirror and walking backward, the spell would be complete (Van Vechten, 1921 pp. 101-2). In the states of Georgia and South Carolina, witches were believed to be able to receive power from particular bones from a black cat. A concoction to see what others cannot was to mix the bile of a male cat and the fat of an entirely white hen and anoint the eyes with it (Kieckhefer, 2000). Another measure used to gain unusual power was to pet a cat, and by so doing it was believed that it could help a woman find a husband. Likewise, eating a cat would cause a girl to become pregnant. In 1929, it was reported in a Pennsylvania newspaper that the whole county of York had been taken over by witchcraft, evidenced by a lack of black cats which had been boiled alive in order to procure a special bone to use as a protective amulet against Satan (Oldfield, 2003).

In summary, during both the Dark and Middle Ages, weak corrupt woman and the maligned misunderstood cat had fallen into the nether world of men's fears. Cat and woman, whose fates had been intertwined from the very beginning of history, fell from graced goddesses to vilified symbols of the devil, witchcraft and magic. Their degradation and persecution would be complete, but once these fears began to wane, over time both cat and woman would slowly rise from this reviled abyss. But yet, they would never again be regarded as the powerful goddesses they had once been.

Chapter Six

THE EARLY MODERN PERIOD

The Early Modern Period (1500-1700), was an era marked by global exploration, the rebirth of classical thought and religious reformation. Christopher Columbus' ships were the first to sail across the world in 1492, probably carrying cats to kill mice and rats, much as the ancient Phoenician vessels did centuries before on their first voyages around the Mediterranean. And just as the cat spread its domain through Phoenician trade, cats aboard Columbus' ships most likely stayed on land to become the first to colonize the Americas. If not, records indicate our seafaring feline certainly accompanied the Jamestown settlers in 1607, but undoubtedly met a grim fate during the period of starvation when the settlers ate whatever they could. Pocahontas, who saved the life of John Smith, was given a domesticated cat, and cats accompanied the Pilgrims on the Mayflower in 1620. Upon landing in the New World, at least one adventurous feline must have scurried over Plymouth Rock.

The Renaissance and the Cat in Art

As the Renaissance brought forth new ideas based on the merging of classical philosophy, mythology and Christianity, the Early Modern Period also became a time for enlightened thinkers to excel at art and literature. Moving away from the vacuousness of the Dark and Middle Ages meant the beginning of a rebirth for the cat as well. However, as with all movements forward, there were sporadic lapses which hung heavy upon progress. As people's fears and superstitions continued, the cat was still to carry its unjustified burden of being a representative of the devil far into this era, evidenced by unrelenting witch trials that lasted into the 1700's. The Reformation, too, produced many instances of cruelty to cats as did other episodes of religious and social unrest. Even so, the cat, an enduring emblem of the ability to overcome torture and suffering, continued to survive, and one by one progressive thinkers of this era came to respect our domestic feline for its untamed and inscrutable nature.

The Renaissance, which ushered in a rebirth of classical thought, first started in Italy and then spread to the whole of Europe. Renaissance artists such as Bosch, Dürer, Ghirlandaio, DaVinci and many others produced exquisite paintings that included the cat as a symbol of domesticity, fertility-lust, treachery and evil. Most often cats found their place in religious paintings, but towards the end of the century they also became the pampered companions of women in portraits and necessary additions to realistic domestic scenes.

Figure 6.1. The Garden of Earthly Delights (Detail), Hieronymus Bosch, 1480, Museo del Prado, Madrid

In Hieronymous Bosch's (1450-1516) *The Garden of Earthly Delights (figure 6.1)*, a cat carries off a rat in its mouth at the bottom of the triptych's left panel, which depicts heaven. In the right wing panel of the triptych, *The Temptation of St. Anthony*, the saint, a hermit that was said to be constantly harassed by demons, is in meditation; a cat, while trying to grab a fish, hisses at a nearby naked woman in a bush (*figure 6.2*). Women's licentious[†], evil nature is symbolized by the clawed feet, horns and the snake shaped train of her dress. St. Anthony's, and perhaps our only salvation, is Christ directing our attention to his own crucifixion (Grössinger, 1997, p. 1).

Figure 6.2. The Temptation of St. Anthony (Detail), Hieronymus Bosch, 1480, Museo del Prado, Madrid

Relying heavily upon classical Greek models, the 1504 engraving, *Adam and Eve* by the German, Albrecht Dürer (1471-1528) (*figure 6.3*), captures Eve right at the moment she accepts the apple of knowledge from the serpent. Surrounding both Adam and Eve are a variety of animals that symbolize differing human temperaments. The cat represents the trait of easily angered or irritated; the rabbit as hopeful; the ox as calm; and the elk as melancholy. However, since this picture portrays the instant of original sin, the cat and mouse are also symbols of men and women's sexual lust, while the parrot represents love. The cat's tail touches the back of Eve's heel, associating it with feminine fertility and temptation, while Adam seems to be almost

[†] It was in the 15th century that French words such as *la chatte, le chat, le mine* and even the English pussy cat started to be used as slang terms for female genitalia. A proverb of the time states, "He who takes good care of cats will have a pretty wife" (Brenner, 1999).

stepping on the mouse's tail in a sort of cat and mouse yin and yang.

In a much later version, a voluptuous Adam and Eve happily involved in the sensualities of life, and totally unconcerned with the consequences of their actions, highlight Hendrik Goltzius', *The Fall of Man* (1616) *(figure 6.4).* Much like Albrecht Dürer's sterner faced

Figure 6.3. Adam and Eve, Albrecht Dürer, 1504, J.P. Morgan Library, New York

Adam and Eve, each animal in the painting holds symbolic significance, and the cat once again takes center stage to prominently represent lust and desire.

Domenico Ghirlandaio specifically painted the *Last Supper* (1480) *(figure 6.5)*, for Dominican Monks that must not be forgotten for their part as inquisition judges, who undoubtedly caused the deaths of many so-called witches and their loving cats. The fresco, located in San Marco, Florence, shows Christ and the apostles sitting on one side of a long banquet table. While Judas, separated from all that is good, sits opposite Christ on a three legged stool, perhaps representative of the trinity. A lone cat, symbolic of Judas's treason and the influence of evil, intently watches nearby.

The greatest of the Renaissance artists, Leonardo da Vinci, found

Figure 6.4. The Fall of Man, Hendrik Goltzius, 1616, National Gallery of Art, Washington, D.C.

Figure 6.5. The Last Supper, Domenico Ghirlandaio, 1480, Fresco, Monastery San Marco, Florence

the cat an intriguing subject that he captured in many sketches and paintings. For example, a cat is present in the 1478 sketch, *Study of the Madonna and Child with Cat (figure 6.6),* and even more prominent in his 1513 sketch of twenty cats in various poses *(figure 6.7).* From da Vinci's many depictions of cats, and a quote attributed to him which states, "Even the smallest feline is a masterpiece," we can assume that the great Renaissance man both respected and liked cats very much. Da Vinci, a known vegetarian, wrote in his notebook that humanity is not "king of the animals" but only "king of the beasts". The visionary also wrote, "The time will come when men such as I will look upon the murder of animals as they now look on the murder of men."

Figure 6.6. Study of the Madonna with Child and Cat, Leonardo da Vinci, 1478, The British Museum, London

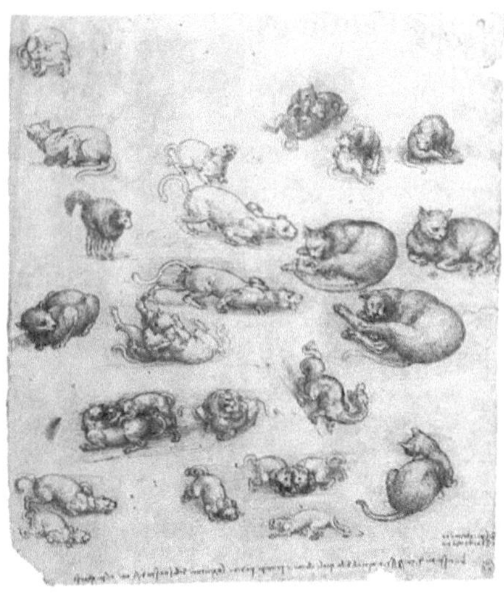

Figure 6.7. Study Sheet with Cats, Leonardo da Vinci, 1513-1515, Royal Library, Windsor

Reminiscent of the cats seen on ancient Egyptian tomb walls sitting under women's chairs, a whitish grey cat sits underneath Mary's chair as a symbol of fertility and motherhood, and perhaps as a reference to Isis, in Bernardino Butinone's (1436-1507) *Adoration of the Magi.*

Figure 6.8. Adoration of the Magi, Bernardino Butinone, 1485-1495, Bequest of Helen Babbott Sanders, Brooklyn Museum, New York

The Cat in Mannerist Paintings

Hans Baldung Grien (1484-1545), a student of Albrecht Dürer, usually known for his renditions of profane witches, in a later allegorical Mannerist work entitled, *Music* (1529) *(figure 6.9)*, a harmless white cat sits next to an elongated figure of a young woman with a book in her left hand, leaning on a musical instrument with her right. Grien probably based this painting on the symbolism of Isis/Bast and her sistrum.

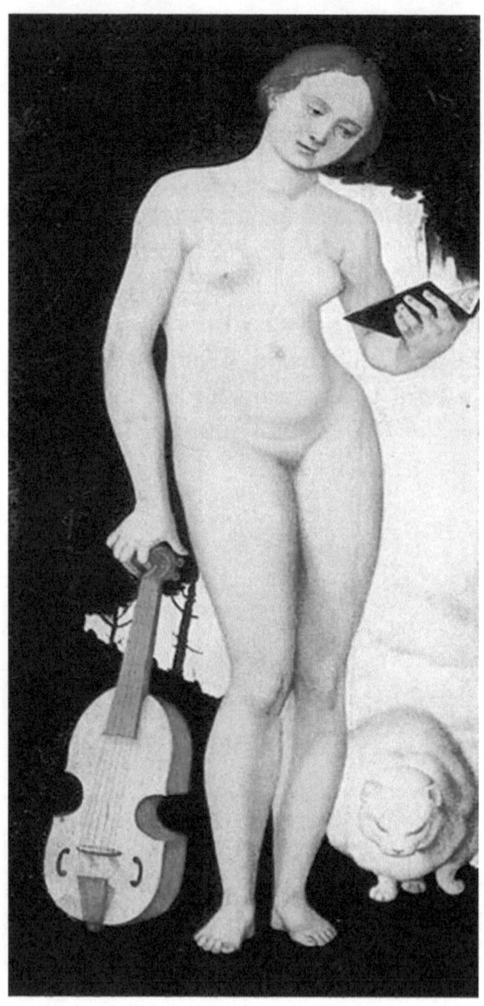

Figure 6.9. Music, Hans Baldung Grien, 1529, Alte Pinakothek, Munich

Paintings in the Mannerist style, an artistic movement which blossomed from the Renaissance, focused less on naturalistic portrayals. In Jan de Beer's 1520 *Annunciation (figure 6.10),* a white cat with the face of a lamb sits peacefully as an angel flies by. In sharp contrast to de Beer's *Annunciation,* in Lorenzo Lotto's Venetian version, *(figure 6.11)* painted seven years later, the angel Gabriel inspires fear and hesitancy as Mary, seen with her hands up, turns away from him as he appears to her in her bedroom. Outside the window on a cloud, God points a demanding finger at her, insinuating that Mary is the chosen one. In back of her, a small brown cat jumps away from the angel in seeming fright, sympathetically mirroring Mary's own feelings. The message is that Mary must accept her fate, and accept the role she has been given by God.

Figure 6.10. Annunciation, Jan de Beer, 1520, Museo Thyssen-Bornemisza, Madrid

Figure 6.11. Annunciation, Lorenzo Lotto, 1534, Museo Civico, Recanati, Italy

Ten years later in 1585, Barocci's pen and ink drawing of the *Annunciation (figure 6.12)* is much different. Here the angel seems kind, and Mary, with a halo over her head, is pleased to be in his presence. The situation is so peaceful that a cat, positioned in the left hand side foreground, contentedly takes a nap; very different from the frightened cat seen in Lotto's *Annunciation.* The symbolic merging of Isis/Bast into Mary is obvious in many of the paintings of the Assumption where Mary, with a crescent moon often painted below her feet, is associated with the sun, stars and moon (Oldfield, 2003).

Figure 6.12. The Annunciation, Federico Barocci, 1585, The Art Institute of Chicago

Cats appear in many of the paintings of the *Supper at Emmaus,* produced in the early to mid-1500's. Painters such as Pontormo, Titian, Tintoretto and Bassano imparted the domesticity of a scene by adding a cat and/or dog usually at odds over some sort of food, and sometimes just an empty bowl *(figures 6.13, 6.14).*

Figure 6.13. Supper at Emmaus, Titian, 1530-1533, Musée du Louvre, Paris

Figure 6.14. Supper at Emmaus, Francesco Bassano, 1570, Museo Nacional del Prado, Madrid

Francesco Bacchiacca's *Portrait of a Young Woman Holding a Cat*, 1525 *(figure 6.15)*, reflects the woman's wild unpredictable animal nature that matches her companion's. The woman's feral eyes tempt us; the colors of her hair and the cat's are similar; and her dress matches its spots. As she tenderly embraces the cat, she peers out at us in a captivating, feline manner. In another portrait of a woman holding a cat, Bacchiacca interestingly has the woman caressing the cat with two fingers extended; the others folded under, a distinct reference to the sign of the cross *(figure 6.16)*.

Figure 6.15. Portrait of a Young Woman Holding a Cat, Francesco Bacchiacca, 1525-1530, Private Collection

Figure 6.16. Woman with a Cat, Francesco Bacchiacca, 1540, Staatliche Museen Berlin

In a much different style from Bacchiacca's, Hans Asper's 1538 portrait of *Cleophea Holtzhalb (figure 6.17),* shows her holding a cat in her left arm and patting a dog with her right hand. The dog bares its teeth antagonistically, while the cat glares menacingly as it stretches out its claws. Cat and dog represent opposites: male devotion and female deceit.

Figure 6.17. Portrait of Cleophea Holzhalb, Hans Asper, 1538, Kunsthaus, Zurich

The 1563 *Wedding at Cana* by Paolo Veronese *(figure 6.18)*, originally commissioned by the Benedictine Monastery of San Giorgio of Maggiore in Venice, highlights both the sacred and profane. On the right side of the painting, a brown and white cat lies on its side, playfully grabbing a face on a large urn with almost human like hands, oblivious to the potential danger of a lithe greyhound, in the middle of the picture, that has spotted it.

Figure 6.18. Wedding at Cana, Paolo Veronese,1563, Musée du Louvre, Paris

Figure 6.18a. Wedding at Cana, Detail of Cat

In Federico Barocci's 1575 *Madonna of the Cat (figure 6.19),* John the Baptist sits next to Mary and teases a cat with a goldfinch, a symbol of Christ's passion. While Joseph looks on, Mary cradles the baby Jesus in her left arm.

Figure 6.19. The Madonna of the Cat, Federico Barocci, 1575, National Gallery, London

The Cat in Baroque Art

By the 1590's, the Baroque style was just beginning to spread across Europe. Noted for its dramatic use of line and vivid color, the style, through its energy and movement, expressed power and control. Favored by the church, the main patron of art at the time, the easily understood Baroque style conveyed the church's religious, moral and ethical messages to the common people.

In Annibale Carracci's *Two Children Teasing a Cat (figure 6.20),* a boy and a girl hover over a cat on a table and dangle a crayfish in front of it. The lesson: if you play with fire, you will get scratched. In much the same manner as Carracci's painting, Judith Leyster, a Dutch genre painter, reveals the same message in her 1635 *Boy and Girl with a Cat and an Eel (figure 6.21).* Here, the boy holds an eel up in order to entice a cat; the girl pulls the cat's tail. Undoubtedly upset, it is almost certain that the cat will eventually scratch and bite them both.

Figure 6.20. Two Children Teasing a Cat, Annibale Carracci, 1590, Metropolitan Museum of Art, New York

Figure 6.21. A Boy and Girl with a Cat and Eel, Judith Leyster, 1635, National Gallery, London

In *Still Life with Dead Game and Fruit and Vegetables* (1614) *(figure 6.22)* by Frans Snyders, the animals represent virtue and vice, good and evil. A barely visible predatory black cat, with piercing yellow eyes, eagerly peers out from under a table watching two cocks fight —the loser, his intended victim.

The German painter, Chrisoph Paudiss, caught an unusual domestic scene wherein an old man seems to be irritatingly interrupted from reading by a playful cat. In an entirely different vein, in Giovanni Lanfranco's 1620, *Naked Man Playing with a Cat in Bed (figure 6.23),* the cat represents woman, lust, and desire in a rather risqué painting for the time.

The Dutch painters of the golden age turned to realism instead of religious subjects, as portrait painting was much more lucrative. Dutch genre paintings tend to illustrate everyday life at all levels of society, and cats, essential to most households, are often in these still lifes and portraits.

Figure 6.22. Still Life with Dead Game, Fruits and Vegetables, Frans Snyders, 1614, Art Institute of Chicago

Figure 6.23. Naked Man Playing with a Cat in Bed, Giovanni Lanfranco, 1620, Commerce d'Art, London

In *The Katzen Familie* (1650), the Dutch painter Jan Steen *(figure 6.24)* captures a lively group of people playing instruments, singing and drinking. Amidst this raucous din, our gaze gravitates to two women in the upper left hand corner of the painting, who have turned their attention to a mother cat and her kittens.

Figure 6.24. The Katzen Familie, Jan Steen, 1650, Magyar Szepmuveszeti Muzeum, Budapest

In Steen's *The Dancing Lesson (figure 6.25)*, four children sit on and around a table. One older boy holds a cat up by its front paws, so it can stand on its back legs to dance to the tune the girl in the foreground plays on a flute. The children are laughing; the dog barking. Polite society at this time did not condone dancing, so it is likely that the cat is a metaphor for lust and lechery, and to accentuate this attitude, at the very top of the picture, a man looks down judgmentally. In a somewhat similar scene, in Steen's *The Family Concert,* a joyous group sits together at a table, playing their various instruments, while a cat crouches over an empty bowl with a dog approaching in the foreground.

Figure 6.25. The Dancing Lesson, Jan Steen, 1665-1668, Rijksmuseum, Amsterdam

Dutch genre paintings did not always mirror happy and gay scenes; they also touched upon the everyday domestic problems that had to be dealt with. In *The Idle Servant (figure 6.26)* by Nicolaes Maes, a mistress confronts issues arising from having an inept housemaid. A cat, in the upper right hand corner of the picture, is making away with a bird, symbolic of the chaos in the house, while the housemaid and her employer contemplate the mess of dishes on the floor.

Figure 6.26. The Idle Servant, Nicolaes Maes, 1655, National Gallery, London

In the Dutch Baroque painting of Gabriël Metsu, (1629-1667) *Woman Feeding her Cat (figure 6.27),* a woman sits with a plate on her lap, a dead chicken in the forefront and a fallen flower from a bouquet both symbolizing death. She offers a dark striped cat, begging at her knee, a morsel. The viewer cannot help but be affected by this dim, lonely scene.

Figure 6.27. Woman Feeding her Cat, Gabriël Metsu,1662-1665, Rijksmuseum, Amsterdam

Etchings also conveyed dramatic energy, as seen in *Man with Cat on Shoulder and Mouse in Hand* by Cornelius Danckerts (1630-40). The man looks almost frightened by what the cat will do to get the mouse he holds in his hand; whereas in *Two Children with Cat*, the two boys laugh heartily, while holding a more contented feline *(figures 6.28, 6.29).*

Figure 6.28. Man with a Cat on Shoulders and a Mouse in Hand, Cornelius Danckerts, 1630-1640, Rijksmuseum, Amsterdam

Figure 6.29. Two Children with a Cat, Cornelius Danckerts, after Frans Hals, 1630-1640, Rijksmuseum, Amsterdam

In the Italian Baroque painting of Giuseppe Recco (1634-1695), *Cat Stealing Fish (figure 6.30),* a cat sits atop a crate, and true to its nature, claws at a fish fallen from the box. The lighting is intense and the action of the cat grabs our attention.

Figure 6.30. Cat Stealing Fish, Giuseppe Recco, Metropolitan Museum of Art, New York

In the French genre painting, *Peasant Interior with an Old Flute Player*, (1642) *(figure 6.31)* by Louis Le Nain, a cat sits peacefully to the right of the matriarch's chair; opposite sits a dog. Again, the animals are added to accentuate the idea of happy domesticity. Ironically, it was Champfluery, author of *Cats Past and Present,* who through his friendship with Courbet, managed to get Le Nain's paintings into the Louvre in the 1800's due to a revived interest in peasant life.

Cats Portrayed on Ceramics

Not only were cats in paintings, but they were also copied onto ceramic ware. In the late 1600's, a cat jug made from Delftware,

Figure 6.31. Peasant Interior with an Old Flute Player, Louis Le Nain, 1642, Kimbell Art Museum, Fort Worth

which originated in the Netherlands, must have been enjoyed in a well-to-do household. A cat portrayed on a Burselem dish from 1680, with an almost human face, looks straight at us, its tail almost camouflaged by the lines on its body. A brave mouse runs up the right side of the plate near the cat's head (Grigsby, 2000).

The Reformation

Shadowing the great rebirth of the Renaissance was the Reformation. When in 1517 Martin Luther nailed his 95 theses to the door of the Castle Church in Wittenburg, a reform movement sprang up, Protestantism. The cat, somehow representative of Catholicism, and always a victim of man's abuse, became a key symbol for English reformist protests. Often the cat represented priests and clergy, as in a horrifying episode of animal cruelty that occurred in Cheape, England, recounted in a chronicle of the time. "The same 8th April being then Sunday, a cat with her head shorne, and the likenesse of a vestment cast over her, with her fore feet tied together, and a round piece of paper like a singing cake[†] between them, was hanged on a gallows in Cheape, near the cross in the parish of St. Matthew; which cat, being taken down, was carried to the Bishop of London, and he caused the same to be showed at

Figure 6.32. A Cat Hung up in Cheapside, Habited like a Priest, From Fox's Book of Martyrs, 16th Century

[†] It is interesting to note that the 'cake' can also be a reference to a cathouse or prostitution since the cat is referred to as 'her' (Patterson, 1993, p. 146).

Paul's Cross by the preacher, Dr. Pendelton" (cited in: Jardine, 1847, p. 46) *(figure 6.32)*. Protestants also burnt effigies of the pope stuffed with live cats that would shrilly cry in pain, somehow pleasing the mad crowds. "Belling a cat", *(figure 6.33)* first mentioned in *Bidpay* and then in *Aesop's Fables*, during the Reformation, came to mean that there was a need to depose a Bishop, and would pose the question who would be brave enough to do it?

Figure 6.33. Belling the Cat, (Detail) Pieter Bruegel, 1559, from Netherlandish Proverbs

Protestants, as an insult to Catholics, published various engravings of friars and nuns in compromising circumstances. In one engraving a friar teaches cats to sing. In the center of the picture, a friar stands with a cat on both his shoulders and one on his head. Three more cats are on the table in front of him with their paws on sheets of music.

The lyrics are: The organs are disliked I'm wonderous sorry,
For the music is our romish Church's Glory.
And ere that it shall music want I'll try,
To make these cats sing and that want supply
(Hattaway, 2002, p. 363).

Other strange abominations occurred, such as the eventual Bishop of London, John Stokesly, being charged with baptizing a cat in order to find lost treasure in his parish of Calley Weston, Northamptonshire. Even though he was cleared of the charges, he would be called "heretic-hemtu" or "bloody bishop christen-cat" (Cressy, 2000). Another Bishop, Matthew Wren, was highly upset at the fact that protesters roasted a live cat on a spit outside his church during the New Year's Day service, which disrupted his sermon with the unlucky animal's tortured screams.

The cat quickly became the victim of not only Protestant politics, but Catholic as well. In the mid-1600's, the Catholics used the cat to protest against the Roundheads. They shaved the poor feline's head and cut off its ears and proclaimed it a Roundhead. This was the ultimate insult. By associating the Roundheads with animals, the Catholics maligned them as inferior to man (Fudge, 2004).

Strange incidences of cat cruelty as well as other absurdities continued, and in 1662, in Henley, Oxfordshire, as a silly prank, five young men baptized a cat in the church's font and named him Tom. Meanwhile, games such as "cat clubbing" were enjoyed by the Dutch. A cat was placed in a barrel that was hung from a tree; and the players would try to break it, and set the cat free, in order to chase it down and capture it again, and have the whole episode replayed (Klein, 2006). Another cruel Dutch tradition, which was mainly practiced for newlyweds, was *Ketelmusik*. A group of musicians, in a crude effort to serenade newlyweds, beat pots and pans and pulled the fur of cats so that their screams accompanied the music. This ritual spread to Germany, where it was called *Katzenmusik*, and even to France, as *fair le chat* (Ruff, 2001).

To top these bizarre happenings, according to an old Germanic law, cats could attend trials and serve as witnesses against thieves and murderers. In fact, in a 16th century trial, a French lawyer, Bartholomew Chassenée, defended rats against the charge of destroying a barely crop. He claimed that the rats could not appear in court for fear of a cat hindering their trip (Evans, 1906).

Not all of the cat's adventures during the Early Modern Period are marked by cruelty and absurdity. Interspersed between tales of horrible abuses, stories and poems of gratitude to the cat have survived.

Sir Izaak Walton (1593-1683) in 1653 wrote in *The Compleat*

Angler, or, the Contemplative Man's Recreation, "When my cat and I entertain each other with mutual apish tricks, as playing with a garter, who knows but that I make my cat more sport than she makes me? Shall I conclude her to be simple, that has her time to begin or refuse to play as freely as I myself have? Nay, who knows but that it is a defect of my not understanding her language (for doubtless cats talk and reason with one another) that we agree no better? And who knows but that she pities me for being no wiser than to play with her, and laughs and censures my folly for making sport for her, when we two play together?"

Cats in Literature

Cats made their mark upon men's hearts, whether for better or for worse, throughout the literature of the Early Modern Period. John Skelton (1460-1529), a poet laureate under Henry VII and Henry VIII's Jester, wrote a poem much like Agathias did in AD 550 entitled, Philip Sparrow.

Philip Sparrow

When I remember again
How my Philip was slain,
Never half the pain
Was between you twain,
Pyramust this be, (tragic lovers in the tale by Ovid)
As then befell me.
I wept and I wailed,
But nothing it availed
To call Philip again,
Whom Gib[†] our cat had slain.

Oh Cat of churlish kind,
The fiend was in your mind
When thou my bird untwin'd!
I would thou hadst been blind!
The leopards savage,
The lions in their rage

[†] Gib is a reference to an old tom cat, derived from a contraction of the name Gilbert.

Might catch thee in their paws,
And gnaw thee in their jaws!
The serpents of Libany
Might sting thee venomously!
The dragons with their tongues
Might poison thy liver and thy lungs!
The manticors of the mountains
Might feed upon thy brains!

An it were a Jew,
It would make one rue,
To see my sorrow new.
These villainous false cats
were made for mice and rats.

From me was taken away
By Gib, our cat savage,

That in furious rage
Caught Philip by the head
And slew him there stark dead!
(Payne & Hunter, 2003, pp. 3-11).

In addition, Joachim du Bellay (1525-60) greatly loved and grieved the loss of his cat if only just because it offered him some respite from the gnawing rats and mice that plagued his mattress at night.

Eptiah on a Pet Cat

My life seems dull and flat,
And, as you'll wonder what,
Magney, has made this so,
I want you first to know
It's not for rings or purse
But something so much worse:
Three days ago I lost
All that I value most,
My treasure, my delight,
I cannot speak, or write,

Or even think of what
Belaud, my small grey cat
Meant to me, tiny creature,
Masterpiece of nature
In the whole world of cats,—
And certain death to rats!—
Whose beauty was worthy
Of immortality.

Then a detailed description of Belaud—

My only memory
Of him annoying me
Is that, sometimes at night
When rats began to gnaw
And rustle in my straw
Mattress, he'd waken me
Seizing most dexterously
Upon them in their flight.

Now that the cruel right hand
Of death comes to demand
My bodyguard from me,

My sweet security
Gives way to hideous fears;
Rats come and gnaw my ears,
And mice and rats at night
Chew up the lines I write!
(Gooden, 1946, pp. 26-31)

The English poet George Turberville (1540-97) proclaimed his love for his mistress by transforming into a cat.

The Lover, whose Mistress Feared
A Mouse, Declareth that he would
Become a cat if he might Have His Desire.
....I would become a Cat,
to combat with the creeping Mouse,
and scratch the screechy Rat.

I would be present, aye,
And at my Ladie's call,
To gard her from the fearfull Mouse,
In Parlour and in Hall;
In kitchen, for his Lyfe,
He should not show his hed;
The Pease in Poke should lie untoucht
When she were gone to Bed.

The Mouse should stand in Feare,
So should the squeaking Rat;
All this would I doe if I were
Converted to a Cat
(Gooden, 1946, p. 32).

The tutor to Louis XIV, Francoise de la Mothe Le Voyer (1588-1672) wrote an epitaph for the Duchess' of Maine's cat.

Puss passer-by, within this simple tomb
Lies one whose life feel Atropho's hath shred;
The happiest cat on earth hath heard her doom,

And sleeps forever in a marble bed.
Alas! What long delicious days I've seen!
O Cats of Egypt, my illustrious sires,
You who on altars, bound with garlands, green,
Have melted hearts, and kindled fond desires,
Hymns in your praise were paid, and offerings too,
But I'm not jealous of those rights divine,
Since Ludovisa loved me, close and true,
Your ancient glory was less proud than mine.
To live a simple pussy by her pride
Was nobler far than the deified"
(Gooden, 1946, p. 33).

Even the first great poet of Japanese Haiku, Basho Matsuo (1644-1694), mentions a cat.

> Why so scrawny, cat?
> starving for fat fish

or mice....
or Backyard love? (Yasuda, 1957)

Cat in Love
The lover cat
over a crumbled stone
comes and goes (Ueda & Basha, 1995 p. 39)

Cats' love
When it is over, hazy
moonlight in the bedroom
(Ueda & Basha, 1995, p. 337)

And the cat of course is mentioned in nursery rhymes.

"Jack Spratt
Had a cat;
It had but one ear;
It went to buy butter,
When butter was dear" (Van Vechten, 1921).

References to the cat in this period are not confined to poetry but also frequently appear in the very first pieces of literature. In Ludovico Ariosto's Italian farce, *The Pretenders* (1509), his character Carione states, "As if the six months that you have at home—and seven with the cat—" (Beecher, 2008, p. 64). The cat is already an important companion. In another comedy, *Cortigiana*, the author Aretino has his character Rosso state, "She was talking to Don Cerimonia the Spaniard. They were talking about going to some vineyard for supper—I don't know which one and I acted like Massino's cat." Parabolano asked, "What did Massion's cat do?" Rosso replied, "She closed her eyes to keep from catching mice" (Beecher, 2008, p. 126). Certainly, the woman does not want to be seduced. In another episode, Togna says to Ercolano angry that he has not been home, "I always have to eat with the cat." And in yet another play, *Piccolonini,* the character Vincenzio states, "—a cat would never fool with a mouse if he didn't expect to eat it in the end" (Beecher, 2008, p. 173).

Beware the Cat, the First English Novel

Perhaps not so surprising, the first novel written in English is entitled *Beware the Cat* by William Baldwin (1515-1563), and includes cats as the main characters. What dog could live up to this claim to fame? First published in 1570, during the Reformation, and set in Ireland, it is a satire on Catholicism; an attack on what Protestants considered superstitious religious rites. The character Streamer narrates the three part story, which is based on the premise that animals are capable of speech and reasoning, and that man can learn to understand them, albeit through some complicated magical spell. The plot revolves around the trial of the main female cat character, Mouse-slayer, who is charged with not abiding by the laws of the cat world, and shunning the advances of her admirer. Throughout the story, for the first time in any literature, the cats act like cats that possess great evil powers, unlike the character Tibert, in *Reynard the Fox*, who acts like a person. The story begins with an Irish soldier killing Grimalkin[†], the chief cat. A soldier and his servant, after stealing a cow and a sheep, take refuge in a church yard and kill and cook the sheep. When the meat is done, a cat comes begging. The soldier and servant give the cat some of their food until it is all gone. The insatiable cat eats the cow as well. The men, fearing for their own lives, run away. The cat chases them, and the soldier resorts to throwing a spear that hits and kills Grimalkin. After Grimalkin dies, a clowder of cats appears; and in revenge, they attack and kill and then, even eat the servant boy. The soldier, after escaping this horrifying experience, finally arrives home, and recounts the whole story to his wife, but little does he realize that his own cat is listening. His cat asks him, "Hast thou killed Grimalkin?!" (Hadfield, 2007, p. 142). Once hearing that he has in fact killed Grimalkin, his own infuriated cat jumps on the ill-fated soldier and strangles him. Here, the invincibility of the cats is a metaphor for the undying power of the Catholic Church, which ultimately cannot be destroyed.

Cats were not just included in novels, but also found their way into various plays. A cat literally had its first onstage role in the comedic play, *Gammer Gurton's Needle*, produced in the late 1500's. Gammer Gurton loses her needle while trying to stop a cat from drinking up the family's milk, and the poor feline, viewed as a

---

[†] Shakespeare took the name of Grimalkin from Baldwin (Ringler, 1979).

trouble-maker, is blamed for swallowing the needle. While the character Hodge is looking for the needle, he is frightened by the cat's eyes which appear like black burning coals. The cat then runs upstairs and Hodge breaks his leg while trying to catch it. The cat "— is left to fend for himself in a world that regards him as best a nuisance and at worst a portent. In this regard he may be viewed as a fairly typical early modern English cat" (Beecher, 2011, p. 110).

The Cat in Shakespeare

Many of Shakespeare's 37 plays have references to the cat, albeit always negative ones. And it was Shakespeare who borrowed the name Tybalt from the fable *Reynard the Fox,* and used it in his play *Romeo and Juliet,* wherein Mercutio insultingly remarks that Tybalt is a "rat catcher" and the "king of cats". He also refers to the cat's ability to have nine lives when, again, Mercutio remarks, "Good king of cats, nothing but one of your nine lives." The first witch in *MacBeth* says, "Thrice the brindled cat hath mew'd." And in another passage the witch says, "I come, Graymalkin." In *Henry IV* Falstaff says, "—I am melancholy as a gib cat—". In *The Merry Wives of Windsor,* Falstaff remarks that Pistol has "cat-a-mountain" looks, a reference to the term "gato-montes" derived from Spanish meaning wild cat. If the word cat was used, it was most likely a term of contempt, as in the *Tempest,* when Antonio states, "For all the rest, they'll take suggestion as a cat laps milk," and when Shylock says, "A harmless necessary cat". And also, in *A Midsummer Night's Dream*, where Lysander says, "Hang off, thou cat." Once more too, in *Coriolanus* it has the same meaning.

"Twas you incensed the rabble;
Cats, that can judge as fitly of his worth,
As I can of those mysteries which heaven
Will not have earth to know."

In *Much Ado About Nothing,* Shakespeare refers to the game practiced in Scotland, which was mentioned previously, where a cat was hung up on a cross beam between two high poles in a small barrel half filled with soot, and then men on horseback would ride back and forth trying to hit the barrel and break it, in order to release the cat for further torture and ultimate death. Benedick says, "Hang me in a bottle like a cat and shoot at me." Undoubtedly Shakespeare was not a fan of cats, but he did make many mentions of them in his plays, mostly using them as metaphorical tools to express the opinions of women and to describe their nature.

Puss in Boots

The popular story that we know today as *Puss in Boots,* originated as a fable written by Giovanni Straparola (1480-1557), as part of his *Facetious Nights.* The fable recounts the plight of three poor boys whose mother, Soriana, has only three possessions of value: a kneading trough, a pastry board and a cat. Knowing that she is soon to die, Sorianna gives away her possessions to her sons. The kneading trough she gives to the oldest son, Dusolino; the pastry board to the middle son, Tesifone; and the cat to the youngest son, Costantino Fortunato. From his name we can probably guess that his life will end happily. But the tale continues with the cat, a disguised fairy, feeling sorry for Costantino and promising to help him, "Costantino, do not be cast down, for I will provide for your well-being and sustenance, and for my own as well." The wily cat manages to kill a leveret[†] and takes it to the King of Bohemia as a gift from Costantino Fortunato. The king is pleased and asks the cat to stay to dine, and the loyal cat takes food home to Costantino where his brothers become jealous of his good fortune. The cat continues this ritual of offering the king game until one day he comes up with a plan. He asks Costantino to go to a nearby river, strip off his clothes and get in. Costantino does as the cat asks. When he is in the river, the cat starts yelling that his master is drowning. The sly cat knew that the king would be passing close by and would hear the cries for help. The king came to the rescue and invited Costantino back to his palace. Thinking that Costantino was rich, he decided that his daughter, Elisetta, should marry him. After they were married, Costantino worried that he had no house. The fairy cat managed to take care of that detail as well. Soon after the King died; Costantino was declared

---

[†] a young hare

Figure 6.34. Illustration of Charles Perrault's Puss in Boots, Gustav Doré, 1867

the new king of Bohemia, and lived happily ever after with his wife and children. At the end of this original version, the fairy cat is not mentioned at all.

In Giambasttista Basile's *Tale of Tales (Pentamerone)*, yet another version of the same story, some simple changes occur. The mother becomes a father; the main character's name changes to that of Cagliuso;[†] and the cat is referred to as "Her Royal Catness". The story follows essentially the same plot as Straparola's version, but varies in small details. More importantly, the characters are rougher,

[†] nest shitter

ruder and, perhaps, meaner. An example is when Cagliuso attends the banquet given by the King, he constantly worries about the rags that he had to take off after being in the river water. He says to the cat, "My little kitty, keep an eye on those rags of mine, for I wouldn't want anything bad to happen to them." And the cat answers, "Be quiet, shut your trap, don't talk about such trifles!" Obviously Cagliuso was not as smart as the cat and would ruin the plan. Cagliuso thanked the cat many times for his good fortune and promised that when she died, he would have her stuffed and put into a golden cage in his bedroom. The cat, not completely trusting of Cagliuso's promise, three days later pretended to be dead. When Cagliuso found the cat dead, he proclaimed, "Better her than us! And may every evil accompany her." When his wife asked what she should do with her body, Cagliuso answered, "Take her by her foot and throw her out the window!" The cat, hearing this, revives and runs away only after chastising Cagliuso. The moral that summarizes the story is, "May God save you from the rich who become poor and from the beggar who has worked his way up" (Canepa, 2007, pp. 167-68).

Puss in Boots by Charles Perrault (1628–1703), the story that we are familiar with today, is generally the same as the other versions, but does not offer the same moral. It instead offers a lesson that seems to hinge on the benefits of lying and being wealthy *(figure 6.34).*

The Cat in Spain

The Spanish writer Miguel de Cervantes mentions cats as devil possessed beings that frighten the windmill-chasing Don Quixote.

" —all of a sudden from a gallery above, that was exactly over his (Quixote's) window, they let down a cord with more than a hundred bells attached to it, and immediately after that discharged out a great sack full of cats, which also had bells of smaller size tied to their tails. Such was the din of the bells and the squalling of the cats...that...the contrivers of the joke...were startled by it, while Don Quixote stood paralyzed with fear; and as luck would have it, two or three cats made their way in through the grating of his chamber, and flying from one side to the other, made it seem as if there was a legion of devils at large in it. They extinguished the candles that were burning in the room and rushed about seeking some way of escape...Don Quixote sprang to his feet and, drawing his sword, began making passes at the grating, shouting out,

'Avaunt, malignant enchanters! Avaunt, ye witchcraft working rabble!'

...and turning upon the cats that were running about the room, he made several cuts at them. They dashed at the grating and escaped by it save one that...flew at his face and held on to his nose with tooth and nail" (de Cervantes, 2, 499).

But it is also a gold cat, with the word *Miau* under it, with which Cervantes adorns Timonel of Carcajon, Prince of New Biscay's shield, supposedly in honor of Miaulina, daughter of the Alfeniquen of the Algarve (Van Vechten, 1921).

Surely not to be included as great literature, in another Spanish book, *Libro de Cocina*, by Roberto de Nola, cook for the King of Naples, is a recipe for roast cat: *Gato asado como se quiere comer*. The recipe is as follows: First, catch the cat and then slit its throat, and cut off its head and throw it away (It was very important to throw the head away as it was believed that if the cat's brains were eaten, the person would go mad). Next, skin the cat and then wrap it in a cloth and bury it in the ground. After a day, dig up the cat and baste it with garlic and olive oil and roast it over an open fire. When completely cooked, again sauté with the garlic and olive oil (Ife, 1999).

The Cat in France

All animals were to suffer as a result of the philosophy of René Descartes (1596-1650), as according to Descartes, no animal had a soul or the ability to feel. In essence, they were just mechanical beings without emotion. His philosophy was highly influential in the 17th century, and caused animals to endure much pain and torture. Descartes reversed the philosophy of Michel de Montaigne (1533-1592) who believed that animals and humans were equal; in other words, no species was superior to another. This idea had in fact been explored in Montaigne's *An Apology for Raymond Sebond* (1576), wherein he writes, "When I play with my cat, how do I know that she is not passing time with me rather than I with her?" (Waddell, 2003).

Despite living during the same time as Decartes and the enduring witch trials, Cardinal Richelieu *(figure 6.35)*, Armand Jean du Plessis (1585– 1642), Louis XIII's chief minister, loved cats very much. So

Figure 6.35. Cardinal Richelieu with three kittens on his lap. Photograph by T.W Ingersoll, St. Paul, 1908, Library of Congress, Washington, D.C.

much so that he built a cattery at Versailles and even left money for the welfare of his cats after his death. Alexandre Landrin writes in *Le Chat*, "With Richelieu the taste for cats was a mania; when he rose in the morning and when he went to bed at night he was always surrounded by a dozen of them with which he played, delighting to watch them jump and gamble. He had one of his chambers fitted up as a cattery, which was entrusted to overseers, the names of whom are known. Abel and Teyssandier came, morning and evening, to feed the cats with patés fashioned of the white meat of chicken. At his death Richelieu left a pension for his cats and to Abel and Teyssandier so that they might continue to care for their charges. When he died, Richelieu left fourteen cats of which the names were: Mounard le Fougueux, Soumise, Serpolet, Gazette, Ludovic le Cruel, Mimie Piaillon, Felimare, Lucifer, Lodoiska, Rubis sur l'Ongle, Pyrame, Thisbé, Racan, and Perruque. These last two received their names from the fact that they were born in the wig of Racan, the academician"(Landrin, 1894, p. 93).Gaston Percheron writes, "History records that Richelieu with one hand caressed a family of cats which played on his knees, while with the other he signed the order for the execution of (Marquis de) Cinq-Mars" (Landrin, 1894).

The Plague of London

Unfortunately, cats and dogs were blamed for the spread of the great plague of London in 1665. Consequently, around 40,000 dogs and 200,000 cats were wantonly slaughtered. Domestic cats and dogs were thought to carry the effluvia or infections in their fur. Hence an order was issued by the Lord Mayor that they should be immediately exterminated. Even so, most did not abide by the order. Daniel Defoe observed that most homes in London had at least five or more cats (Defoe, 1722/1983, pp. 136-7).

The schizophrenic behavior of the Early Modern Period, on the one hand, preserved and glorified the cat as a useful symbol in art, literature and plays with mischievous pets even being immortalized in poetic epitaphs. However, on the other hand, the cat was still thought to be a pariah, a devil, a loathsome thing to be feared and hence tortured and killed. Even so, as either revered or reviled the ubiquitous cat had permeated men's psyches and had begun to re-establish itself as an integral part of society and art from which it could never again be displaced.

Chapter Seven

THE ENLIGHTENMENT

The threat of plague and witchcraft waned in the 18th century, and the poverty and pestilence of earlier centuries slowly receded, making way for a new era full of new possibilities. Man's condition advanced with a concern for sanitation, and as the importance of good hygiene gained a foothold in major urban areas, health improved; an inoculation for smallpox in 1720 allowed the population to grow and thrive. No longer preoccupied with the basic needs of life, men were able to pursue education, and were thereby able to raise their financial and social status. A growing educated bourgeoisie class blossomed into writers, scientists, and social activists. These intellectuals and artists, who sought knowledge for the betterment of society, gave the century its name: the Enlightenment, for it was certainly a period of light after so much darkness and suffering. This light did not shine on man alone, but consequently on the cat as well. As man's condition progressed, so did that of the cat. No longer seen solely as a symbol of witchcraft and the devil, the cat became an icon of cleanliness in a time when cleanliness was truly next to godliness. Thus, the cat became an acceptable companion for royalty, the upper classes, and the bourgeoisie, and not least of all, the rising group of intellectuals composed of philosophers, writers, politicians and statesmen. Even though the cat's greatest enemies: the ignorant, poor and superstitious would continue to threaten its existence (as they still do today), the cat moved on to a period of pampered acceptance in upper class educated circles, protected by a previously unheard of concern for animal welfare.

Philosophers and Cats

Philosophers of the time promoted these changes and espoused such concepts as the pursuit of happiness and the love of nature. The concern for happiness and a return to the importance of nature were the essential ingredients of the Enlightenment. Dennis Diderot (1713-84), one of the first Enlightenment philosophers, made happiness a legitimate goal for all people. According to Diderot, freedom, and the ability to accumulate goods, led to happiness. These literally became revolutionary ideas, and Diderot became the ideological father of both the French and American revolutions. Furthermore, during this time, the beliefs of the ancient pagans were reborn. The philosophy of Jean Jacques Rousseau (1712-78) proclaimed that God and nature were one. The thrust of philosophical thought had returned to the old pagan idea of Pantheism, and with it, a new-found respect for animals and their treatment emerged. Reflecting this renewed respect for nature, Pantheism seeped into every aspect of the arts. Later, Romanticism would be based on this new philosophy, and music, art and literature would also mirror this close relationship. Scientists, too, from Copernicus to Newton[†] contributed to this awakening by spawning a tolerance for other cultures and ideas by moving away from the dictates of the once all-powerful church.

In his famous *Essay on Man*, 1733-4, Alexander Pope asserted that man was not that different from animals and should, therefore, treat them in a compassionate manner. In a Guardian article of 1713, he said that animals were abused and "—have the misfortune, for not manner of reason, to be treated as common enemies wherever found. The conceit that a cat has nine lives has cost at least nine lives in ten of the whole race to them: scarce a boy in the streets but has in this point outdone Hercules himself, who was famous for killing a monster that had but three lives" (Steele & Addison, 1829, p. 95).

Building on Diderot's earlier philosophy, Jeremy Bentham's (1748-1832) English philosophy of Utilitarianism was also based on the belief that all actions should lead to happiness: "—it is the greatest happiness of the greatest number that is the measure of right

[†] Newton was, unsurprisingly, a cat lover and had a cat when he was at Cambridge named CC whom he fed off his dinner tray, (Westfall, 1980 p. 103-104), and it was perhaps for this cat that he invented the first cat flap in 1700. In addition, during this time, a constellation named, "Felis" appeared in an atlas by J. E. Bode (Engels, 2001, p. 171).

and wrong". Undoubtedly, as a cat owner, he must have considered and included the happiness of animals. A well-known misanthrope, as many cat lovers are, he named his favorite cat Langbourne and proceeded to give him the title: Reverend Sir John Langbourne, DD. Such irreverence surely caused consternation. One of the first proponents of animals' rights, Bentham avidly fought against the idea that if they (people and animals) did not have reason, they could not suffer. "If reason alone were the criterion by which we judge who ought to have rights, human infants and adults with certain forms of disability might fall short, too" (Bentham, 1789/2005). Through Bentham's writings we see that he cared a great deal for his own macaroni eating cat. "I had a remarkably intellectual cat, who never failed to attend one of us when we went round the garden. He grew quite a tyrant, insisting on being fed, and on being noticed...His moral qualities were most despotic-his intellect extraordinary; but he was a universal nuisance" (Bentham, 1789/2005, p. 80). In his protests against animal cruelty, Bentham wrote, "It is proper...to forbid every kind of cruelty towards animals, whether by way of amusement, or to gratify gluttony...Why should the law refuse its protection to any sensitive being? The time will come when humanity will extend its mantle over everything which breathes" (Bentham, 1789/2005, p. 562).[†]

Academics and writers of the age expressed their love and respect for the cat as well. François-Augustin de Paradis de Moncrif (1687-1770), a member of the *Académie Française* and the royal historiographer to Louis XV, was the first person to ever write a book specifically about cats, originally entitled *Les Chats*[††] and published in 1727 *(figure 7.1)*. Unfortunately, "—it (*Les Chats*) at once became the subject of satires and skits...a comedy had been presented entitled *Gulliver dans L'Isle de la folie*, by Dominique and Romagnesi...It contained a scene between Gulliver and a musician, who boasted of writing 'a magnificent Cantata to the honour and glory of Cats...The stuff of the lyrics was taken directly from Moncrif, and the piece was performed with enthusiastic mewings"...for which he would be ever afterward ridiculed (de Paradis de Moncrif, 1727/1965, pp. 10-11). However, according to

[†] Oddly enough he had himself mummified and sits in a cabinet at the University of London. No one knows where his cat is, or if it was in fact mummified too.
[††] A later edition would be entitled *Histoire des Chats.*

Maurepas' memoirs, it was upon Moncrif's election to the *Academie Française* that an aspiring comedian let lose in the crowd a cat which started to make the most horrendous howling noises. The audience immediately mimicked it and turned the whole gathering into chaos (de Paradis de Moncrif, 1727/1965, p. 12). Even so, perhaps Moncrif had the last laugh, as his exceptional book is still being published today. "....somebody said of him, when he was famous as the laureate of the cats, that he had risen in life by never scratching, by always having velvet paws, and by never putting up his back, even when he was startled"(Gosse, 1891, p. 174).

Figure 7.1. Etching of Moncrif and a Cat from his book Les Chats, 1727

Samuel Johnson, the father of the first English dictionary, had a cat named Hodge for whom he cared deeply. James Boswell, Johnson's friend and biographer, found Johnson's relationship with Hodge so important that he included a description of this bond in Johnson's biography.

"Nor would it be just under this head, to omit the fondness which he shewed for animals which he had taken under his protection. I never shall forget the indulgence with which he treated Hodge, his cat; for whom he himself used to go out and buy oysters, lest the servants, having that trouble, should take dislike to the poor creature. I am, unluckily one of those who have an antipathy to a cat, so that I am uneasy when in the room with one; and I own, I frequently suffered a good deal from the presences of this same Hodge. I recollect him one day scrambling up Dr. Johnson's breast, apparently with much satisfaction, while my friend smiling and half-whistling, rubbed down his back, and pulled him by the tail; and when I observed he was a fine cat, saying why, yes, Sir, but I have had cats whom I liked better than this; and then as if perceiving Hodge to be out of countenance, adding, but he is a very fine cat, a very fine cat indeed" (Boswell, 1820, p. 824) *(figure 7.2)*.

Figure 7.2. Dr. Johnson and his Cat Hodge, 19th century engraving

The Cat in Poetry

Percival Stockdale, a not very famous poet, but an avid reformer against slavery, and most importantly, Johnson's friend, wrote an elegy to poor deceased Hodge *(figure 7.3)*.

An Elegy on The Death of Dr. Johnson's Favourite Cat

Percival Stockdale 1778

Let not the honest muse disdain
For Hodge to wake the plaintive strain.
Shall poets prostitute their lays
In offering venal Statesmen praise;
By them shall flowers Parnassian bloom
Around the tyrant's gaudy tomb;
And shall not Hodge's memory claim

Of innocence the candid fame;
Shall not his worth a poem fill,
Who never thought, nor uttered ill;
Who by his manner when caressed
Warmly his gratitude expressed;
And never failed his thanks to purr
Whene'er he stroaked his sable furr?
The general conduct if we trace
Of our articulating race,
Hodge's, example we shall find
A keen reproof of human kind.
He lived in town, yet ne'er got drunk,
Nor spent one farthing on a punk;
He never filched a single groat,
Nor bilked a taylor of a coat;
His garb when first he drew his breath
His dress through life, his shroud in death.
Of human speech to have the power,
To move on two legs, not on four;
To view with unobstructed eye
The verdant field, the azure sky
Favoured by luxury to wear
The velvet gown, the golden glare -
—If honour from these gifts we claim,
Chartres had too severe a fame.
But wouldst though, son of Adam, learn
Praise from thy noblest powers to earn;
Dost thou, with generous pride aspire
Thy nature's glory to acquire?
Then in thy life exert the man,
With moral deed adorn the span;
Let virtue in they bosom lodge;
Or wish thou hadst been born a Hodge

(Stockdale, P. (1809/2012, p. 79).

Another poem included in Repplier's, *The cat: Being a Record of the Endearments and Invectives Lavished by Many Writers Upon an Animal Much Loved and Abhorred* written by Susan Coolidge is about Johnson's famous relationship with his cat, Hodge.

Hodge the Cat

Burly and big his books among,
    Good Samuel Johnson sat,
With frowning brows and wig askew,
His snuff strewn waistcoat far from new;
So stern and menacing his air,
That neither "Black Sam" nor the maid
To know or interrupt him dare;
Yet close beside him, unafraid,
Sat Hodge the cat.

"This participle," the Doctor wrote,
"the modern scholar cavils at,
But,"---even as he penned the word,
A soft protesting note was heard:
The Doctor fumbled with his pen,
The dawning thought took wings and flew,
The sound repeated come again,
It was a faint reminding "Mew!"
From Hodge, the cat.

"Poor Pussy!" said the learned man,
Giving the glossy fur a pat,
"It is your dinner time, I know,
And, ---well, perhaps I ought to go;
For if Sam every day were sent
Off from his work your fish to buy,
Why, men are men, he might resent,
And starve or kick you on the sly;
Eh! Hodge, my cat?"

The Dictionary was laid down,
The Doctor tied his vast cravat,
And down the bussing street he strode,
Taking an often –trodden road,
And halted at a well know stall:
"Fishmonger," he spoke the Doctor gruff,
"give me six oysters, that is all;

Hodge knows when he has had enough,
Hodge is my cat."

Then home Puss dined, and while in sleep
He chased a visionary rat,
His master sat him down again,
Rewrote his page, renibbed his pen;
Each I was dotted, each t was crossed,
He labored on for all to read,
Nor deemed that time was waste or lost
Spent in supplying the small need—
Of Hodge, the cat.

The dear old Doctor! fierce of mien,
Untidy, arbitrary, fat
What gentle thoughts his name enfold!
So generous of his scanty gold,
So quick to love, so hot to scorn,
Kind to all sufferers under heaven,
A tenderer despot ne'er was born;
His big heart held a corner even
For Hodge, the cat
(Repplier, 1918, pp. 80-82).

Composing poetry to deceased beloved companion cats was a trend of the times. Just as Johnson had mourned the death of Hodge, Bentham and many others would mourn the deaths of their beloved companion cats. The following are some examples from the *London Magazine* of 1733, but interestingly enough these poems are anonymous, probably because the authors were concerned about being ridiculed as Moncrif had been.

The Poet's Lamentation for the Loss of His Cat, Which He Used to Call His Muse
Anonymous

Oppressed with grief,
In heavy strains I mourn
The partner of my studies from me torn

Figure 7.3 Statue of Hodge in the courtyard outside Dr. Johnson's House, 17 Gough Square, London, Photograph by Jim Linwood

How shall I sing?
What numbers shall I choose?
For in my favorite cat I've lost my muse…
In acts obscene she never took delight
No catterwawls disturbed our sleep by night…
She never thirsted for the chicken's blood;
Her teeth she only used to chew her food;
Harmless as satires which her master writes,
A foe to scratching,
And unused to bites.
She in the study was my constantinate;
There we together many evenings sat.
Whene'er I felt my tower fancy fail,
I stroked her head, her ears, her back and tail;
And, as I stroked, improved my dying song
From the sweet notes of her melodious tongue.
Her purrs and mews so evenly kept time,
She purred in metre and she mewed with rhyme.
My cat is gone, ab!
Never to return
Now in my study all the tedious night,
Alone I sit, and unassisted write;
Look often around
And view the numerous labors… ;
Those quires of words arrayed in pompous rhyme;
Which brav'd the jaws of all devouring time
Now undefended and unwatched by cats,
Are doomed a victim to the teeth of rats
(Green, 1733, p. 579).

An Epitaph

Here lies beneath this verdant hill
Tom, a favorite cat
Who when alive, did never spill
The blood of mouse or rat,
Yet many a bird and many a nest
His cruel claws befit

The partridge too could find not rest,
Nor escaped the leveret.
For callow young he fought the filed,
And often made a feast,
While fluttering round, the dam beheld,
And mourned the sad repast…
Ye pretty songsters, clap the wing,
Let every partner know;
Let every wood and valley ring,
The death of Tom your foe.
Now build your nests, now hatch your young,
And whistle to and fro;
Let every hill and dale return
The death of Tom your foe.
But mourn his death, ye vermin kind,
And shriek, ye mice and rats,
For such a friend ye ne'er shall find
In all the race of cats
(Anonymous, 1769, p. 48).

An Epitaph on A Favorite Cat Named Blewet

Here lies entombed poor honest Blewet
Poor honest Blewet, Pray who's that
Some tippling poet? No, a cat…
It was a loving, lovely creature
Compleat in every grace and feature.
What gooseberry eyes, and what velvet fur!
Ye gods what a melodious pur!...
When on patrole about the house,
What cat less pus-illanimous?
But a description yet would suit his
person, and parts, for subject new 'tis requires, a cat-alogue of beauties.
To tell in brief his worth and mien,
But death, whose never erring dart
makes dogs, and cats, and men to part,
Our friend to realms of silence bore,

And honest Blewet purs no more…
In dismal discords all agree.
To moan this sad cat-astrophe
A cat whom merit thus indears,
Demands a cat-aract of tears
(Anonymous, 1775, pp. 654-655).

William Stukeley, a famous antiquarian of the time, had a cat named Tit. He loved his cat so much that when she died, he wrote a heartfelt eulogy for her. "The creature had a sense so far superior to her kind; had such inimitable ways of testifying her love to her master and mistress, that she was as a companion, especially so to me…From the admirable endowments of the cat I took a great liking to her, which gave me so much pleasure, without trouble. Her death I grieved for exceedingly" (Piggott, 1985, p. 124). When the gardener buried her under a mulberry tree in Stukeley's garden, Stukeley refused to go anywhere near it, stating, "I never cared to come near that delightful place; nor so much as to look toward it" (Piggott, 1985, p. 124).

In 1747, Horace Walpole's (1717-97) cat, Selima, drowned in a large Chinese porcelain goldfish tank. Walpole was distraught and his friend and poet Thomas Gray, with whom he had spent much time traveling, wrote an elegy for the poor goldfish loving cat. The poem became a well-loved sensation and important enough to be one of the not very prolific poet's only thirteen poems published in his lifetime. Ironically, it certainly was not a serendipitous discovery for his cat to slip and fall into the goldfish tank. He coined the word *serendipity* which offered a lesson to those thinking all that glitters is gold *(figure 7.4).*

Ode on the Death of a Favourite Cat, Drowned in a Tub of gold Fishes

Thomas Gray

T'was on a lofty vase's side,
Where China's gayest art had dyed
The azure flowers, that blow;

Demurest of the tabby kind,
The pensive Selima reclined,
Gazed on the lake below.

Her conscious tail her joy declared;
The fair round face, the snowy beard,
The velvet of her paws,
Her coat, that with the tortoise vies,
Her ears of jet, and emerald eyes,
She saw; and purred applause.

Still had she gazed; but 'midst the tide
Two angel forms were seen to glide,
The genii of the stream:
Their scaly armour's Tyiian hue
Through richest purple to the view
Betrayed a gold gleam.

The hapless nymph with wonder saw:
A whisker first and then a claw,
With many an ardent wish,
She stretched in vain to reach the prize.
What female heart can gold despise?
What cat's averse to fish?

Presumptuous maid! With looks intent
Again she stretched, again she bent,
Nor knew the gulf between.
(Malignant fate sat by, and smiled)
The slippery verge her feet beguiled,
She tumbled headlong in.
Eight times emerging from the flood
She mewed to every watery god,
Some speedy aid to send.
No dolphin came, no Nereid stirred;
Nor cruel Tom, nor Susan heard.
A favourite has no friend!

Even hence, ye beauties undeceived,

Know, one false step is ne'er retrieved,
And be with caution bold.
Not all that tempts your wandering eyes
And headless hearts is lawful prize;
Nor all that glistens gold
(Gray, 1902, p. 9).

In every age there was at least one prisoner in the Tower of London who enjoyed the company of a friendly feline. Likewise, Citizen the cat managed to keep John Augustus Bonney company after he had been accused of treason and imprisoned in 1794. Sadly, however, the poor creature died on August 22, 1794, and was buried in the Tower wall inspiring Bonney to write this lovely epitaph about his lost companion.

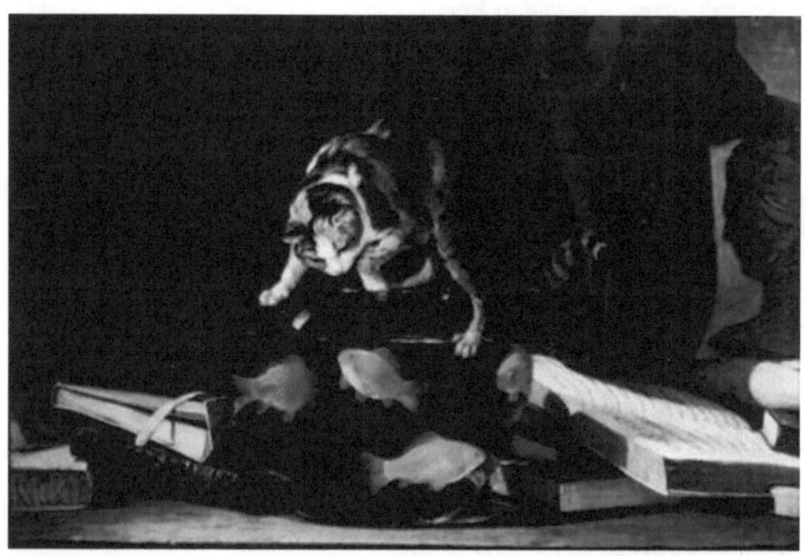

Figure 7.4. Mr. Horace Walpole's Favorite Cat, 1796, Stephen Elmer, Private Collection

Epitaph on a Cat named Citizen

If, led by fancy o'er this sent woe
In search of secrets hid within these walls,
Thine kind eye, kind reader, thou should'st chance to throw
On the small spot where my poor dwelling falls;

Think not, within this cell there is compress'd
Ought which the world could envy, nor could fear;
Nor stars, nor ribbons deck'd my honest breast?
An humble Citizen lies buried here.
A friend, that could my lonely talents prize,
(At his fond kindness, reader, do not laugh)
Sooth'd my last moments, clos'd my dying eyes.
Dug here my grave, and wrote my epitaph.
But lest these lines they fancy should deceive,
And thou should'st think some patriot claims a tear,
Thy rising anguish let me now relieve:
'Tis only Puss, the Citizen, lies here
(Bayley, 1821, p. 178).

Another anecdote of mourning and remembrance is related by Moncrif of Madamoiselle Dupuy, a harpist, who relied upon her tomcat to guide and inspire her during her musical performances. She very much believed that she owed much of her universal success to the critical evaluations of this feline muse. Quite well-to-do, when she realized that she was dying, she made a bequest to her beloved cat to keep him in the manner to which he had been accustomed, which included covering the costs of the services of a person to wait on him. Unfortunately, the family contested the will, and no one knows what actually became of the poor cat after Mlle. Dupuy's death *(figure 7.5).*

Another French woman who loved her cat above all was Madame de Lesdiguieres. The tombstone is a representation of her cat with the epitaph *(figure 7.6)*:

A lovely Cat lies here:
Her Mistress, who loved no one,
Loved her almost to despair;
Why say so? This will show one.

Figure 7.5. Death of Mlle Dupuy Bequeathing all to her Cats, From Moncrif's Les Chats, 1727

Even so, not everyone was touched by the light of the Enlightenment, and a few scientists such as George Louis Leclerc de Buffon, a dog lover, and author of the *Histoire Naturelle* 1749-67, did not have a very high opinion of cats, and turned away from a reverence for nature, instead valuing animals solely for their purposefulness and submissiveness to man. He wrote, "The cat is a faithless domestic, and only kept through necessity to oppose to another domestic which incommodes us still more, and which we cannot drive away; for we pay not respect to those, who, being fond of all beasts, keep cats for amusement. Though these animals are gentle and frolicsome when young, yet they, even then, possess an

Figure 7.6. Mme de Lesdigieres Cat, Paris, From Moncrif 's Les Chats, 1727

innate cunning and perverse disposition, which age increases, and which education only serves to conceal. They are, naturally, inclined to theft, and the best education only converts them into servile and flattering robbers; for they have the same address, subtlety, and inclination for mischief or rapine. Like all knaves, they know how to conceal their intentions, to watch, wait, and choose opportunities for seizing their prey; to fly from punishment, and to remain away until the danger is over, and they return to safety. They readily conform to the habits of society, but never acquire its manners; for of attachment they have only the appearance, as may be seen by the obliquity of their motions, and duplicity of their looks. They never look in the face those who treat them best, and of whom they seem to be the most fond; but either the nigh fear or falsehood, they approach him by windings to seek for those caresses they have no pleasure in, but only to flatter those from whom they receive them. Very different from that faithful dog, whose sentiments are all directed to the person of his Master, the cat appears only to feel for himself, only to love conditionally, only to partake of society that he may abuse it; and by this disposition he has more affinity to man than the dog, who is all sincerity…It cannot be said that cats, though living in our houses, are entirely domestic. The most familiar are not under any subjection, but rather enjoy perfect freedom, as they only do just what they please, and nothing is capable of returning them in a place which they are inclined to desert" (Buffon, 1792, Vol. 6, pp. 1-10) *(figure 7.7)*.

In line with Buffon's view of the cat, the *Encyclopaedia Britannica*, 3rd edition, 1787, reads, "The *domesticus,* or tame cat, is so well known, that it requires no description. It is a useful, but deceitful domestic. Although when young they are playful and gay, they possess at the same time an innate malice and perverse disposition, which increases as they grow up, and which education learns them to conceal, but never to subdue. Constantly bent upon theft and rapine, though in a domestic state, they are full of cunning and dissimulation; they conceal all their designs; seize every opportunity of doing mischief, and then fly from punishment. They easily take on the habits of society, but never its manners; for they have only the appearance of friendship and attachment. This disingenuity of character is betrayed by the obliquity of their movements and the ambiguity of their looks. In a word, the cat is totally destitute of friendship; he thinks and acts for himself alone."

Cat Massacre

In addition to these negative images of the cat, a well-documented incident in Paris of a working class mob torturing and murdering cats because the rabble rousers were unhappy with their economic situation, proved that not all mentalities had changed.

In 1730, workers revolted in a print shop in Saint Séverin, Paris, where they massacred the innocent cats of Jacques Vincent's wife. The story goes that Vincent's wife fed and pampered many cats while

Figure 7.7. Cat, Oeuvres complètes de Buffon,1830

their own print shop workers went hungry. The jealous workers grew upset when the cats constantly howled, keeping them awake during the night. In revenge for the noise and for the kindness the Vincents had shown the cats, the workers at first pretended to be cats and howled in order to wake up the Vincents. Unable to sleep because of the din produced by the workers, the printer and his wife asked them to remove all the cats except her favorite, *La grise*. Presumably due to their overall dissatisfaction with their working conditions, the workers, in a fit of sadism and contempt, instead killed the wife's favorite cat, *La grise*, by breaking its back. The other feline victims, after being severely beaten, were thrown into sacks and given mock trials. Once the workers had pronounced their inevitable guilty sentences, they garroted or hanged the innocent creatures. The working class, perhaps due to their own continued social suffering, were not affected by the bourgeois concern for animal welfare and persisted in their torture of animals, especially the cat. Again, the cat became a symbol and victim of social unrest. This time used as a pawn by the workers against the bourgeoisie (Darnton, 1984, p. 87).

Other incidents of cat torture persisted in France especially during religious events. During Mardi Gras, boys joyfully threw cats up in the air and pulled their hair so as to hear them howl. Sometimes the evil ruffians set cats on fire and chased them through the streets, *cour amiaud,* and on St. John the Baptist day cats were burned. Only in 1765, was the burning of dozens of cats in Metz outlawed (Darnton, 1984, p. 104).

The evil mantle that the cat had borne through history owing to Greeks and early Christians was exploited by the French workers, and was then manipulated into a source of individual profit by a Prussian magician, Katterfelto (1743-1799). In order to entice crowds to his show, he used a "Famous Moroccan Black Cat" in his act, which he advertised as "evil". After luring in the gullible audience, he confessed that the cat was as innocent of evil as himself. Katterfelto said that his cat "—so much excited the attention of the public, as to induce several gentlemen to make bets respecting its TAIL, as by the wonderful skill of Katterfelto she in one moment appears with a big tail and the next without any, to the utter astonishment of the spectators" (Paton-Williams, 2008, p. 81). One of Katterfelto's advertisements read, "Wonders! Wonders! Wonders! Are to be seen by Katterfelto and his Black cat, worth 30,000 pounds, let out of the bag by the Philosopher himself, who has discovered a secret more valuable and astounding than the Philosopher's Stone, the art of extracting god from the body of the cat."[†] One news announcement written about his fabulous cat, reads "—his celebrated Black Cat, who has nine times more excellent properties than any nine cats among those nine-lived animals, was safely delivered of NINE kittens, seven of which are black and two are white." Katterfelto's cat became so popular that royalty eagerly awaited the ownership of one of the kittens. Marie Antoinette was even rumored to have received one of these special kittens in 1783 (Paton-Williams, 2008, p. 84). With the kittens he kept, Katterfelto made good use. "...one of the gentlemen present asked the Doctor what he had done with his black cat and kittens; the Doctor, to great surprise of the whole company conveyed one of the kittens into the Welsh gentleman's waistcoat pocket at 6 yards distance, purposely to make that gentleman believe he was the Devil" (Paton-Williams, 2008, p. 87). That he chose to keep "conveying the cats into people's pockets taking money and watches out of them, as well as stopping and starting these time pieces were some of Katterfelto's favorite tricks" (Paton-Williams, 2008, p. 88) *(figure 7.8).*

Figure 7.8. Katterfelto with Black Cat, from The Quacks of Old London by Charles John Samuel Thompson, Bretano, London, 1928

[†] A reference to the cat being a goddess in ancient Egypt.

The Cat in Poetry and Literature

By and large, the cat was highly thought of during this age especially by those eccentrics who were judged to be a bit mad. William Cowper (1751-1800), who had bouts of madness and depression was no less a great poet. His first volume of poems published in 1782, was, by his death in 1800, so popular that it had already been reprinted ten times. Cowper espoused the Pantheistic belief of the time which was a love of nature and thereby a love of animals. In *The Retired Cat,* written in 1791, the plight of his cat that has become trapped in a dresser drawer seems a good opportunity for a moral.

Retired Cat

A POET'S cat, sedate and grave,
As poet well could wish to have,
Was much addicted to inquire
For nooks, to which she might retire,
And where, secure as mouse in chink,
She might repose, or sit and think.
I know not where she caught the trick—
Nature perhaps herself had cast her
In such a mould PHILOSOPHIQUE,
Or else she learn'd it of her master.
Sometimes ascending, debonair,
An apple-tree or lofty pear,
Lodg'd with convenience in the fork,
She watched the gard'ner at his work;
Sometimes her ease and solace sought
In an old empty wat'ring-pot,
There, wanting nothing, save a fan,
To seem some nymph in her sedan,
Apparell'd in exactest sort,
And ready to be borne to court.
But love of change it seems has place
Not only in our wiser race;
Cats also feel as well as we
That passion's force, and so did she.

Her climbing, she began to find,
Expos'd her too much to the wind,
And the old utensil of tin
Was cold and comfortless within:
She therefore wish'd instead of those,
Some place of more serene repose,
Where neither cold might come, nor air
Too rudely wanton with her hair,
And sought it in the likeliest mode
Within her master's snug abode.
A draw'r,—it chanc'd, at bottom lin'd
With linen of the softest kind,
With such as merchants introduce
From India, for the ladies' use,—
A draw'r impending o'er the rest,
Half open in the topmost chest,
Of depth enough, and none to spare,
Invited her to slumber there.
Puss with delight beyond expression
Survey'd the scene, and took possession.
Recumbent at her ease ere long,
And lull'd by her own hum-drum song,
She left the cares of life behind,
And slept as she would sleep her last,
When in came, housewifely inclin'd,
The chambermaid, and shut it fast,
By no malignity impell'd,
But all unconscious whom it held.
Awaken'd by the shock (cried puss)
Was ever cat attended thus!
The open draw'r was left, I see,
Merely to prove a nest for me,
For soon as I was well compos'd,
Then came the maid, and it was closed:
How smooth these 'kerchiefs, and how sweet,
O what a delicate retreat!
I will resign myself to rest
Till Sol, declining in the west,
Shall call to supper; when, no doubt,

Susan will come and let me out.
The evening came, the sun descended,
And puss remain'd still unattended.
The night roll'd tardily away,
(With her indeed 'twas never day)
The sprightly morn her course renew'd,
The evening gray again ensued,
And puss came into mind no more
Than if entomb'd the day before.
With hunger pinch'd, and pinch'd for room,
She now presag'd approaching doom,
Nor slept a single wink, or purr'd,
Conscious of jeopardy incurr'd.
That night, by chance, the poet watching,
Heard an inexplicable scratching,
His noble heart went pit-a-pat,
And to himself he said—what's that?
He drew the curtain at his side,
And forth he peep'd, but nothing spied.
Yet, by his ear directed, guess'd
Something imprison'd in the chest,
And doubtful what, with prudent care,
Resolv'd it should continue there.
At length a voice, which well he knew,
A long and melancholy mew,
Saluting his poetic ears,
Consol'd him, and dispell'd his fears;
He left his bed, he trod the floor,
He 'gan in haste the draw'rs explore,
The lowest first, and without stop,
The rest in order to the top.
For 'tis a truth well known to most,
That whatsoever thing is lost,
We seek it, ere it come to light,
In ev'ry cranny but the right.
Forth skipp'd the cat; not now replete
As erst with airy self-conceit,
Nor in her own fond apprehension
A theme for all the world's attention,

But modest, sober, cur'd of all
Her notions hyperbolical,
And wishing for a place of rest
Any thing rather than a chest:
Then stept the poet into bed,
With this reflection in his head:

MORAL
Beware of too sublime a sense
Of your own worth and consequence!
The man who dreams himself so great,
And his importance of such weight,
That all around, in all that's done,
Must move and act for him alone,
Will learn in school of tribulation,
The folly of his expectation (Milford, 1905, pp. 407-409).

In another of Cowper's poems, *Familiarity Dangerous*, he writes of a cat and her mistress who are playing, but the mistress is scratched. The moral: don't play with dangerous things.

Familiarity Dangerous

As in her ancient mistress' lap,
The youthful tabby lay,
Alike dispos'd to play.

But strife ensues. Puss waxes warm,
And with protruded claws
Ploughs all the length of Lydia's arm,
Mere wantonness the cause.

At once, resentful of the deed,
She shakes her to the ground
With many a threat, that she shal bleed
With still a deeper wound.
But Lydia, bid thy fury rest!
It was a venial stroke;
For she, that will with kittens jest,
Should bear a kitten's joke (Gooden, 1946, p. 50).

Another poet who went mad reportedly suffering from some sort of religious mania, was the English poet Christopher Smart, (1722-1771). Not even his good friend Samuel Johnson, who did not believe that Smart should be confined for merely wanting people to pray with him, could keep him out of the asylum. Smart eventually ended up in a debtor's prison where he died. But before that sad end, he wrote the poem *Jubilate Agno,* which remained unpublished until 1939. The poem, written primarily about his cat Jeoffry, is an example of nature and God as one, Pantheism. In the poem, Smart describes the Cat as a servant of God, worshipping in his own way.

Jubilate Agno

For I will consider my Cat Jeoffry.
For he is the servant of the Living God duly and daily serving him.
For at the first glance of the glory of God in the East he worships in his way.
For this is done by wreathing his body seven times round with elegant quickness.
For then he leaps up to catch the musk, which is the blessing of God upon his prayer.
For he rolls upon prank to work it in.
For having done duty and received blessing he begins to consider himself.
For this he performs in ten degrees.
For first he looks upon his forepaws to see if they are clean.
For secondly he kicks up behind to clear away there.
For thirdly he works it upon stretch with the forepaws extended.
For fourthly he sharpens his paws by wood.
For fifthly he washes himself.
For sixthly he rolls upon wash.
For seventhly he fleas himself, that he may not be interrupted upon the beat.
For eighthly he rubs himself against a post.
For ninthly he looks up from his instructions.
For tenthly he goes in quest of food.
For having consider'd God and himself he will consider his neighbor.
For if he meets another cat he will kiss her in kindness.
For when he takes his prey he plays with it to give it a chance.

For one mouse in seven escapes by his dallying.
For when his day's work is done his business more properly begins.
For he keeps the Lord's watch in the night against the adversary.
For he counteracts the powers of darkness by his electrical skin and glaring eyes.
For he counteracts the Devil, who is death, by brisking about the life.
For in his morning orisons he loves the sun and the sun loves him.
For he is of the tribe of Tiger.
For the Cherub Cat is a term of the Angel Tiger.
For he has the subtlety and hissing of a serpent, which in goodness he suppresses.
For he will not do destruction, if he is well-fed, neither will he spit without provocation.
For he purrs in thankfulness, when god tells him he's a good Cat.
For he is an instrument for the children to learn benevolence upon.
For every house is incomplete without him and a blessing is lacking in the spirit.
For the Lord commanded Moses concerning the cats at the departure of the Children of Israel from Egypt.
For every family had one cat at least in the bag.
For the English Cats are the best in Europe.
For he is the cleanest in the use of his forepaws of any quadruped.
For the dexterity of his defense is an instance of the love of God to him exceedingly.
For he is the quickest to his mark of any creature.
For he is tenacious of his point.
For he is a mixture of gravity and waggery.
For he knows that God is his Savior.
For there is nothing sweeter than his peace when at rest.
For there is nothing brisker than his life when in motion.
For he is of the Lord's poor and so indeed is he called by benevolence perpetually-Poor Jeoffry! Poor Jeoffry! The rat has bit thy throat.
For I bless the name of the Lord Jesus that Jeoffry is better.
For the divine spirit comes about his body to sustain it in complete cat.
For his tongue is exceeding pure so that it has in purity what it wants in music.
For he is docile and can learn certain things.

For he can set up and gravity which is patience upon approbation.
For he can fetch and carry, which is patience upon proof positive.
For he can spraggle upon waggle at the word of command.
For he can jump from an eminence into his master's bosom.
For he can catch the cork and toss it again.
For he is hated by the hypocrite and miser.
For the former is afraid of detection.
For the latter refuses the charge.
For he camels his back to bear the first notion of business.
For he is good to think on, if a man would express himself neatly.
For he made a great figure in Egypt for his signal services.
For he killed the Ichneumon-rat very pernicious by land.
For his ears are so acute that they sting again.
For from this proceeds the passing quickness of his attention.
For by stroking of him I have found out electricity.
For I perceived God's light about him both wax and fire.
For the Electrical fire is the spiritual substance, which God sends from heaven to sustain the bodies both of man and beast.
For God has blessed him in the variety of his movements.
For, tho he cannot fly, he is an excellent clamberer.
For his motions upon the face of the earth are more than any other quadruped.
For he can tread to all the measures upon the music.
For he can swim for life.
For he can creep (Smart, 1763/1939).

Jonathan Swift, (1667-1745), the author of *Gulliver's Travels* and many other notable works even found time to pen a poem about a cat, albeit not a very favorable one.

A Fable of the Widow and Her Cat

A widow kept a favourite cat.
At first a gentle creature;
But when he was grown sleek and fat,
With many a mouse, and many a rat,
He soon disliked his nature.

The fox and he were friends of old,
Nor could they now be parted;

They nightly slunk to rob the fold,
Devoured the lambs, the fleeces sold,
And puss grew lion-hearted.

He scratched her maid, he stole her cream,
He tore her best laced pinner;
Nor Chanticleer upon the beam,
Nor chick, nor duckling 'scapes, when Grim
Invites the fox to dinner.
The dame full wisely did decree,
For fear he should dispatch more,
That the false wretch should worried be:
But in saucy manner he
Thus speeched it like a Lechmere.
"Must I, against all right and law,
Like a pole-cat vile be treated?
I! Who so long with tooth and claw
Have kept domestic mice in awe,
And foreign foes defeated!

"Your golden pippins, and your pies,
How oft have I defended?
'Tis true, the pinner which you prize
I tore in frolic; to your eyes
I never harm intended.

"I am a cat of honour---" "Stay,"
Quoth she, "no longer parley;
Whate'er you did in battle slay,
By laws of arms become your prey,
I hope you won it fairly.

"Of this, we'll grant you stand acquit,
But not of your outrages:
Tell me, perfidious! was it fit
To make my cream a *perquisite*,
And steal to mend your wages!

"So flagrant is thy insolence,

So vile thy breach of trust is;
That longer with thee to dispense,
Were want of power, or want of sense:
Here, Towser!---Do him justice" (Bryant, 1999, pp. 117-119).

Sir Walter Scott (1771-1832) owned a cat named Hinx *(figure 7.9)* and once made a comment to Washington Irving, "Ah! Cats are mysterious kind of folk. There is more passing in their minds than we are aware of. It comes no doubt from their being so familiar with warlocks and witches" (Van Vechten, 1921, p. 81). He had the pleasure of meeting the Archbishop of Toronto, Naples, who had quite a reputation for loving cats. Scott himself observed that the archbishop's only passion was in fact for his cats. Likewise, amused by the archbishop's passion for cats, a Lady Morgan recorded her meeting with the ailourophile. "'You must pardon my passion for cats,'" said the archbishop, "but I never exclude them from my dining room and you will find they make excellent company..." Between the first and second courses, the door opened, and several enormously large beautiful Angora cats were introduced by the names, Pantalone, Desdemona, and Othello. They took their places on chairs near the tables, and were as silent, as quiet, as motionless,

Figure 7.9. Sir Walter Scott at his Desk with Cat, Engraved portrait of Sir Walter Scott at his desk by R. C. Bell after J. Watson Gordon, [Portraits], Sir Walter Scott in His Study (Castle Street, Edinburgh) John Watson Gordon, 1871, University of Edinburgh

and as well behaved as the most *bon-ton* table in London could require. On the Bishop requesting one of the chaplains to help the Signora Desdemona, the butler stepped to his lordship, and observed, "'My lord, la Signora Desdemona will prefer waiting for the roasts'" (Van Vechten, 1921, pp. 280-281).

Poetry about cats was not confined to the West. The great Japanese Haiku master and Buddhist monk Kobayashi Issa (1763-1827), wrote several Haiku about cats concentrating on the cat's nature and world around it.

After a long nap,
The cat yawns, rises, and goes out
Looking for love.

Goes out
Comes back---
The loves of a cat.

The winter fly
I caught and finally freed
The cat quickly ate.

The spring rain;
A little girl teaches
The cat to dance.

Flopped on the fan,
The big cat
Sleeping.
(Issa, n.d.)

Cats in Art

Conspicuous as ever, the ubiquitous cat posed for the painters of the century. The typical paintings of a cat trying to steal fish or meat, or having a duel with a dog, were accompanied by the cat's more refined presence in portraits, especially of children and/or ladies. In the 1713 Dutch Baroque painting, *A Woman and a Fish Pedlar in a Kitchen* by Willem Van Mieris (1662-1747) *(figure 7.10),* a cat sits at the bottom of the picture looking up at a dead duck as the woman and the peddler perhaps haggle over a price.

In the 1728 painting by Jean-Baptiste-Siméon Chardin, *The Ray (figure 7.11)* we see the same sort of realism as in Van Mieris' work, but here the cat is the sole actor on the canvas, greedily treading over oysters probably unable to decide where to start first. Chardin greatly impressed Diderot when he proclaimed that painting was done with emotions not just colors. "Who told you that one paints with colors? One makes use of colors, but one paints with emotions." Even though painted with emotion, most of Chardin's paintings relay peacefulness and profess no real message.

Figure 7.10. Fish Peddler in Kitchen, Willem Van Mieris, 1713, National Gallery, London

In another of his paintings, *Still Life with Cat and Fish (figure 7.12)*, painted the same year as *The Ray*, the cat takes center stage again surrounded by a veritable feast of fish. The expression of expectation on the cat's face in *Partridge, Hare and Cat* (1730*) (figure 7.13)* again shows the cat as the only living thing on the canvas, looking up, ready to steal the partridge which lies next to a dead hare. In a different attitude, a cat sits patiently in the foreground of *The Washerwoman*, 1735 *(figure 7.14)* a symbol of domesticity, while a lone woman washes

Figure 7.11. The Ray, Jean-Baptiste Siméon Chardin, 1728, Musée du Louvre, Paris

clothes.

Not only did the cat perch next to the poor and common folk in these early portraits, but it also accompanied royalty, as well as the rich and famous on canvases. An early portrait of Ivan VI of Russia (1740-1764), artist unknown *(figure 7.15),* has the young boy sitting barefooted wearing a bright red gown with his left hand resting on the head of a black and white cat. Again we have to note the use of a black and white cat which symbolizes good luck.

Another portrait of a high ranking child is that of Louis Philippe Joseph, Duke of Montpensier, (1750) by François Boucher. Here the young Duke sits with a small white kitten on his lap, undoubtedly symbolic of his innocence *(figure 7.16).*

Figure 7.12. Still Life with Cat and Fish, Jean-Baptiste Siméon Chardin, 1728, Museo Thyssen-Bornemisza, Madrid

Figure 7.13. Partridge, Hare and Cat, Jean-Baptiste Siméon Chardin, 1730, Adolph Menzel Museum, Berlin

The English painter, William Hogarth, (1697-1794), who was highly critical of the lax social mores of the time, set out to draw and paint about issues of which he felt strongly, and used the cat symbolically in many of his works. A versatile artist, Hogarth was both a painter and engraver. Some of his most famous engravings are of a prostitute named Moll Hackabout. Based loosely on the life of a real prostitute, Kate Hackabout, the series of six engravings tells her life story. When she first arrives in London in hopes of getting a job as a seamstress, she is instead set upon by members of the grimy underside of society and is unsuspectingly duped into becoming the mistress of a wealthy businessman. By Plate 3 in the series, Moll has gone from being a mistress to a common prostitute with a Madame

Figure 7.14. Washerwoman, Jean-Siméon Chardin, 1735, Toledo Museum of Art, Ohio

to look after her. The small cat in the foreground with its bottom raised in a rather suggestive way serves as only one of many symbols of her imminent downfall and licentiousness *(figure 7.17).*

Figure 7.15. Ivan VI of Russia with a Cat, 1740-1741, Artist unknown, Private Collection

Figure 7.16. Louis Philippe Joseph, Duke of Montpensier, François Boucher, 1749, Private Collection

Figure 7.17. The Harlot's Progress, William Hogarth, 1732, Private Collection

In the end, Hogarth creates a very strong moral condemnation of the depravity that was rampant in London. In another group of engravings entitled, *The Four Stages of Cruelty*, Hogarth depicts his disgust for animal cruelty and the high crime rate amongst the poor of London. The pictures, issued on affordable paper, were to be distributed to the lower classes as educational material. In the engraving, *First Stage of Cruelty (1751) (figure 7.18),* we meet Tom Nero, an infamous torturer of animals, whom we see doing unspeakable things to a dog. Not only does the dog suffer but several other animals as well, including two fighting cats who are hanged by their back legs from a tall pole just within reach of each other. In the bottom left corner, a dog is attacking a cat, and in the background of the picture, a cat tied to two bladders to weigh it down is being

Figure 7.18. The First Stage of Cruelty, William Hogarth, 1751, Engraving, London Evening Post

thrown from a high window.

When not producing these vivid moralistic works, Hogarth was painting portraits of the social elite†. *The Graham Children* (1742) *(figure 7.19)* displays several symbols of mortality, and a tribute to the baby in the picture who had actually died before the picture was completed. The cat looks longingly at the bird wishing for its death, the scythe on the clock, and the hour glass all allude to the finiteness of life.

† The father of the Graham children was the apothecary to the King.

Figure 7.19. The Graham Children, William Hogarth, 1742, National Gallery, London

The French painter Jean Baptiste Perronneau (1715-1783), specialized in portraits which were more prestigious and lucrative than landscapes. *Girl with a Kitten (figure 7.20),* painted in 1745, shows a very pretty young girl holding a long haired grey cat, one of its paws held gently in her hand. The grey of the cat matches the blue of her dress, and the eyes of the cat and the girl's are almost the same color leading us to recognize a distinct affinity between the two.

In another similar portrait, *Young Girl with a Cat (figure 7.21),* the girl is daintily stroking the cat's head. Yet another 'blue'[†] portrait is of *Mme Pinceloup de la Grange.* She stares off into space in a regal fashion holding a somewhat perplexed feline, which resembles a Charteux.

[†] 'Blue' because most of the portraits were painted in blue and white colors.

Figure 7.20. Girl with a Kitten, Jean-Baptiste Perronneau, 1745, National Gallery, London

Figure 7.21. Young Girl with a Cat, Jean-Baptiste Perronneau, 1747, National Gallery, London

These portraits stand in marked contrast to Giuseppe Maria Crespi's (1665-1747) *Girl with Cat (figure 7.22).* Instead of an upper class woman, we see a peasant, with her hair wrapped up, holding a black cat which she teases with a mouse. Even the color scheme is dark, unlike the light images of Perronneau's.

Alexandre-François Desportes (1661- 1743), was a French painter and decorative designer who specialized in animals. In *Cat with Dead*

Game, we see a black and white cat stretching up to reach what looks like a dead chicken. In a second painting, *Still Life with Cat*, Desportes' main character, the cat, extends a greedy paw hoping to grab one of the fresh oysters laid out on the table while its owner has briefly stepped away, indicated by one eaten oyster with a fork nearby

Figure 7.22. Girl with a Cat, Giuseppe Maria Crespi, Fitzwilliam Museum, University of Cambridge

Cats were often depicted as uninhibited scavengers and stealthy thieves. However, Desportes, seemingly a cat fancier, did not confine the content of his paintings to their less desirable side, but also painted *Kittens at Play* which captures the light hearted creatures happily amusing themselves.

The English painter Thomas Gainsborough painted *Six Studies of Cats* (1765-70), now in the Rijksmuseum, Amsterdam, which is reminiscent of Leonardo da Vinci's studies of cats. Even though Gainsborough preferred painting landscapes, he was famous for his portraits. An example of which is *The Artist's Daughters with a Cat* (1759)*(figure 7.23)*. The painting's main colors are brown, beige and grey tones which camouflage the cat so well that it seems to be a part of the older girl's dress. Although the cat is barely visible, we see that it looks like it might be trying to bite the younger sister's shoulder. Perhaps there is some deeper meaning to the painting regarding the two sisters' relationship.

Figure 7.23. The Artist's Daughters with a Cat, Thomas Gainsborough, 1759-61, National Gallery, London

The Swiss artist, Gottfried Mind, also known as the Raphael of Cats (1758-1814), was a genius at capturing every nuance of a cat's attitude. He loved cats very much and left behind dozens of pictures of them in various poses and situations. In the painting *Katzen*, a mother cat sits above her two kittens on a bench while they play below. Her look is expectant and playful *(figure 7.24).* In yet another painting, *Cat in a Cage*, a cat sits in a bird cage surrounded by mice, indicative of Mind's sense of humor and irony.

Figure 7.24. Katzen, Gottfried Mind, 1800

Jean Honoré Fragonard and his sister-in-law Marguerite Gérard both painted *L'Élève intéressante (figure 7.25)* in which a young girl admires a painting while a mischievous cat tries to attack a dog sitting on a stool behind her. In another portrait in blue and white tones, Fragonard again pits cat against dog but this time in the arms of a beautiful girl in *Girl Playing with a Dog and Cat* said to be a portrait of Marie-Madeleine Colombe.

Figure 7.25. L'Élève intéressante, Jean Honoré Fragonard and Marguerite Gérard, Private Collection

Francisco Goya (1746-1828), used cats as symbols and allegories in his etchings and paintings. In the 1799 etching *Alla va eso,* or in English, *There it Goes,* part of the Caprichos group of etchings, a witch holds on to the devil who is holding some sort of staff which a cat bites. Goya often used witches as a form of social criticism and is said to have commented, "There goes a witch, riding on the little crippled devil. This poor devil, of whom everyone makes fun, is not without his uses at times." In another famous etching, *The Dream (or Sleep) of Reason Produces Monsters*, we see the artist himself, Goya, fitfully asleep at his desk while above him are bats and owls representative of necromancy. Next to his chair an oversized cat stares at the sleeper who is desperate for reason to triumph over superstition. For Goya the cat is still the iconic symbol of the devil and witchcraft. At the very end of the 18th century Goya painted Manuel Osorio Manrique de Zuñiga, the son of the Count and Countess of Altamira *(figure 7.26)*. In the child's portrait, three cats (the third is barely visible behind the two) intently stare at a pet magpie which holds Goya's calling card. The cat is a contrast to the child's innocent gaze and the birds symbolize the soul and death.

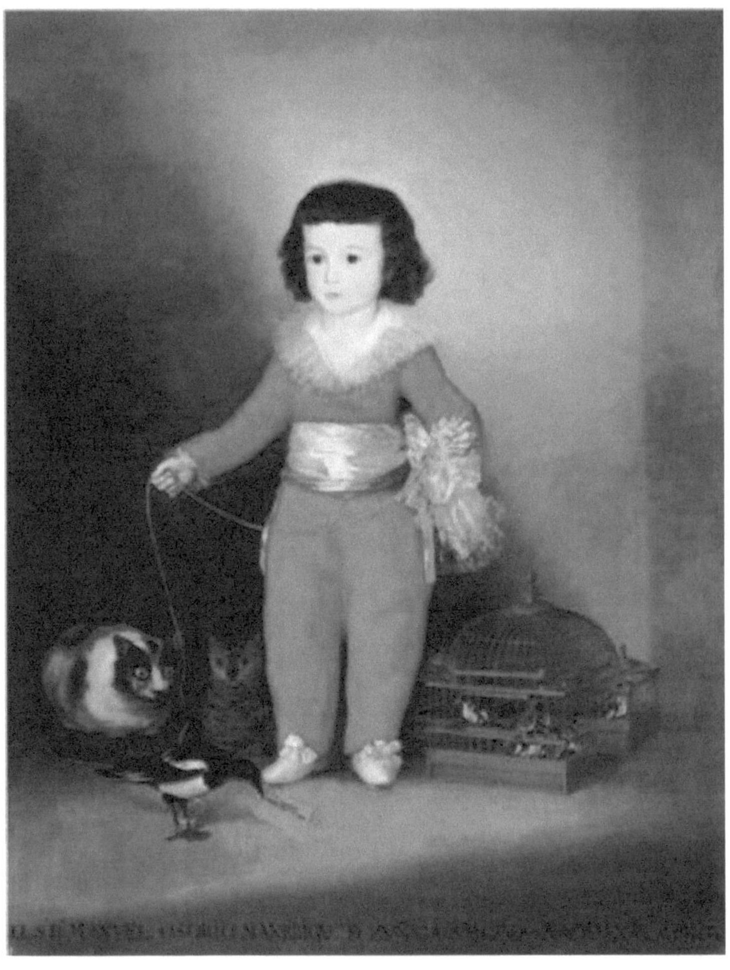

Figure 7.26. Manuel Osorio Manrique de Zúñiga, Franciso Goya, 1787-1788, Metropolitan Museum of Art, New York

Europeans were not the only ones painting our famous beast. Japanese and Chinese painters also included the cat in many of their paintings of the 18th century. *Children with a Cat and Mouse,* 1768-69, by the Japanese painter Suzuki Harunobu (1725-1770), shows a young boy holding a rather large white cat while his mother and sister look on *(figure 7.27).*

Figure 7.27. Children with Cat and Mouse, Suzuki Harunobu, Japanese Edo Period, Museum of Fine Arts, Boston

In another painting, Harunobu captures the princess Nyosan-no-Miya with her cat at her feet, a typical pose for the time. Gan Ku, influenced by the Chinese Nagasaki style, created a rather ornate realistic scroll painting where a black and white cat has just killed a bird (1782). In another work from the Edo period, again a black and white cat sits up to smell some peonies; it is appropriately entitled *Cat and Peonies*. Another attributed to Isoda Koryûsai, and also of the Edo period, is *Cat Looking at Three Butterflies*. The oblong representation shows a calico cat looking up at three pinkish butterflies. In *Cat and a Goldfish Bowl*, 1765-1780 also by Koryûsai, a black and white cat stealthily balances on the rim of the bowl to look down at his hapless victims. In *Woman Holding a Cat* a woman holds a black and white cat at arm's length above her head as if it were a child with whom she were playing or admiring.

The colors black and white have similar meanings in both Japanese and Western cultures. Black represents foreboding, doom, and death and white purity and goodness. The symbolism of the cats being black and white might represent the duality between good and evil, or the balance of good and evil, or perhaps the Chinese concept of yin and yang.

Moving away from the peaceful coexistence with nature that the Japanese prints depict, the 18th century Indian painting, *A Lady Chases a Cat with a Stick*, reveals a rude violence that sharply contrasts with Japanese paintings and prints *(figure 7.28)*.

Figure 7.28. Indian Lady Chasing a Cat with a Stick, 18th Century, Artist Unknown

Painters in Korea and China also found the cat to be an irresistible subject. In *Cats and Sparrows* by Byeon Sang-byeok, a black and white cat and a tabby and white cat look at each other as one climbs a tree filled with birds *(figure 7.29)*. Both Korean and Chinese paintings captured the cat in natural settings, usually highlighting its innate hunting abilities.

The 18th century had brought about a new vision, and the cat had become even more ubiquitous than ever before. With dozens of poems penned in grief of its death, the cat lived on in minds as an icon to the beginnings of an advancement in man's humanity to his fellow creatures. The next century would bring the cat even closer to the pinnacle of a goddess risen.

Figure 7.29. Myojakdo (Cats and Sparrows), Byeon Sang-byeok, Joseon Dynasty, National Museum of Korea, Seoul

Chapter Eight

THE VICTORIAN CAT IN THE 19TH CENTURY

The gradual shift towards the humane treatment of animals that had started in the 17th and 18th centuries among the upper and middle classes became even more widespread in the 19th century. Urban planners concerned with the issues of cleanliness and sanitation now, in the 19th century, outwardly proclaimed the cat to be the primary mascot for their advertising campaigns. Advertisements for soap with neatly dressed little girls and boys accompanied by a cute kitty became the most frequently seen *(figure 8.1)*.

Figure 8.1. Baby's Own Soap Trade Card, Albert Toilet Soap Makers, Early 20th Century

Cats, finally prized for their cleanliness and neatness, were also honored for their godly past. Napoleon's scientific expedition to Egypt 1798-1801, and the eventual publication of the monumental 23 volume series, *Le Description de L'Égypte,* from 1809-1828, as well as the discovery of over 80,000 mummified cats in the Egyptian town of Beni Hasan, opened up the world of Egyptian magic and mysticism, and at last documented the cat's past as the cat goddess Bast.

With the beginning of the Victorian era, cats, and animals in general, gained even more popularity and status in society. The Victorian home would not be complete without plants, animals, and eventually even fish. Pet keeping became a symbol of the modern household, and represented the ability to control what seemed uncontrollable. Compensating for their inability to control the dangerous lower working classes, the upper and middle classes asserted their power over nature and domestic pets. In an effort to establish and perpetuate their own values, they projected them onto pets so that "…cleanliness, order and rationality marked bourgeoisie pet keeping" (Kete, 1994, p. 138).

As a result of this new-found acceptance of pets, there came a movement to establish their rights as living, feeling beings. In 1850, The Grammont Law prohibited the public abuse of all animals in France. Even so, the private torture of vivisection for supposed medical advancement continued unabated. An unnecessary process that tortured primarily dogs because of their docility and ability to be easily caught, luckily enough, did not often affect cats because of their aloofness and feral viciousness. Artists and writers such as Victor Hugo (1802-1885) spoke out against vivisection as a malevolent treatment of animals calling it "—a crime"(Kete, 1994, p. 138). However, it was the women of the age that took the lead in setting up sanctuaries for these maltreated animals. "The ladies occupied themselves with rescuing dogs and cats, spending all their small resources on the creation of animal shelters" (Besse, 1895, pp. 239-256).

The bond between women and cats became even more pronounced during the 19th century. Many attributed the new-found care that women lavished upon needy animals, in particular cats, as a refuge from "…the brutality they endured from men" (Zeldin, 1981, p. 156). But many men saw the situation differently and equated women with cats in a profoundly negative manner, often referring to the two as having the disposition of prostitutes. Alphonse Toussenel wrote in *Passional Zoology* (1852), "An animal so keen on maintaining her appearance, so silky, so tiny, so eager for caresses, so ardent and responsive, so graceful and supple….; an animal that makes the night her day, and who shocks decent people with the noise of her orgies, can have only one single analogy in this world, and that analogy is of the feminine kind." He went on to add, "Lazy and frivolous and spending entire days in contemplation and sleep, while pretending to be hunting mice….incapable of the least effort when it comes to anything repugnant, but indefatigable when it is a matter of pleasure, of play, of sex, love of the night. Of whom are we writing, of the (female) cat or of the other?" (Kete, 1994, p. 120) The other here of course is woman. Continuing, Toussenel wrote, "The female cat attaches herself to the dwelling and not to the people who live there, proof of her ingratitude and aridity of her heart" (Kete, 1994, p. 127). Similar negative views about cats that eventually came to be equated with women can be traced all the way back to Aristotle who wrote in his *History of Animals* that "the females are very lascivious, and invite the male, and make a noise during intercourse" (Aristotle, trans. 1897, p. 103) *(figure 8.2)*.

Figure 8.2. Tintype portrait of 4 women with a cat, 1865, Smithsonian Institute, Washington, D.C.

Society as a whole began to change because of the taming and acceptance of domestic pets, and with this change came many firsts. The first public aquarium opened in London in 1875. And due to the fruition of an idea of the cat loving Harrison Weir, the first cat show was held in London's Crystal Palace in 1871 *(figures 8.3 and 8.4),* and in 1895, New York's Madison Square Garden welcomed the first cat show in the United States.

Figure 8.3. First cat show at The Crystal Palace, 1871, London

Prize Cats at the Crystal Palace Cat Show, 1871.

Figure 8.4. Prize-winners, The Crystal Palace, 1871, London

The first pet cemetery, *Cimetière des Chiens et Autres Animaux Domestiques,* in the small city of Asnières-sur-Seine just outside Paris, was founded in 1899 *(figure 8.5).* And to accommodate this widespread love of household pets in the middle of the 19th century, veterinarians began to care for the welfare of cats and other domestic animals.

Figure 8.5. Asnières cimetière chiens, Antique Postcard

The first pet vendors appeared in London, and a lucrative trade in domesticated pets blossomed to a record 20,000 sellers (Ritvo, 1987). With this rise in pet ownership, a new product, canned dog food, soon followed *(figure 8.6).*

The First Cat Ladies

Not long after this increasing interest in pet ownership began, the first cat ladies became known. Appearing in children's literature in such stories as, *Dame Wiggins of Lee* and *Dame Trot and her Cat, (figure 8.7)* cat ladies seemed acceptable and taught children moral and ethical lessons.

Figure 8.6. Cats' Meat Man, 1920, London

However, in reality cat ladies were punished for their excesses. In 1887, one of the first cat ladies, the Countess de la Torre, was charged with having too many cats in her rooms in Lille-road, Fulham. A well-known cat lover, to the utter consternation of her neighbors, by 1885 she had acquired twenty-one cats. Newspapers were filled with lengthy articles regarding her odd behavior such as one published in the *Te Aroha News* of 1884 documenting the subsequent turn of events.

Figure 8.7. Dame Trot and her Comical Cat, 1880

The Countess and Her Cats

One day recently the Countess de la Torre, who is famous in London as the owner of a large number of cats, was summoned in a Police Court and ordered to destroy her pets, as they had become a nuisance to her neighbours. On this the "Pall Mall Gazette" sent their enterprising interviewer to see the Countess, with the following result:

CURIOUS INTERIOR. *I pulled the bell at 35, Pembroke Square, but it offered no resistance and made no sound. I knocked with my knuckles, but there* *was no answer. The lower sitting room seemed to be empty, and the house, above and below, gave no sign of life. The door was evidently new, and had received a first coat of red paint. It was without a knocker, or a handle, or a number. I was beginning to think that I had come to the wrong house when a boy who was playing in the square cried out, "Look out! She's coming!" and I heard steps, and, after some unbarring of bolts, the door was cautiously opened."The Countess de la Torre?" "I am the Countess. Come in." The door was carefully closed behind me, and I found myself in the narrow passage which would be called a hall by courtesy, half lighted by a long window opening on to the staircase. What little space there was was blocked with dishes, bottles, and bundles of newspapers. I followed the Countess into the sitting-room. She seated herself in a low chair near the window, guarded by wooden shutters drawn close together for protection from stray stones and iron, which sometimes came crashing through. She motioned me to a low oak chair, the only remnant of luxury in the room. The floor was carpetless. In one corner was a small heap of blankets; at my feet was a small open hamper half filled with straw, the bed of one of her cats. Between us stood a deal box, which might be used as a table, but was occupied by various cats during my sitting of two hours. By her side was another box filled to overflowing with letters and papers, to which she constantly referred. The wall was papered. The mantel-piece was littered with an undiscribable(sic) mass of odds and ends; a few empty shelves were fixed in one corner, and that was all. Through the open folding-doors I saw another room, containing a plain iron bed with a few bed clothes, the only piece of furniture, unless one counted boxes and jugs, and plates of rod disinfecting powder. That, I presume, was the bedroom.*

THE COUNTESS'S BIOGRAPHY

In her chair by the window, in that bare room, surrounded by her cats in council, sat the Countess, her face in the shade. She is apparently about forty-five years old, with a pale, intellectual face, furrowed by much trouble, a broad high forehead, from which her dark grey hair is brushed away. Her face lightens up when excited, and the wildness of her brown eyes softens when her cats jump up on her lap. A grey knitted shawl was fastened round her neck and fell to her waist, where it was joined by a well-worn cotton dress. "Perhaps," she began, "I inherited my fondness for animals from my father. He had a passion for cats. Whenever I take a poor starved creature in I think of my father, and fancy that I am paying a tribute to his memory. I have no other tie in the world but my cats, no one to care for, no one to care for me." The Countess was born in the purple. Her father was Italian and her mother a Scotchwoman, but she herself is cosmopolitan, and speaks fluently English, German, Italian, and French. The united fortunes of herself and her husband made a most handsome income, but much of it was gambled away, and the Countess has lavished her own share with a free hand. Garibaldi was indebted to her for large sums of money, and that the Countess, who has paid so much for the cause of Italian freedom, should be reduced to her present extremities, should serve as a warning to intending patriots; for, alas! she has not found the gratitude which she expected. "I have spent gold enough to fill this room — aye, and more — to benefit my fellow-beings. They have proved to be ingrates. My charity has been abused. Animals are more grateful than my fellows. I now devote my small means to the cause of suffering cats and dogs and dumb creatures." The Countess, it may be added, besides devoting much of her large fortune to the cause of Italian freedom, took charge of one of the hospitals during the war, and when in charge of the ambulance was twice wounded. Her sobriquet was the Italian Nightingale, in allusion not to her powers of singing, but of nursing. In 1870 she was busy again at Versailles nursing the German wounded. "I come of a military family. I shall stick to my post. At present I am in a state of siege. l am ordered to abate the nuisance, and daily I am subject to a fine of ten shillings a day until I do so. I keep my doors locked, so that my enemies shall not enter if I can help it. Will, oh! will the law allow them to come and kill my cats?" And here there was a flood of tears. The little boys and girls — wicked urchins — who deserve to be devoured by wolves like the rogues who mocked at the prophet, cry at her: "Hoh ! hoh ! mother of dogs and cats ! Thou shouldst be burned, thou wicked one ! Harbourer of unclean animals, thou shouldst be drowned as a witch" "Are we living in the Middle Ages? Will they duck (drown) me? or will the ordeal be by fire ?"

THE STRYCHNINE AT WORK.

An animal smell pervaded the house, but without I did not detect anything unusual, however one might regard the Countess as a next-door neighbour, it is ridiculous to say that her establishment is a nuisance to the whole square. Since the decision of the magistrate on Saturday, poison has made sad havoc among the cats. The Countess burst into tears as she told of the death of her red cat "Ruby," of the tabby Manx "Rosie," of the decease of "Jumbo," of "Bella," and another whose name has escaped me. Post-mortems have revealed the strychnine. How have they come by their death? Is it the neighbours? For, strange to say, after the appeal case, which went against the Countess, poison carried off two of the collection, "Bob" and "Cobby," who are now at rest. "I would not have sold them for a hundred pounds apiece," sobbed the Countess, crying bitterly. "How can they inflict this agony upon me? My cats are all I have to care for in the whole world. My left-hand neighbour does not complain; it is the people on my right who are persecuting me. Ask the postmen or the policemen whether my house smells strongly enough to be a nuisance. Why, my windows are always open; my cats are never allowed to go out at night, so that there may be no noise. Every morning at daylight I put on my dressing-gown and let them out. As for the smell, why, my windows are open all day long, with a draught of fresh air constantly ventilating the house, and dishes of carbolic powder in every room. Does the law of England say how many cats or how many dogs I shall keep? No. *Why the pigeons in the square have damaged my roof, but I have said nothing about it. Then why shouldn't I be allowed to have my cats in peace; there are seventy houses round about me; every house has its cat, I daresay, and those seventy are actually allowed to do as they list at night, whilst my poor pets are put under lock and key to preserve the peace."*

FIVE CATS DEAD IN THE COAL-CELLAR.

The Countess then led the way down the steps on to the kitchen floor, down a passage which took us to the area. "Here are my dead pets," she cried, as she pulled open the door of the coal-cellar. On the top of an empty hamper lay two fine black-and-white cats, rigid with the colds of a violent death. These were lifted up, and beneath the hamper were three more fine cats, also dead, apparently from strychnine. With careful step I then went into the strip of garden, a little wilderness with one or two trees, the grass long and uncared for, and the beds choked up with weeds, low party walls separating it from the gardens on each side. The dogs, bright, cheery fellows, barked a welcome, and one or two cats appeared and followed us with every mark of affection. "Ah!" said the Countess with a shriek, "there is something wrong with this poor cat," lifting it up, smelling its mouth, and carrying it indoors. Then we went into the dark kitchen, in which it is easy to picture the Countess, brooding over the ingratitude of the men and women whom she had befriended, and thinking of the treasure that has been thrown so recklessly and so fruitlessly away, seated on a broken-backed chair, with a few embers burning in the grate, and a halfpenny candle stuck in the neck of a bottle. "Let us go upstairs," said the Countess; and, mounting the narrow bare steps, followed by half-a-dozen cats, we entered a room overlooking the square, one window being open, the other closed, with the shutters fastened across. This room is the old nursery. An old sideboard stood in the middle, on which was a waste-paper basket filled with litter, where inclined a big grey cat. A small, low chair, such as passengers use at sea, covered with a bit of sheepskin, stood by the open window. Before the fireplace were the cradles ranged round. On a torn and battered sofa were half a dozen little baskets for the reception of the mothers and their offspring. The room, like the others in the house, had a poverty-stricken air, being altogether given up to the animals. Close against the walls were jugs and pails of water, plates full of the red disinfectant powder, dirty glasses, and an old basket or two.

THE CATS COME TO THE COUNTESS.

"I have now only five of my own left. I have eight or ten stray ones, three dogs, and a few puppies. Do not think that I go to look for them. No, no. They come to me. There is a poor little kitten who came mewing to my door last night. I must give it shelter. Sometimes I have more, sometimes less. It is all the same to me. Letters often come asking me to take charge of a cat whose mistress is going to India, or to some far-off country. 'Will you take my cat, Countess, and care for it? they write. I take it, of course, and when my house gets too full I try to provide homes elsewhere for the poor creatures. Look at Bijou," stroking a pretty cat sitting beside me purring most contentedly. "He was brought to me a few weeks ago by a poor girl, a seamstress, whose garret full of furniture had been sold for a debt. She came to me sobbing as if her heart would break, and beseeched me to take the poor fellow. Bijou came, and you ask about the existence of affection in a cat. Why for many hours he never moved from one position, and refused all food. At last he settled down, but the other day his mistress came here, and the cat made a great spring to her lap, kissing her face, and evincing the greatest joy at her appearance. Some day she will take him away again, poor girl! There is a cat which a lady who has sailed for India sent to me. I had to pay three shillings for its carriage from Brighton," added the Countess with an odd smile. "When a stray cat first joins the circle, starving and wretched, I put her down in the middle of the room before a basin of milk or soup. The others, who have probably gone through the same experience and know quite well how the case is, watch their new comrade from a distance, eyeing her with vigilance taking her food. One by one they approach nearer, looking at me and then at the cat. Gradually they form a circle, and sitting each on her haunches, they regard the new-comer with complacency, never thinking of helping themselves." "Cats," mused the Countess, sadly, "have a prescience of coming death. My dear ones who have just gone hovered round me for the last week closer than ever, clinging to my skirts, and looking up at me with forbodings of evil omen in their eyes. I watched them with all the greater care and tenderness. But I have always noticed this in the cats. Ruby gave two great bounds and jumped to my bosom. She died there, and her last look said, 'Mother, they have poisoned me.'"

THE HABITS OF THE CATS.

"I never allow anyone to feed my cats but myself; no other hand touches their food.

They have bread and milk at times, but I find that soup with biscuit is the best diet. I take a sheep's head, and make a good stock. I then break the biscuit up into it. The food costs me about a penny a day. You see how beautifully clean my cats are; that is by the constant use of the brush. It is most cruel to wash a cat, which abhors water. The greatest insult you can offer to a cat is to throw water at it. If a strange cat comes into a house, and you wish to get rid of it, do not drive it away with a stone or a stick; throw a glass of water over it. You will then see the cat retreat indignantly, and with a haughty indifference to the consequences of a retreat, as much as to say, 'You dare to throw water at me. I leave you. I shake the dust of your house from my paws. Nevermore shall you see me.' It is like pork to a Jew. Of all cats the tortoise-shell is the most intelligent. They are almost human. Prince Krapotkin's experiments, of which I read the other day, I have repeatedly tried myself. I have seen cats look into the mirror, paw it gently, walk right round it, over and over again, puzzled, and eventually beat a retreat, completely at a loss to understand the phenomenon. Now that we are discussing the cat, it is worth noticing that during the whole of one year, with all my cats of both sexes, I have only had one litter of kittens, of which the father and mother have been my own cats. They prefer fresh faces like human beings." The Countess at this moment rose from her chair and called in a soft voice for some of her familiars. They came in from every corner. Upstairs I heard the patter of feet, as they had evidently jumped up from their sleep, and then the sound of their footsteps coming down the steps. (Is the instinct of locality very strong in the cat? Do the cats that are placed in your charge never find their way back to their former homes? "No. I find that cats that have been petted very much and have never been allowed to roam soon settle down." "Surely in your large family it is a little difficult to preserve order"—a question suggested by a very severe lick in the face administered by a sedate-looking black-and-white cat to a too playful kitten. " I call the black-and-white there the Policeman. He settles all quarrels. He is exclusive in his friendships, and keeps order in my house. He is my oldest friend, and is rewarded with an odd mixture of fear and respect." "If I had seventy cats in my house, do you think that they would have the same dispositions?" "No. Cats are as human beings. 'One is sulky, another affectionate, one is spiteful, another combative, one sentimental, another may have a sweet disposition, be soft and gentle, one may be fond of wandering, another prefers the fireside. When a strange cat comes into the house it shows much concern as to its surroundings. It refuses food perhaps, and sits on a box or a chair for hours together, looking intently at me as I sit here. 'Who are you?' 'Are you going to be kind to me!' 'Why do you go out of your way to show me all this kindness ?' That is what the strange cat says to me. Having made up its mind quite suddenly that I am its friend, she makes a great jump at me, and clings to me, purring and caressing me."

CRUELTY TO ANIMALS.

"Countess, have you taught your doctrine of kindness to your cats ? Suppose Bijou there spied a mouse, would she sit contentedly then on the box?" "No, alas! Bijou and Bob, Jumbo and Bella, soft and gentle as they are, are but cats. When the millennium comes then they will play with a mouse no longer. But can you explain the horrible cowardice which shall make a man able to abuse an animal. Now I feed the sparrows in the square with a few handfuls of crumbs, but when they come fluttering to me — for they have learned to know me well— why the boys, urged on by bribes, or by their own innate cruelty, stone them to death. Only the other day they killed one before my eyes with a catapult ; another I rescued, and gave the poor bruised thing a shelter. I put it in the sun, and in two or three hours it revived and took wing. When I hear a woman say, 'Oh ! I hate cats,' I look upon her with contempt. The heart of a woman should be open to the sufferings of animals and all dumb things. A woman who is cruel to an animal would be cruel to a child. A hard hearted woman is an error of nature. Why, I could tell you of many great men and women who have cherished the cat. Mahommed himself when his cat fell asleep on his sleeve, it being time to go to prayers at the mosque, rather than disturb the slumbers of the cat, cut off his sleeve. Richelieu had his portrait painted with cats in his arm; then take Chateaubriand, George Sand, or Victor Hugo. The Princess of Wales once said at a meeting of the Society for the Protection of Animals: ' If I have saved one cat from misery, I shall feel that I have done something.' What a charming answer !" But all animals are fond of the Countess. She has even cherished spiders more for their delicate beauty of their workmanship than for themselves. "I used to bring them to me by a peculiar low hiss."

A LETTER OF SYMPATHY.

Letters of sympathy came pouring in upon this unfortunate lady. Some are genuine enough. Others may be judged of by what follows : "My lady, — I am sorry for the magistrate's decision against you on Saturday, and in case you should wish to find sympathy with the human race, instead of the feline," etc. Certainly neat. The writer then goes on to tell a sad enough story, and winds up by proposing that the Countess shall purchase the pawn-tickets for what follows :" Girls' button boots (nines), 3s. ; flannel petticoat, 4s. 6d. ; black overcoat, 12s. ; light trousers, 6s. ; half-dozen table knives, Gs. ; half-dozen cheese knives, 5s; best plate half dozen table forks, 7s. ; ditto half dozen desert, 6s. ; ivory carver and fork, 7s. ; ditto poultry ditto, 6s. ; silver watch, 15s. ; metal ditto, 7 ; " etc. There is a touch of humour in the postcript, "All warranted good as new and carriage paid. Cash with order, as they have to be redeemed from the pawnbrokers' — suitable for presents {sic)." "Self and wife are members of the Church of England" damns the fellow at once. Then I bade the Countess good-bye, thinking of some of the grim stories which she had poured out, half sadly, half fiercely, of women who had lain in amid those sad surroundings, of families she had succoured within those bare walls; and but over these it is best to draw the veil of oblivion. Her whole life affords another proof of the old saying that truth is stranger than fiction. So ends the story of the Countess and her cats. I met the cat's-meat man with his armful of skewers on the door step. The door closed upon him, but I heard the cats chorusing a devouring welcome. Some day they may devour the Countess. There may be no gratitude either in man or beast. It would be a sublime ending" (as cited in Hartwell, 2014).

The news of the Countess' odd behavior was even reported in *The New York Times,* dated January 22, 1885, and picked up from *The London Daily News* outlining her bad reputation for caring for cats. In addition, there seems to be some outrage at her audacity to put up placards soliciting the prevention of cruelty to animals.

Cat ladies did not just exist in London, but in other cities as well. New York City was to have its own notorious cat hoarder too. Rosalie Waare (nicknamed Catty Goodman-her married name), a Prussian immigrant, purchased a 17th century house in 1871 which came to be called "one of the greatest curiosities in New York". In 1875, a reporter from the *New York Sun* visited Rosalie's house upon rumors that she was a crazy cat lady. When he arrived, he found dozens of cats near the house and even sitting on the eaves and window sills. He also found cats in the courtyard drinking soup and milk out of earthenware dishes. The reporter vividly describes the house as follows:

"As the visitor clambers up the dark, cobwebbed staircases, evidence of cats are perceptible on every hand; cats yellow, cats black, golden and dingy; cats tawny, white, and dubious; cats ringtailed, dovetailed, and notailed; cats with eyes, without eyes, earless, and cats of every description skulk in the black nooks or rush out and disappear in sudden panic. And all the time, from sunrise to sunrise, an aromatic and voluminous cloud of feline exhalation is rafted down the stairs into the street."

Oddly enough, Rosalie was initially afraid of cats until one day she came across "a wee little kitten, a homeless street Arab which she nursed and Christianized. Tiger informed the rest of the neighborhood cats that there was a cat lover nearby and thus started poor Rosalie's reputation as a cat lady. It was only when Tiger was stolen and kept in a basement where he eventually starved to death that Rosalie decided to provide food and homes for the other needy animals.

"I found nothing but his bones, and I buried him, and then I made up my mind that I'd take care of all the cats I could when people turned them out in the cold to starve. It's only people without sense or heart that would turn a helpless animal out in the cold. There ought to be some asylum for such abandoned animals in this country, as there is in England, but there is none, and somebody must look out for them. I don't love the cats yet, but I pity them, and I think when I'm dead they'll have no one to take care of them" (Gavan, n.d.).

Figure 8.8. Rosalie Goodman, Cat Hoarder, 1871

The *New York Sun* published Rosalie Goodman's story on the front page, and soon after other newspapers and their reporters became interested in her strange story. In August 1877, *The New York Tribune* sent a reporter to her house who found her stirring a pot on the stove surrounded by about 50 cats. Rosalie told the reporter that she spent about $1.50 a day feeding her cats the best cakes, sausages, and beefsteaks. As she spoke, she served the cats their dinner from the pot she had been stirring. "The cats ate daintily, as though used to a good living" (The Iola Register, 1877).

Reporters continued to try to get stories about her, but she got tired of being interviewed, and by the summer of 1878, Rosalie was totally fed up with the intrusions and threatened the reporters so that they would leave her and her cats alone. In the end, Rosalie was able to keep her cats, as even though the neighbors continued to complain, the Board of Health found nothing illegal about her trying to help cats. This was a much kinder resolution to the problem than poor Countess de la Torre had to endure *(figure 8.8)*.

Famous Cat Owners

Even though bourgeois society tried to claim the ownership of the cat, by its very nature it was never truly an integral part of bourgeois culture. Instead, the 19th century cat became a constant companion and a symbol of those in the bohemian literary life. Associating with intellectuals, elitists, writers and artists, "The excessively independent cat lived rather as the intellectual did, an existence of bourgeois individualism freed from the constraints of modern life. In the fictional world of creativity, both set themselves outside of family, society, and state, refusing to be dishonored—" (Kete, 1994, p. 126). Unsurprisingly, the cat's truculent amoral attitude fit that of its companion artists and intellectuals.

On the other hand, even sensible Victorians prized the cat because of its ancient symbolic association with motherhood and domesticity, using it to reinforce and model those ideals in women. "Cats were touted as great role models for young girls because of their cleanliness, grace, poise and mothering skills. It was suggested that each girl be given a small female kitten and when it grew up the

the girl would learn about being a devoted mother"[†](Milani, 1993, p. 30)*(figure 8.9)*. The once wild, untamable feline became a loyal and most importantly clean, well-behaved companion. Gone were the representations in paintings of cats stealing food and fighting seen in earlier centuries. Now they were mostly depicted in peaceful, loving scenes as mother cats and kittens as well as loyal docile companions to children, mainly girls.

Figure 8.9. Three Girls, Cats, and a Trike, Library of Congress Prints and Photographs Division, Washington, D.C.

Inevitably the cat became a subject fawned over by writers and artists, but many statesmen, politicians, and other famous personages

[†] Many paintings of girls and cats were created during the 19th century supporting this thesis.

came to be known as cat lovers as well. Abraham Lincoln, the 16th president of the United States, agreed to let his son Tad bring his Tabby cat to the White house as its first feline resident. Lincoln himself held a soft spot for cats. When on a trip to visit General Grant's troops, he came across a litter of kittens and took them back to the White House. Even the Confederate Civil War General Robert E. Lee often referred to his cats in letters to his family, and noted his dog's jealousy of them. In 1878, the first Siamese landed in America as a gift to the wife of the 19th president of the United States, Rutherford B. Hayes. "Siam" as she was called became a cherished pet, but died only nine months after her arrival. Other notable people of the time loved cats such as Hiram Bingham (1789-1869), who was an American missionary who translated the Bible into Hawaiian while accompanied by his cat Barnabus.

The famous British nurse and humanitarian Florence Nightingale (1820-1910) owned more than 60 cats during her lifetime, mostly Persians; some even ventured with her on her many journeys. One of the more memorable of her pets was named Mr. Bismarck. Mr. Bismarck was just one of the reputed 17 cats that shared their lives with Florence Nightingale after she returned to London from the Crimean War. She described him as "the most sensitive of cats" and his paw prints frequently marched across her correspondence. Other members of her feline family included Big Pussie, Tom, Topsy, Tib, Gladstone, Mrs Tit, Mr Muff, and Quiz. Nightingale was chronically ill in later years and took refuge in her cats who, she said, possessed much more sympathy and feeling than human beings. When she died in 1910, it was no surprise to learn that she had made provision for her remaining cats in her will (Bostridge, 2008).

Pope Leo XII (1823-29), loved his cat Micetto. As a kitten, Micetto hid in the Pope's papal sleeve peering out at those being given audiences. Even Queen Victoria (1837-1901), loved cats, especially one named White Heather, a fluffy white Persian or Angora. Queen Victoria is usually portrayed as having been an austere woman and lacking in humor ("we are not amused"). However, she was a noted animal lover, and she and her dearly lamented deceased husband, Prince Albert, offered a warm and loving home to many cats. She truly doted on her last cat, White Heather, who, on her orders, remained living in the lap of luxury at Buckingham Palace long after the queen herself had died.

It was also Queen Victoria who demanded that a cat be included in the picture on the Queen's Medal of Kindness, insisting that something must be done about the general aversion to cats, "which were generally misunderstood and grossly ill-treated" (Rogers, 2006, p. 48).

Cats in Art

Over a 100 artists in the 19th century and through the turn of the 20th century chose to capture the cat not only on canvas but in a myriad of advertisements, greeting cards and sculptures. For the first time in history the cat would find itself as the primary subject of art with such artists as the prolific cat lovers Henriëtte Ronner-Knip, Théophile Alexandre Steinlen and Louis Wain choosing almost exclusively to paint their feline friends, while the well-known photographer Harry Pointer photographed them in strange anthropomorphic poses *(figure 8.10).*

Figure 8.10. Harry Pointer's Pets, c 1880

Cats would become human in dresses, bows and ribbons, wearing pants, and even fighting wars. Wain and Pointer's anthropomorphic representations brought the cat closer to the human heart by depicting it as human. The cat's natural viciousness was gone; instead, it sat primly clothed in dresses sipping tea, a living doll, an eternal child.

Figure 8.11. A Young Girl with Cat, Berthe Morisot, 1886, Private Collection

An avid cat painter, the Dutch artist Henriëtte Ronner-Knip (1821-1901) was born in Amsterdam into a family of painters. Quite precocious, she sold her first painting at age 15. Highly decorated with many medals and honors, and having painted for quite a few of the royalty in Europe, Ronner-Knip is well known for her paintings of domestic pets, primarily cats. Paintings of pets were popular with the wealthy bourgeois in the Victorian era, and her many paintings of cats getting into mischief in domestic scenes proved to be favorites. Mostly sentimental portrayals, her paintings rarely offer any metaphorical meanings, and are focused only on the cats themselves. She studied her cat subjects with avidity and sincerity, even going so far as to construct a specially built glass-fronted studio wherein her cats could freely scamper about, sleep, and get into the type of trouble that only cats can while the prolific Ronner-Knip sketched and painted them *(figure 8.12)*.

Figure 8.12. Playing with Paints, Henriëtte Ronner- Knip, c. 1890, Private Collection

Probably best known today for his posters, the Swiss artist Théophile Alexandre Steinlen (1859-1923) loved cats. As a young boy, Steinlen drew cats in the margins of his books and grew up to live in a house he named "Cat's Cottage". While living in Paris, his house on the Rue Caulaincourt became a well-known gathering place for all the cats in the quartier. Steinlen's depictions of cats consist of simple lines. Unlike the cute Victorian kittens of Ronner-Knip, Steinlen's cats exude a certain feline regality. Ronner-Knip's cats are children's pets, whereas Steinlen's are independent and too proud to be depicted tipping over a lamp or teapot. Their quiet beauty is also profoundly portrayed in the many sculptures that Steinlen produced *(figure 8.13).*

Figure 8.13. Two Cats, Théophile Alexandre Steinlen , La Bodinière, Museum of Fine Arts, Boston

The English artist Louis Wain's (1860-1939) depictions of cats during the Victorian era caused their popularity to rise to a height not known since they were first worshipped as the goddess Bast. Wain was the only boy in a household of five sisters, where he remained until the age of 23 when he married his sisters' governess, Emily Richardson. Sadly, only three years after their marriage, Emily died of breast cancer. Wain's lifelong devotion to cats perhaps started because of Peter, a black and white kitten, whom the couple had taken in as a stray. Peter comforted Emily throughout her illness, and Wain taught the cat various tricks to cheer his wife. He began to draw Peter, and Emily encouraged him to try and have the pictures published. Later Wain was to write, "To him, properly, belongs the foundation of my career, the developments of my initial efforts, and the establishing of my work." Over the next 30 years, Wain would produce hundreds of drawings a year, illustrate about a hundred children's books, publish in magazines and journals and even find time to be the President and Chairman of the newly founded National Cat Club. He also avidly supported several animal charities such as the Governing Council of Our Dumb Friends League, the Society for the Protection of Cats and the Antivivisection Society. Wain was quoted as saying, "I have found as a result of many years of inquiry and study, that people who keep cats and are in the habit of petting them, do not suffer from those petty ailments which all flesh is heir to. Rheumatism and nervous complaints are uncommon with them, and pussy's lovers are of the sweetest temperament. I have often felt the benefit after a long spell of mental effort, of having my cats sitting around my shoulders or half an hour's chat with Peter" (Van Vechten, 1921, p. 116).

Unfortunately, Wain had no head for business and endured financial hardships throughout his lifetime. From the early 1900's, Wain's mental health began to deteriorate. Most have thought that he had schizophrenia, but some today believe he might have had Asperger's Syndrome. Throughout the last years of his life his depictions of cats became more and more surreal, kaleidoscopic *(figure 8.14)*. He was eventually committed to a pauper's mental asylum in 1924. After outcries from H.G. Wells and the Prime Minister, he was moved to a proper hospital where he lived out the remaining years of his life until 1939. H.G. Wells said of him, "He has made the cat his own. He invented a cat style, a cat society, a whole cat world. English cats that do not look and live like Louis Wain cats are ashamed of themselves."

Harry Pointer (1822-1889) was an English photographer who became successful photographing his *Brighton Cats* series. After spending almost twenty years as a soldier in the Life Guards, the Oxfordshire born Pointer arrived in Brighton in 1858 and began working as a military drill instructor. However, in 1866 he established himself as a professional photographer and opened his studio in Bloomsbury Place. Pointer found his niche in photographing cats and kittens in anthropomorphic poses such as having tea and roller-skating or even demanding dinner. Pointer took and published around 200 pictures of cats.

Figure 8.14. Untitled, Called 'Early Irish Indian Cat', Louis Wain, c. 1924-1939

The American Harry Whittier Frees (1879-1953) followed in the wake of Pointer and began a career in cat photography in 1906. He made a successful living producing postcards, calendars and children's books often photographing dead animals that had been rather gruesomely stuffed. Frees wrote in his book *Animal Land on the Air*,

'Rabbits are the easiest to photograph in costume, but incapable to taking many "human" parts. Puppies are tractable when rightly understood, but the kitten is the most versatile animal actor, and possesses the greatest variety of appeal. The pig is the most difficult to deal with, but effective on occasion. The best period of

young animal models is a short one, being when they are from six to ten weeks of age. An interesting fact is that a kitten's attention is best held through the sense of sight, while that of a puppy is most influenced by sound, and equally readily distracted by it. The native reasoning powers of young animals are, moreover, quite as pronounced as those of the human species, and relatively far sure" (Frees, 1929) *(figure 8.15).*

Figure 8.15. The Little Folks of Animal Land, 1915, Harry W. Frees

The great French artists Renoir, Rousseau, Manet, Gauguin, and Cassatt are only a few of the hundreds of 19th century artists that included the cat in their paintings. In Renoir's *Madame Georges Charpentier and her Children*, (1878) *(figure 8.16)* the cat is barely visible on her lap. A very close and careful look at this painting reveals deeper images and meanings. There is a monstrous face on the curtain and skulls in Madame's dress. A cat sits on her lap looking up at her barely visible, disguised, an allusion to the fact that women and cats were still tied together through their association with sexuality and magic. Even though Marcel Proust once commented on the painting as representing the epitome of the bourgeois home, he obviously did not see the secondary images and did not realize that

Figure 8.16. Mme George Charpentier and her Children, 1878, Pierre Auguste Renoir, Metropolitan Museum of Art, New York

Renoir's message was ambiguous.

Henri Rousseau believed, as many cat lovers do today, that a person's character could be judged upon their attitude toward cats. Rousseau reveals this in a conversation with Boswell, who by the way, did not like cats.

"Rousseau : Do you like cats? Boswell : No. Rousseau : I was sure of that. It is my test of character. There you have the despotic instinct of men. They do not like cats because the cat is free and will never consent to become a slave. He will do nothing to your order, as the other animals do. Boswell : Nor a hen, either. Rousseau : A hen would obey your orders if you could make her understand them. But a cat will understand you perfectly and not obey them" (Lunn, 1953, p. 9).

Rousseau was self-taught and much of his life was spent as a customs officer, hence the nickname *Le Douanier*. Having only started painting at age 49, he was greatly ridiculed by most artists of the time. However, Picasso and some surrealists noticed his talent and genius.

His paintings are of the primitive style and usually have a person standing in the forefront of a landscape as in the *Portrait de Mme M. Rousseau*. Rousseau also painted a portrait of the writer and naval officer Pierre Loti, who just happened to be a cat lover as well *(figure 8.17)*. Loti even wrote a short story called *The Lives of Two Cats*. From *The Argus*, a Melbourne paper dated 1923, we have this article:

Pierre Loti's Cats.

Pierre Loti, whose death recently is so deeply deplored, adored cats, the New York "World" tells us. For many years he was president of a society of cat-lovers known as "La Patte de Velours" ("The Velvet Paw"). In the story he wrote "for my son Samuel when he has learned to read," Loti describes how he once saw the soul of a cat reveal itself suddenly for a moment "sad as a human soul and searching for my soul with pleading tenderness." In his "Le Livre de la Pitie et de la Mort" there is a terrible picture of a cat dying of mange. "It must have felt in its awful plight the worst of all sufferings of a cat—that of not being able to make its toilet, to lick its fur, and to groom itself with the care cats always bestow upon this operation." A cat which formed part of the Loti household for ten years had her own visiting cards, inscribed "Mlle Moumoutte."

Figure 8.17. Portrait of Pierre Loti, Henri Rousseau, 1891, Kunsthaus, Zurich

The French artist Édouard Manet sketched and painted cats even decorating his personal letters with them. In a portrait of his wife, their pet cat Zizi nestles contentedly in her lap. In his controversial painting *Olympia, (figure 8.18)* a nude prostitute lies on a bed with a black cat at her feet as a symbol of sexuality and promiscuity. The painting caused quite a stir in the Paris art world of the time.

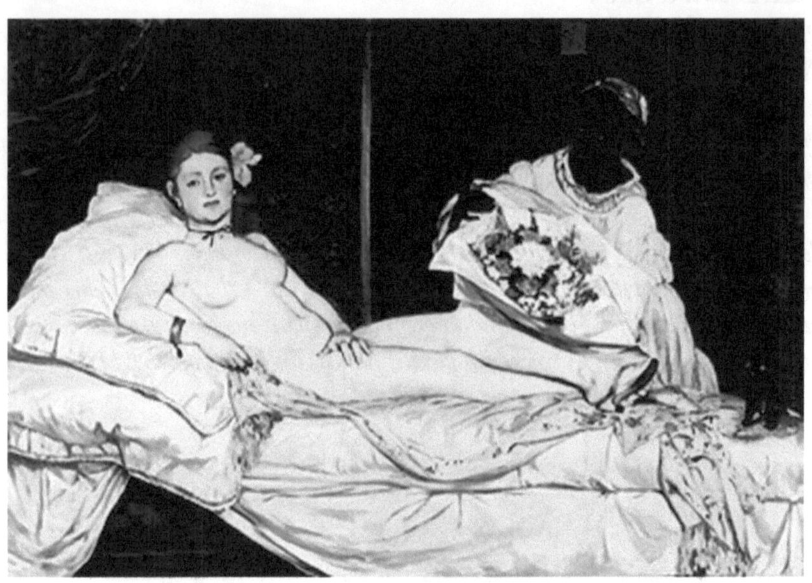

Figure 8.18. Olympia, Édouard Manet, 1863, Musée d'Orsay, Paris

Paul Gauguin (1848-1903) an inspiration to 20th century artists such as Pablo Picasso, Henri Matisse and Félix Vallotton, began painting off and on in 1873 and became friends with Camille Pissarro who also included cats in his works. Influenced by folk art and Japanese prints, Gauguin's new style was termed *Cloisonnism* because of his use of blocks of color divided by lines. During his nine week stay with Van Gogh in 1888, the two artists worked together *(figure 8.19).*

In Gauguin's *A Little Cat* (1888) our eyes are drawn to the cat, as it is the only figure in the painting, and it stands out dramatically against the gold and orange background. In 1888, Gauguin had defined his goal as " ——synthesis of form and color derived from the observation of only the dominant element." Both *A Little Cat* and

Mimi and her Cat can serve as examples of this. After travelling to Tahiti, Gauguin continued to paint, and the indispensable cat is present in many of these works as well. In the painting *Tahitian Woman and Two Children (1901)* a woman sits in a chair with a little boy on her lap while a girl stands in back at her side holding a white cat. Gauguin chose to add only white cats to these Tahitian paintings, perhaps due to the white cat being a symbol of purity and fertility *(figure 8.20)*. In his more Western-oriented paintings, his cats are usually two colors: brown/orange and white or even calico as in *Flowers and Cats* and *Mimi and her Cat.* The only exception is *A Little Cat,* which is black. Even though quite a prolific painter, Gauguin only became popular after his death. However, his use of bold colors and primitive style still continues to influence artists.

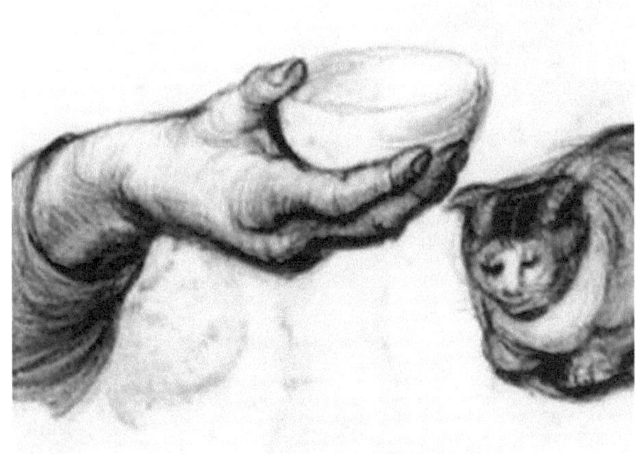

Figure 8.19. Hand with a Bowl and a Cat, Vincent Van Gogh, 1885, Van Gogh Museum, Amsterdam

Men were not the only artists to find the cat a great addition to paintings. Mary Stevenson Cassatt (1844-1926) and other female artists such as Cecilia Beaux used the cat as an age-old symbol of domesticity, motherhood and sexuality in their paintings. Cassatt became close friends with Edgar Degas and Camille Pissarro, and was the private student of Jean-Léon Gérôme. After some time, she was invited to join the Impressionist's group which only had one other female member, Berthe Morisot, another artist who included cats in her paintings, with whom Cassatt became close friends. Cassatt remained with the Impressionists until around 1886, but afterward started experimenting with other techniques, and eventually broke away from the group. The 1890's were her most prolific and creative years. In the 1900's, she began to concentrate almost exclusively on mother and child scenes where a cat is sometimes present to accentuate the idea of motherhood and domesticity *(figure 8.21).*

Figure 8.20. Where Do We Come From? What Are We? Where Are We Going? (Detail), Paul Gauguin, 1897-1898, Museum of Fine Arts, Boston

Nineteenth century French artists who pursued art for art's sake and looked away from the moralizing bourgeoisie found the cat an apt mascot. Because of its historical association with demons and the occult, the cat became the perfect symbol for the artist's rebellion against societal convention. Artists equated their own ability to see through the ordinary with superior perceptiveness to that of the cat's cool, indifferent detachment.

Figure 8.21. Sara Holding a Cat, Mary Cassatt, 1908, Private Collection

Cats and Musicians

Likewise, the great musicians of the age kept cats as pets and often included them in their operatic compositions. Alexander Borodin (1833-1887*)*, Rimsky Korsakov (1844-1908), Giacchino Rossini (1792-1868) and Ignacy Paderewski (1860-1941) loved the cat too. The Russian composers Alexander Borodin and Rimsky Korsakov were friends. Borodin was a well-known cat lover and Rimsky-Korsakov even wrote about Borodin's unruly cats. "Many cats, that the Borodins' lodged, marched back and forth on the table, thrusting their noses into the plates or leaping on the backs of the guests. These felines enjoyed the protection of Catherine Sergueïevna. They all had biographies. One was called Fisher because he was successful in catching fish through the holes in the frozen river. Another, known as Lelong, had the habit of bringing home kittens in his teeth which were added to the household. More than once, dining there, I have observed a cat walking along the table. When he reached my plate I drove him away; then Catherine Sergueïevna would defend him and recount his biography. Another installed himself on Borodin's shoulders and heated him mercilessly. 'Look here, sir, this is too much!' cried Borodin, but the cat never moved" (Van Vechten, 1921).

The Italian composer Giacchino Rossini (1792-1868) who is famous for writing *The Barber of Seville* is also attributed to writing *Duetto Buffo dei due Gatti, ("humorous duet for two cats")*. A popular performance piece for two sopranos, it is often performed as a concert encore. The "lyrics" consist entirely of the repeated word "miau" ("meow") [†].

Ignacy Paderewski was a Polish composer and pianist who became the Prime Minister and Foreign Minister of Poland in 1919, and is claimed to have been calmed by a cat during his first piano concerto. Paderewski was suffering from a bout of stage fright at his first major concert in London when an errant cat jumped into his lap during the performance. Not at all put off, Paderewski allowed the cat to remain in his lap throughout the performance, perhaps being comforted by the purring feline (Lane, 2004).

Cats and Writers

But it was in literature and poetry that the cat found its optimum medium. Almost all of the great writers and poets from all over the world referred to the feline in their writings. From Dickens to Mark Twain, cats were at the sides of the century's writers and poets.

When one of Charles Dickens' (1812-1870) cats, originally named William, gave birth to kittens in his study, she was appropriately

---

[†] While the piece is typically attributed to Gioachino Rossini, it was not actually written by him, but is instead a compilation written in 1825 that borrows from his 1816 opera, *Otello*. The English composer Robert Lucas de Pearsall most probably compiled the piece, and, for this purpose, used the pseudonym "G. Berthold" (Woodstra, Chris. *All Music Guide to Classical Music*, 2005, p. 1126).

renamed Willamena. Dickens was quite fond of one of her female kittens and named her "Master's Cat". While he wrote, she kept him company, sometimes annoyingly extinguishing the candle on his desk. It stands to reason that Dickens is quoted as saying, "What greater gift than the love of a cat." In 1862, Dickens was so distressed by the loss of his cat, Bob, that he had the cat's paw stuffed and mounted rather macabrely on an ivory letter opener engraved with "*C.D., In memory of Bob, 1862*"[†] *(figure 8.22)*. The great writer also made sure to include cats in his literary works. In *Bleak House* and *The Uncommercial Traveller* he used the cat as a metaphor for a cruel usurious society. Bleak House's cat, Lady Jane (originally bought for her skin) is loved by Krook who carries her around on his shoulder, but yet he is upset that the cat clingingly follows him, 'winding her lithe tail and licking her lips'. When the cat stares at Miss Flite's cage of birds, she represents a predatory society. Both Krook and the cat can be metaphors for warlock and familiar. Krook's mysterious knowledge and his spontaneous combustion suggest occult powers, and Lady Jane is by his side as an evil familiar (Rogers, 2006, p. 66).

Dickens negatively equated cats and women in *The Uncommercial Traveller* (1860) where he called the cats sluttish housewives and women feral cats.

"…so the cats of shy neighborhoods exhibit a strong tendency to relapse into barbarism. Not only are they made selfishly ferocious by ruminating on the surplus population around them, and on the densely crowded state of all the avenues to cat's meat; not only is there a moral and politico-economical haggardness in them, traceable to these reflections; but they evince a physical deterioration. Their linen is not clean, and is wretchedly got up; their black turns rusty, like old mourning; they wear very indifferent fur; and take to the shabbiest cotton velvet, instead of silk velvet. I'm on terms of recognition with several small streets of cats, about the Obelisk in St. George's Fields, —In appearance they are very like the women among whom they live. They seem to turn out of their unwholesome beds into the street, without any preparation. They leave their young families to stagger about the gutters, unassisted, while they frowzily quarrel and swear and scratch and spit, at street corners…. I remark that when they are about to increase their families (an event of frequent recurrence) the resemblance is

[†] The letter opener is on display at the New York Public Library in the Berg Collection of English and American Literature.

strongly expressed in a certain dusty dowdiness, down-at-heel self-neglect, and general giving up of things" (Dickens, 1860, p. 103).

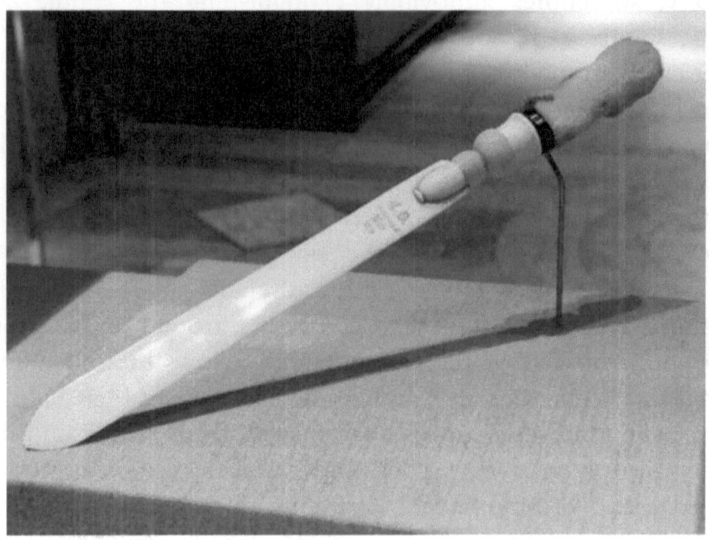

Figure 8.22. Charles Dicken's Cat Paw Letter Opener, Berg Collection, New York Public Library

Edward Lear (1812-1888), known for writing *The Owl and the Pussy Cat,* came from a large family, the 20th of 21 children. His father had been well off but lost his money in stocks and the family became impoverished. When he was 15, he started selling sketches to shopkeepers for "bread and cheese". Two years later he became well-known for his drawings of animals and birds at the London Zoo, and by age 19, he had compiled a monograph on parrots which was recognized as the first of its kind. From the age of 15 to 25, Lear suffered from depression, asthma and bronchitis as well as epilepsy.

In 1873, Lear met the kitten, Foss. Foss was a tabby who had had his tail shortened by the servants in the belief that it would keep him from straying away. As Foss aged, he came to have a rotund body and with his shortened tail was deemed an unattractive cat. Even so, Lear loved his cat and made many drawings of him *(figure 8.23).*When it became necessary for Lear to move, he requested that the architects design an exact duplicate of his former abode so that Foss would not be upset by the relocation (Vinegar, 2012). At the age of 17, Foss died in November, 1887. Lear devotedly buried him in his Italian garden at San Remo with a large tombstone to commemorate his life. Lear himself died only two months later in January, 1888.

He has many friends, lay men and clerical,
Old Foss is the name of his cat;
His body is perfectly spherical,
He weareth a runcible hat.

The Owl and the Pussy-Cat

I

The Owl and the Pussy-cat went to sea
  In a beautiful pea-green boat,
They took some honey, and plenty of money,
  Wrapped up in a five-pound note.
The Owl looked up to the stars above,
  And sang to a small guitar,
"O lovely Pussy! O Pussy, my love,
  What a beautiful Pussy you are,
    You are,
    You are!
What a beautiful Pussy you are!"

II

Pussy said to the Owl, "You elegant fowl!
  How charmingly sweet you sing!
O let us be married! too long we have tarried:
  But what shall we do for a ring?"
They sailed away, for a year and a day,
  To the land where the Bong-Tree grows
And there in a wood a Piggy-wig stood
  With a ring at the end of his nose,
    His nose,
    His nose,
  With a ring at the end of his nose.

III

"Dear Pig, are you willing to sell for one shilling
  Your ring?" Said the Piggy, "I will."
So they took it away, and were married next day

By the Turkey who lives on the hill.
They dined on mince, and slices of quince,
Which they ate with a runcible spoon;
And hand in hand, on the edge of the sand,
They danced by the light of the moon,
The moon,
The moon,
They danced by the light of the moon (Lear, 1894).

Figure 8.23. Edward Lear and Foss

Even though the cat had gained love and respect from some, the uneducated still clung to the superstitions of previous centuries, as Elizabeth Gaskell describes in her novel *North and South* (1855), in which an old peasant woman learns that Betty Barnes has stolen her cat and roasted it alive in a magical spell to appease her husband's anger. She believes that the cat's cries would summon the dark demons much as they were claimed to do during Taigherm (Rogers, 2006, p. 51).

English poets of the age found the cat a most willing subject for their poetic musings. Rosamond Marriott Watson (1860-1911) a Victorian poet dedicated a poem to her cat.

To My Cat

HALF loving-kindliness and half disdain,

Thou comest to my call serenely suave,
With humming speech and gracious gestures grave,
In salutation courtly and urbane;
Yet must I humble me thy grace to gain,
For wiles may win thee though no arts enslave,
And nowhere gladly thou abidest save
Where naught disturbs the concord of thy reign.
Sphinx of my quiet hearth! who deign'st to dwell
Friend of my toil, companion of mine ease,
Thine is the lore of Ra and Rameses;
That men forget doest thou remember well,
Beholden still in blinking reveries
With somber, sea-green gaze inscrutable (Stedman, 1895; Watson, 1892).

James William Elliott (1833-1915) collected nursery rhymes and set them to music. Famous for having written the *Mother Goose Nursery Rhymes*, the following rhyme was completed in 1870. The rhyme instructs children on how *not* to annoy a cat.

I love little pussy,
Her coat is so warm,
And if I don't hurt her,
She'll do me no harm.
So I'll not pull her tail,
Nor drive her away,
But pussy and I,
Very gently will play.

She shall sit by my side
And I'll give her some food;
And pussy will love me
Because I am good.

I'll pat pretty pussy,
And then she will purr;
And thus show her thanks
For my kindness to her.

I'll not pinch her ears,

Nor tread on her paw,
Lest I should provoke her
To use her sharp claw.
I never will vex her
Nor make her displeased:
For pussy don't like
To be worried and teased (Elliot, 1870).

The romantic English poet John Keats (1795-1821) penned the following poem *To Mrs. Reynold's Cat.* Even though not fully appreciated during his lifetime, his odes, especially *Ode on a Grecian Urn*, became quite famous.

To Mrs. Reynolds' Cat

Cat! who hast pass'd grand climacteric,
How many mice and rats hast in thy days
Destroy'd? How many tit bits stolen? Gaze
With those bright languid segments green,
  and prick
Those velvet ears – but pr'y thee do not stick
They latent talons in me—and upraise
Thy gentle mew – and tell me all thy frays,
Of fish and mice, and rats and tender chick.
Nay, look not down, nor lick thy dainty wrists –
For all thy wheezy asthma – and for all
Thy tail's tip is nicked off – and though the fists
Of many a maid have given thee many a maul,
Still is that fur as soft, as when the lists
In youth thou enter'dest on glass-bottled wall (Keats, 1884).

One of the earliest poems written by the poet Percy Bysshe Shelley (1792-1822) is *A Cat in Distress.* Written sometime between 1809-1811 when he was just ten years old, the poem describes his concern for the local tenant farmers as well as his love of nature. His sister Elizabeth copied the poem out and painted the watercolor picture of the cat on top and most probably gave it to their younger sister, Hellen, as a gift. Hellen then mentioned it to Percy Shelley's biographer, "I have in my possession a very early effusion of

Bysshe's, with a cat painted on the top of the sheet, I will try and find it: but there is not promise of future excellence in the lines, the versification is defective." The poem was first published in Thomas Jefferson Hogg's *Life of Percy Bysshe Shelley* (1858).

A Cat in Distress
Verses On A Cat

I.
A cat in distress,
Nothing more, nor less;
Good folks, I must faithfully tell ye,
As I am a sinner,
It waits for some dinner
To stuff out its own little belly.

II.
You would not easily guess
All the modes of distress
Which torture the tenants of earth;
And the various evils,
Which like so many devils,
Attend the poor souls from their birth.

III.
Some a living require,
And others desire
An old fellow out of the way;
And which is the best
I leave to be guessed,
For I cannot pretend to say.

IV.
One wants society,
Another variety,
Others a tranquil life;
Some want food,
Others, as good,
Only want a wife.

V.
But this poor little cat
Only wanted a rat,
To stuff out its own little maw;
And it were as good
Some people had such food,
To make them hold their jaw!

Quite often poets composed poems in remembrance of their beloved cats. Christina Rossetti (1830-1894) was a British romantic poet who dearly missed her cat and wrote the following poem.

On the Death of a Cat

Who shall tell the lady's grief
When her Cat was past relief?
Who shall number the hot tears
Shed o'er her, belov'd for years?
Who shall say the dark dismay
Which her dying caused that day?

Come, ye Muses, one and all,
Come obedient to my call;
Come and mourn with tuneful breath
Each one for a separate death;
And, while you in numbers sigh,
I will sing her elegy.

Of a noble race she came,
And Grimalkin was her name
Young and old fully many a mouse
Felt the prowess of her house;
Weak and strong fully many a rat
Cowered beneath her crushing pat;
And the birds around the place
Shrank from her too close embrace.
But one night, reft of her strength,
She lay down and died at length;
Lay a kitten by her side

In whose life the mother died.
Spare her line and lineage,
Guard her kitten's tender age,
And that kitten's name as wide
Shall be known as hers that died.
And whoever passes by
The poor grave where Puss doth lie,
Softly, softly let him tread,
Nor disturb her narrow bed (Rossetti, 1904, p. 89).

The famous writer Thomas Hardy (1840-1928) who also had a fondness for cats immortalizes a beloved feline companion in *Last Words to a Dumb Friend.*

Last Words to a Dumb Friend

Pet was never mourned as you,
Purrer of the spotless hue,
Plumy tail, and wistful gaze
While you humoured our queer ways,
Or outshrilled your morning call
Up the stairs and through the hall -
Foot suspended in its fall -
While, expectant, you would stand
Arched, to meet the stroking hand;
Till your way you chose to wend
Yonder, to your tragic end.

Never another pet for me!
Let your place all vacant be;
Better blankness day by day
Than companion torn away.
Better bid his memory fade,
Better blot each mark he made,
Selfishly escape distress
By contrived forgetfulness,
Than preserve his prints to make
Every morn and eve an ache.

From the chair whereon he sat
Sweep his fur, nor wince thereat;
Rake his little pathways out
Mid the bushes roundabout;
Smooth away his talons' mark
From the claw-worn pine-tree bark,
Where he climbed as dusk embrowned,
Waiting us who loitered round.

Strange it is this speechless thing,
Subject to our mastering,
Subject for his life and food
To our gift, and time, and mood;
Timid pensioner of us Powers,
His existence ruled by ours,
Should - by crossing at a breath
Into safe and shielded death,
By the merely taking hence
Of his insignificance -
Loom as largened to the sense,
Shape as part, above man's will,
Of the Imperturbable.

As a prisoner, flight debarred,
Exercising in a yard,
Still retain I, troubled, shaken,
Mean estate, by him forsaken;
And this home, which scarcely took
Impress from his little look,
By his faring to the Dim
Grows all eloquent of him.

Housemate, I can think you still
Bounding to the window-sill,
Over which I vaguely see
Your small mound beneath the tree,
Showing in the autumn shade
That you moulder where you played (Hardy, 1994, p. 621).

The English poet and novelist Algernon Charles Swinburne (1837-1909) was generally regarded in his youth as a decadent rebel, but after a serious illness, he settled down to a life of social respectability. In his poem *To a Cat* Swinburne captures the cat's independence and beauty, and compares its innate superiority to the commonness of the dog.

To a Cat

STATELY, kindly, lordly friend,
Condescend
Here to sit by me, and turn
Glorious eyes that smile and burn,
Golden eyes, love's lustrous mead,
On the golden page I read.

All your wondrous wealth of hair,
Dark and fair,
Silken-shaggy, soft and bright
As the clouds and beams of night,
Pays my reverent hand's caress
Back with friendlier gentleness.

Dogs may fawn on all and some
As they come;
You, a friend of loftier mind,
Answer friends alone in kind.
Just your foot upon my hand
Softly bids it understand.

Morning round this silent sweet
Garden-seat
Sheds its wealth of gathering light,
Thrills the gradual clouds with might,
Changes woodland, orchard, heath,
Lawn, and garden there beneath.

Fair and dim they gleamed below:
Now they glow
Deep as even your sunbright eyes,

Fair as even the wakening skies.
Can it not or can it be
Now that you give thanks to see?

May not you rejoice as I,
Seeing the sky
Change to heaven revealed, and bid
Earth reveal the heaven it hid
All night long from stars and moon,
Now the sun sets all in tune?

What within you wakes with day
Who can say?
All too little may we tell,
Friends who like each other well,
What might haply, if we might,
Bid us read our lives aright.

Wild on woodland ways your sires
Flashed like fires;
Fair as flame and fierce and fleet
As with wings on wingless feet
Shone and sprang your mother, free,
Bright and brave as wind or sea.

Free and proud and glad as they,
Here to-day
Rests or roams their radiant child,
Vanquished not, but reconciled,
Free from curb of aught above
Save the lovely curb of love.

Love through dreams of souls divine
Fain would shine
Round a dawn whose light and song
Then should right our mutual wrong---
Speak, and seal the love-lit law
Sweet Assisi's seer foresaw.

Dreams were theirs; yet haply may
Dawn a day
When such friends and fellows born,
Seeing our earth as fair at morn,
May for wiser love's sake see
More of heaven's deep heart than we (Swinburne, 1911, p. 255).

Ever cherishing nature, William Wordsworth (1770-1850) was an integral part of the romanticist movement. Perhaps influenced by Lady Sydney Morgan (1783-1859) who said, "The playful kitten with its pretty little tigerish gambole is infinitely more amusing than half the people one is obliged to live with in this world." Wordsworth wrote the following poem to a kitten in 1804. The kitten symbolizes the struggle that the tree must endure as the kitten plays with the leaves. The new vigorous life of the kitten is juxtaposed against the death of the tree's leaves. There is also a hint of the typical symbolism of the cat being a magical creature in the line, "Now she works with three or four like an Indian conjuror."

The Kitten and the Falling Leaves

THAT way look, my Infant, lo!
What a pretty baby-show!
See the Kitten on the wall,
Sporting with the leaves that fall,
Withered leaves--one--two--and three--
From the lofty elder-tree!
Through the calm and frosty air
Of this morning bright and fair,
Eddying round and round they sink
Softly, slowly: one might think,

From the motions that are made,
Every little leaf conveyed
Sylph or Faery hither tending,--
To this lower world descending,
Each invisible and mute,
In his wavering parachute.
----But the Kitten, how she starts,

Crouches, stretches, paws, and darts!
First at one, and then its fellow
Just as light and just as yellow;

There are many now--now one--
Now they stop and there are none.
What intenseness of desire
In her upward eye of fire!
With a tiger-leap half-way
Now she meets the coming prey,
Lets it go as fast, and then
Has it in her power again:
Now she works with three or four,
Like an Indian conjurer;

Quick as he in feats of art,
Far beyond in joy of heart.
Were her antics played in the eye
Of a thousand standers-by,
Clapping hands with shout and stare,
What would little Tabby care
For the plaudits of the crowd?
Over happy to be proud,
Over wealthy in the treasure
Of her own exceeding pleasure!

'Tis a pretty baby-treat;
Nor, I deem, for me unmeet;
Here, for neither Babe nor me,
Other play-mate can I see.
Of the countless living things,
That with stir of feet and wings
(In the sun or under shade,
Upon bough or grassy blade)
And with busy revellings,
Chirp and song, and murmurings,
Made this orchard's narrow space,
And this vale so blithe a place;
Multitudes are swept away

Never more to breathe the day:
Some are sleeping; some in bands
Travelled into distant lands;
Others slunk to moor and wood,
Far from human neighbourhood;
And, among the Kinds that keep
With us closer fellowship,

With us openly abide,
All have laid their mirth aside.
Where is he that giddy Sprite,
Blue-cap, with his colours bright,
Who was blest as bird could be,
Feeding in the apple-tree;
Made such wanton spoil and rout,
Turning blossoms inside out;
Hung--head pointing towards the ground--
Fluttered, perched, into a round

Bound himself, and then unbound;
Lithest, gaudiest Harlequin!
Prettiest Tumbler ever seen!
Light of heart and light of limb;
What is now become of Him?
Lambs, that through the mountains went
Frisking, bleating merriment,
When the year was in its prime,
They are sobered by this time.
If you look to vale or hill,
If you listen, all is still,
Save a little neighbouring rill,
That from out the rocky ground
Strikes a solitary sound.
Vainly glitter hill and plain,
And the air is calm in vain;
Vainly Morning spreads the lure
Of a sky serene and pure;
Creature none can she decoy
Into open sign of joy:

Is it that they have a fear
Of the dreary season near?
Or that other pleasures be
Sweeter even than gaiety?
Yet, whate'er enjoyments dwell
In the impenetrable cell
Of the silent heart which Nature
Furnishes to every creature;
Whatsoe'er we feel and know
Too sedate for outward show,

Such a light of gladness breaks,
Pretty Kitten! from thy freaks,--
Spreads with such a living grace
O'er my little Dora's face;
Yes, the sight so stirs and charms
Thee, Baby, laughing in my arms,
That almost I could repine
That your transports are not mine,
That I do not wholly fare
Even as ye do, thoughtless pair!

And I will have my careless season
Spite of melancholy reason,
Will walk through life in such a way
That, when time brings on decay,
Now and then I may possess
Hours of perfect gladsomeness.
--Pleased by any random toy;
By a kitten's busy joy,
Or an infant's laughing eye
Sharing in the ecstasy;

I would fare like that or this,
Find my wisdom in my bliss;
Keep the sprightly soul awake,
And have faculties to take,
Even from things by sorrow wrought,
Matter for a jocund thought,

Spite of care, and spite of grief,
To gambol with Life's falling Leaf (Wordsworth, n.d., p. 255).

Not unlike William Wordsworth, the Scottish poet Joanna Baillie (1762-1851) was also a lover of nature and animal life. Baillie, a cat lover, was never married and lived with her sister for much of her adult life. Her poem *The Kitten* follows the life of a cat from its kitten-hood to old age, and it shares some similarities to Wordsworth's *The Kitten and Falling Leaves.*

The Kitten

WANTON droll, whose harmless play
Beguiles the rustic's closing day,
When, drawn the evening fire about,
Sit aged crone and thoughtless lout,
And child upon his three-foot stool,
Waiting till his supper cool,
And maid, whose cheek outblooms the rose,
As bright the blazing faggot glows,
Who, bending to the friendly light,
Plies her task with busy slight;
Come, shew thy tricks and sportive graces,
Thus circled round with merry faces.
Backward coiled and crouching low,
With glaring eyeballs watch thy foe,
The housewife's spindle whirling round,
Or thread or straw that on the ground
Its shadow throws, by urchin sly
Held out to lure thy roving eye;
Then stealing onward, fiercely spring
Upon the tempting faithless thing.
Now, wheeling round with bootless skill,
Thy bo-peep tail provokes thee still,
As still beyond thy curving side
Its jetty tip is seen to glide;
Till from thy centre starting far,
Thou sidelong veer'st with rump in air
Erected stiff, and gait awry,

Like madam in her tantrums high;
Though ne'er a madam of them all,
Whose silken kirtle sweeps the hall,
More varied trick and whim displays
To catch the admiring stranger's gaze.
Doth power in measured verses dwell,
All thy vagaries wild to tell?
Ah no!--the start, the jet, the bound,
The giddy scamper round and round,
With leap and toss and high curvet,
And many a whirling somerset,
(Permitted by the modern muse
Expression technical to use)
These mock the deftest rhymester's skill,
But poor in art though rich in will.
The featest tumbler, stage bedight,
To thee is but a clumsy wight,
Who every limb and sinew strains
To do what costs thee little pains;
For which, I trow, the gaping crowd
Requite him oft with plaudits loud.
But, stopped the while thy wanton play,
Applauses too thy pains repay:
For then, beneath some urchin's hand
With modest pride thou takest thy stand,
While many a stroke of kindness glides
Along thy back and tabby sides.
Dilated swells thy glossy fur,
And loudly croons thy busy pur,
As, timing well the equal sound,
Thy clutching feet bepat the ground,
And all their harmless claws disclose
Like prickles of an early rose,
While softly from thy whiskered cheek
Thy half-closed eyes peer, mild and meek.
But not alone by cottage fire
Do rustics rude thy feats admire.
The learned sage, whose thoughts explore
The widest range of human lore,

Or with unfettered fancy fly
Through airy heights of poesy,
Pausing smiles with altered air
To see thee climb his elbow-chair,
Or, struggling on the mat below,
Hold warfare with his slippered toe.
The widowed dame or lonely maid,
Who, in the still but cheerless shade
Of home unsocial, spends her age
And rarely turns a lettered page,
Upon her hearth for thee lets fall
The rounded cork or paper ball,
Nor chides thee on thy wicked watch,
The ends of ravelled skein to catch,
But lets thee have thy wayward will,
Perplexing oft her better skill.
Even he, whose mind of gloomy bent,
In lonely tower or prison pent,
Reviews the coil of former days,
And loathes the world and all its ways,
What time the lamp's unsteady gleam
Hath roused him from his moody dream,
Feels, as thou gambol'st round his seat,
His heart of pride less fiercely beat,
And smiles, a link in thee to find,
That joins it still to living kind.
Whence hast thou then, thou witless puss!
The magic power to charm us thus?
Is it that in thy glaring eye
And rapid movements, we descry--
Whilst we at ease, secure from ill,
The chimney corner snugly fill--
A lion darting on his prey,
A tiger at his ruthless play?
Or is it that in thee we trace
With all thy varied wanton grace,
An emblem, viewed with kindred eye,
Of tricky, restless infancy?
Ah! many a lightly sportive child,

Who hath like thee our wits beguiled,
To dull and sober manhood grown,
With strange recoil our hearts disown.
And so, poor kit! must thou endure,
When thou becomest a cat demure,
Full many a cuff and angry word,
Chased roughly from the tempting board.
But yet, for that thou hast, I ween,
So oft our favoured play-mate been,
Soft be the change which thou shalt prove!
When time hath spoiled thee of our love,
Still be thou deemed by housewife fat
A comely, careful, mousing cat,
Whose dish is, for the public good,
Replenished oft with savoury food.
Nor, when thy span of life is past,
Be thou to pond or dung-hill cast,
But, gently borne on goodman's spade,
Beneath the decent sod be laid;
And children shew with glistening eyes
The place where poor old Pussy lies
(Baille, 1840, p. 194).

The cranky cynic Mark Twain (1835-1910), kept the company of up to 19 cats at a time with such names as Sour Mash, Appollinaris, Zoraster, Blatherkite, and Beelzebub, preferring their company to that of humankind. There are quite a few quotations attributed to Twain regarding cats, as well as a few photos of him with his feline companions. One photo appearing in a magazine shows him playing billiards accompanied by a kitten who sits on the table and tries to stop the balls as they approach the corner pocket *(figure 8.24).*Twain writes in a letter, "If I can find a photograph of my 'Tammany' and her kittens, I will enclose it in this. One of them likes to be crammed into a corner-pocket of the billiard table---which he fits as snugly as does a finger in a glove and then he watches the game (and obstructs it) by the hour, and spoils many a shot by putting out his paw and

Figure 8.24. Mark Twain with Kitten Playing Pool, Courtesy of the Mark Twain Project, The Bancroft Library, University of California, Berkeley

changing the direction of a passing ball."

A well-known incident proving Twain's true love of cats occurred when Bambino *(figure 8.25)*, who had been a gift from his daughter Clara, disappeared. Twain put a "Lost Cat" ad in the *New York American* offering a $5 reward for his return with this description:

Mark Twain Has Lost a Black Cat.
From the *New York American.* *Have you seen a distinguished looking cat that looks as if it might be lost? If you have take it to Mark Twain, for it may be his.*

The following advertisement was received at the *American* office Saturday night:

A CAT'S LOST - FIVE DOLLARS REWARD for his restoration to Mark Twain, No. 21 Fifth Avenue. Large and intensely black; thick, velvety fur; has a faint fringe of white hair across his chest; not easy to find in ordinary light.
- reprint in *Kansas City Star*, April 5, 1905

Katy Leary, who worked for Twain, recounts the incident in her book, *A Lifetime with Mark Twain.*

"One night he got kind of gay, when he heard some cats calling from the back fence, so he found a window open and he stole out. We looked high and low but couldn't find him. Mr. Clemens felt so bad that he advertised in all the papers for him. He offered a reward for anybody that would bring the cat back. My goodness! The people that came bringing cats to that house! A perfect stream! They all wanted to see Mr. Clemens, of course.

Two or three nights after, Katherine heard a cat meowing across the street in General Sickles' back yard, and there was Bambino — large as life! So she brought him right home. Mr. Clemens was delighted and then he advertised that his cat was found! But the people kept coming just the same with all kinds of cats for him — anything to get a glimpse of Mr. Clemens!" (Lawton, 2003/1925)

His daughter Clara writes of Bambino in *My Father, Mark Twain*:

"In the early autumn Father rented a house on Fifth Avenue, corner of Ninth Street, number 21, where he, Jean, the faithful Katie, and the secretary settled down for the winter. I was taken to a sanatorium for a year. During the first months of my cure I was completely cut off from friends and family, with no one to speak to but the doctor and nurse. I must modify this statement, however, for I had smuggled a black kitten into my bedroom, although it was against the rules of the sanatorium to have any animals in the place. I called the cat Bambino and it was permitted to remain with me until the unfortunate day when it entered one of the patient's rooms who hated cats. Bambino came near giving the good lady a cataleptic fit, so I was invited to dispose of my pet after that. I made a present of it to Father, knowing he would love it, and he did. A little later I was allowed to receive a limited number of letters, and Father wrote that Bambino was homesick for me and refused all meat and milk, but contradicted his statement a couple of days later saying: "It has been discovered that the reason your cat declines milk and meat and lets on to live by miraculous intervention is, that he catches mice privately" (Clemens, 1931).

Twain summed up the cat's personality in his short story, *The Refuge of the Derelicts (1905)*, *"That's the way with a cat, you know -- any cat; they don't give a damn for discipline. And they can't help it, they're made so. But it ain't really insubordination, when you come to look at it right and fair – it's a word that don't apply to a cat. A cat ain't ever anybody's slave or serf or servant, and can't be -- it ain't in him to be. And so, he don't have to obey anybody. He is the only creature in heaven or earth or anywhere that don't have to obey somebody or other, including the angels. It sets him above the whole ruck, it puts him in a*

Figure 8.25. Twain's Cat Bambino, Courtesy of the Mark Twain Project, The Bancroft Library, University of California, Berkeley

class by himself. He is independent. You understand the size of it? He is the only independent person there is. In heaven or anywhere else. There's always somebody a king has to obey -- a trollop, or a priest, or a ring, or a nation, or a deity or what not -- but it ain't so with a cat. A cat ain't servant nor slave to anybody at all. He's got all the independence there is, in Heaven or anywhere else, there ain't any left over for anybody else. He's your friend, if you like, but that's the limit -- equal terms, too, be you king or be you cobbler; you can't play any I'm-better-than-you on a cat -- no, sir! Yes, he's your friend, if you like, but you got to treat him like a gentleman, there ain't any other terms. The minute you don't, he pulls freight" (Twain, 1980, p. 282).

The tormented American poet and writer Edgar Allan Poe (1809-1849), had a beloved pet cat named Catterina. Catterina often perched on his shoulders while he wrote as if overseeing his work and would remain there, observed a visitor, "—purring as if in complacent approval of the work proceeding under [her] supervision". Catterina also kept Poe's wife Virginia, who was dying of tuberculosis, company by lying next to her in bed. Poe acknowledged that Catterina was "—one of the most remarkable black cats in the world---and this is saying much; for it will be remembered that black cats are all of them witches" (Poe, 1978, p. 479).

However, it was perhaps on his cat Peter that Poe based his character Pluto in *The Black Cat* (1843). An excerpt from Poe's novel has the narrator stating, *"Pluto—this was the cat's name- was my favorite pet and playmate. I alone fed him, and he attended me wherever I went about the house. It was even with difficulty that I could prevent him from following me through the streets."* Originally a genteel man, the narrator becomes an alcoholic and starts to abuse his once beloved black cat, Pluto. The clever cat then begins to avoid him, and when the narrator tries to grab him, the cat naturally scratches him, and in retaliation the narrator gouges out one of his eyes. The narrator, in a fit of guilt at the realization of how cruelly corrupted he had become, eventually hangs the once loved cat. Not long after this horrendous crime, another almost identical black cat appears. At first, the narrator is pleased to have a new cat, but he soon becomes fearful when it persists on showing him its feline affection. He guiltily thinks that it is persecuting him for his previous crime, understanding the natural behavior of the cat as a threat. In the narrator's eyes the cat is Pluto's reincarnation and is seeking revenge. Ironically, it is his fear of this cat that causes him to commit the crime that will destroy him. As he goes downstairs, the cat weaves between his legs and drives the narrator to attempt to hit the defenseless animal with an axe. As his wife grabs his arm to stop him, he swings at her as well and accidentally kills her. He hides her body behind the cellar wall and would have gotten away with the murder if the cat, who had been accidentally walled up with her, had not alerted the police by its crying. The cat is an avenger that leads the narrator to murder his wife. The cat here is seen as a supernatural being, an evil agent of satan. However, it is the narrator's evil passions, not the cat's that bring him to his unfortunate end (Rogers, 2006, pp. 65-66).

The American author Harriet Beecher Stowe (1811-1896), famous for her novel *Uncle Tom's Cabin,* had a Maltese cat named after her husband Calvin. When Stowe had to move, she gave the large cat to Charles Dudley Warner (1829-1900), who grew to love Calvin and even wrote an entire chapter devoted to the life of the cherished animal, *Calvin (A Study of Character) from my Summer in a Garden* in 1870.

Even the romantic poet Emily Dickinson, around 1862, penned a poem about a cat.

She Sights a Bird – she chuckles—
She sights a Bird – she chuckles-
She flattens – then she crawls –
She runs without the look of feet –
Her eyes increase to Balls –

Her Jaws stir – twitching – hungry

Her Teeth can hardly stand –
She leaps, but Robin leaped the first –
Ah, Pussy, of the Sand,

The Hopes so juicy ripening –
You almost bathed your Tongue –
when bliss disclosed a hundred
Toes –
And fled with every one –
(Johnson, 1955)

As was the fashion of the time, cat poems and stories were essential to the upbringing of children. The short children's readers *Dame Trot* and *Dame Wiggins of Lee,* mentioned earlier, led the way in children's literature. However, many other poems were written.

Eugene Field, a newspaper journalist and poet (1850-1895), wrote the following poem that teaches the lesson that arguing can go badly for both sides.

The Duel

THE GINGHAM dog and the calico cat

Side by side on the table sat;
'Twas half-past twelve, and (what do you think!)
Nor one nor t' other had slept a wink!
The old Dutch clock and the Chinese plate
Appeared to know as sure as fate
There was going to be a terrible spat.

(I wasn't there; I simply state
What was told to me by the Chinese plate!)

The gingham dog went "bow-wow-wow!"
And the calico cat replied "mee-ow!"
The aire was littered, an hour or so,

With bits of gingham and calico,
While the old Dutch clock in the chimney-place
Up with its hands before its face,
For it always dreaded a family row!
(Nevermind: I'm only telling you
What the old Dutch clock declares is true!)

The Chinese plate looked very blue,
And wailed, "Oh, dear! What shall we do!"
But the gingham dog and the calico cat
Wallowed this way and tumbled that,
Employing every tooth and claw
In the awfullest way you ever saw—
And, oh! how the gingham and calico flew!
(Don't fancy I exaggerate ---
I got my news from the Chinese plate!)
Next morning where the two had sat
The found no trace of dog or cat;
And some folks think unto this day
That burglars stole that pair away!
But the truth about the cat and pup
Is this: they ate each other up!

Now what do you really think of that!
(The old Dutch clock it told me so,
And that is how I came to know.)
(Lounsbury, 1912).

The French novelist, George Sand (1804-1876), her real name Amantine Aurore Lucile Dupin Dudevant, is said to have written much of her work in bed and shared her breakfast bowl with her cat, Minou.

A cat, François, plays an integral part in Émile Zola's (1840-1902) novel *Thérèse Raquin* (1867), seemingly assuming diabolical supernatural powers, as it sits and observes the two main characters commit a murder which leads to their own self destruction. The murderer, the superstitious Laurent, sees Françoise, Madame Raquin's pet cat, as a witness to his crime. "Dignified and motionless, he (François) stared with is round eyes at the two lovers, appearing to examine them carefully, never blinking, lost in a kind of devilish ecstasy." Once the conspiring lovers drown Camille, the cat's behavior, while always realistic, accentuates their guilt and anxiety. On the night of their marriage, they hear a scratching at the door and believe that it is the drowned man who has come back to haunt them, but they realize that it is only the cat, François. François then "…bounded onto a chair, where with bristling fur and legs stiff he stood looking at his new master with a hard, cruel stare". Laurent understood the cat's actions as an attempt at revenge (Rogers, 2006 p. 67). The novel almost mirrors the use of the cat Pluto in Poe's *The Black Cat,* wherein both the murderous main characters come to view the cat as a satanic nemesis.

In Paul Verlaine's (1844-1896) poem *Woman and Cat* (1866) both woman and cat are demonic. He uses the age-old idea of witch and familiar and equates the woman and cat as reflections of each other. The last line of the poem refers to the eyes of the woman and cat and the bright light that emanates from them. Phosphor means morning star and is a reference to Lucifer.

Woman And Cat

(Poèmes Saturniens: Caprices I, Femme et Chatte)

She was playing with her cat:
And it was lovely to see

The white hand and white paw
Fight, in shadows of eve.

She hid – little wicked one! –
In black silk mittens
Claws of murderous agate,
Fierce and bright as kittens'.

The other too was full of sweetness,
Sheathing her sharp talons' caress,
Though the devil lacked nothing there…

And in the bedroom, where sonorous
Ethereal laughter tinkled in the air,
There shone *four* points of phosphorus.

On the other hand, the publisher of the French dictionary, Pierre Larousse viewed the cat in a more positive light, writing, "The cat is attractive, adroit, clean, and voluptuous: he likes his leisure, he searches out only the softest furniture to sleep and play on." "The philosophes of the last century affirmed on good authority no doubt, that a pronounced taste for cats in certain people was indication of superior merit" (Kete, 1994, pp. 118, 123).

The short-lived French poet Charles Baudelaire (1821-1867), had much in common with Edgar Allan Poe. Both would die young, and both were interested in the macabre and supernatural. Baudelaire and Poe suffered from depression, drug and alcohol abuse and were sensitive men who enjoyed the company of cats. Baudelaire was often known to enter a house and give his full attention to any cat available, completely ignoring his human companions. Baudelaire was not unaccustomed to scandal and his penchant for giving felines more of his attention was ridiculed perhaps almost as much as his immoral poems. He described himself as "A voluptuous wheedling cat, with velvety manners."

The publication of Baudelaire's collection of poems, *The Flowers of Evil* in 1857 created a public scandal. The French court ruled it to be an obscene collection, and some of the poems had to be deleted in subsequent editions. *The Cats* was first published in the journal *Le Corsaire* in 1847, and was ultimately included in Baudelaire's collection of 1857, known in English as *The Flowers of Evil.* In the following poems Baudelaire is symbolically equating cats with women and their ambiguity, a symbol of both the sacred and profane.

The Cats

The lover and the stern philosopher
Both love, in their ripe time, the confident
Soft cats, the house's chiefest ornament,
Who like themselves are cold and seldom stir.
Of knowledge and of pleasure amorous,
Silence they seek and Darkness' fell domain;
Had not their proud souls scorned to brook his rein,
They would have made grim steeds for Erebus.
Pensive they rest in noble attitudes
Like great stretched sphinxes in vast solitudes
Which seem to sleep wrapt in an endless dream;
Their fruitful loins are full of sparks divine,
And gleams of gold within their pupils shine
As 'twere within the shadow of a stream (Squire, 1909).

The Cat (II)

I.

In my mind it strolls
As well as in my apartment,
A cat, strong, sweet and delightful.
When it meows, one scarcely hears it,

Its timbre is so tender and discreet;
Whether a growl or an appeasement,
It is always rich and deep?
That is its charm and its secret.

That voice, which pearls and filters
To the darkest recess of my purse
Delights me like a philtre
And fills me like the rhythms of a verse.

It lulls the most cruel pains to sleep
And contains all ecstasies,
It has not the need of words to speak
The lengthiest phraseologies.

There is no bow that tears so profound
On my heart's perfect strings,
No sovereign instrument vibrant with sound
Could stronger in me sing

Than your voice, mysterious
Seraphic, blissful cat? in form an angel,
Strange cat? in which all is
As harmonious as it is subtle.

II.

Out of its fur, brown and blonde
Rose a perfume so sweet I nearly
Dissolved in its scent, one night, embalmed
When I caressed it once, once only.

It is the familiar mien of a sire;
It judges, it presides, it inspires
All things in its empire;
Is there a fairy, is there a God, in its eyes fires?

When my eyes finally tire and pull away,
Turned around as by a magnet they veer
From this cat that I love, and gently
Look at myself in the mirror,

I see to my astonishment
The fire of its pale pupils inside me
Like beacons, lively opals clear and dominant
Contemplating me fixedly.(Baudelaire, 1868)

The Cat

Come, superb cat, to my amorous heart;
Hold back the talons of your paws,
Let me gaze into your beautiful eyes
Of metal and agate.

When my fingers leisurely caress you,
Your head and your elastic back,
And when my hand tingles with the pleasure
Of feeling your electric body,

In spirit I see my woman. Her gaze
Like your own, amiable beast,
Profound and cold, cuts and cleaves like a dart,

And, from her head down to her feet,
A subtle air, a dangerous perfume
Floats about her dusky body (Aggeler, 1954).

Guy de Maupassant, even though not much of a cat lover, mentioned Baudelaire's love of cats in an essay he wrote about cats[†]. Maupassant wrote, "A woman is a perfidious tricky cat, with claws and fangs, an enemy in love who will bite him when she is tired of kisses" (Maupassant, 1955).

Honoré de Balzac (1799-1850) had a cat that greeted him at the door every night. In his short story, *Passion in the Desert*, a lost French soldier and a panther form an interesting love relationship. In another short story, *The Afflictions of an English Cat,* or also known as *Peines de Cour d'une chatte anglaise (Complaints of the Heart of an English Cat),* the cat is used more as a metaphor in the satire on British society. Loosely based on Balzac's play, an adapted opera was written and performed in 1983.

Alexander Dumas (1802-1870) called the cat a "traitor, deceiver, theif...egoist…ingrate. Her egoism is proof of her superiority: the dog's willingness to hunt for man demonstrates his stupidity, while the cat has an excuse. When she catches a bird, for she means to eat it herself" (Aberconway, 1968). Even so, Dumas had a cat, Mysouff,

[†] Guy de Maupassant, *On Cats*, 1886

who he said, "…would jump up on my knees as if he were a dog, then run off and turn then take the road home, returning at a gallop" (Kete, 1994, p. 129).

The French poet and writer Théophile Gautier (1811-1872), truly adored cats. Many of his poems include them, and they were his beloved companions. An excerpt from the *Daily Telegraph* of 1895, describes his passionate affection for his felines.

'Théophile Gautier, one of the most famous and artistic French authors of the present century, had an especial fondness of all animals, but cats were his particular favorites. In his book called 'La Menagerie Intime' he describes his household pets.

One of the first was Childebrand, a short-haired, fawn colored beauty, striped with black velvet, like the clown in Hugo's 'Roi s'Amuse'. He had great green eyes, almond-shaped, and surrounded by bands of black.

Madame Théophile was another favorite, reddish and white breasted, pink-nosed and blue-eyed. She dwelt with him on terms of great intimacy, sleeping with him, sitting on the arm of his chair when he wrote, following him on his walks through the garden and always present at meals, when she sometimes stole attractive bits from his plate.

He tells an amusing tale about her and a parrot left in his charge for a short time by an absent friend. Madame Théophile had never beheld a parrot, and it astonished her greatly by its gyrations and beak and claw and the strange motions of its awkward green body. She sat for a long time as still as an Egyptian mummied cat, watching it with meditation, for she had never seen such a peculiar example of natural history. Finally she seemed to say: 'I have it now; it is a green chicken!' Meanwhile the parrot watched the cat with increasing alarm, ruffling its feathers and whacking its beack uneasily against its cage. Presently the cat seemed to say: 'Well, even if it is a green chicken, very likely it is good to eat.'

'I watched the scene,' says Gautier. 'Her paws gradually spread and contracted, she gave alternative purrs and growls, and prepared for a spring. The parrot, perceiving the danger, said in a deep bass voice: 'Have you breakfasted, Jacquot?'

The blare from a trumpet, a pistol shot, an earthquake, could not have frightened her more. All her ornithological ideas were upset. 'What more,' said the parrot, 'the king's roast beef?'

The cat's face expressed terror. 'He is not a bird; he is a monsieur,' she seemed to say. The green creature then sang a French couplet about good wine, and the cat, fleeing for her life, took refuge under the bed.

Madame Théophile had all the tastes of a great French lady, being especially fond of perfumes, but patchouli and vertivert would throw her into ecstasies. She liked music, too, but sharp, high notes affected her and she would put her paw upon a singer's lips when such a high note distressed her.

A third favorite was brought to Gautier from Havana by a friend. This was an Angora, as white as a swan, the founder of the 'White Dynasty.' He received the name of Pierrot, and as he grew older and more dignified this was extended to Don Pierrot de Navarre. He always loved to be with people, adored Gautier's literary friends, and used to sit silently when they discussed great questions, sometimes putting his head on one side and occasionally making a little cry. He used to play with the books, turning over the leaves with his paws and going to sleep on top of them. Like Childebrand, he used to sit by the author when he was at work and watch his pen move across the paper with intense interest. He never went to bed until Gautier returned home, and no matter how late it was he would bound out in the dark to greet him, and as soon as the candle was lit scamper ahead like a page. His companion was a beautiful puss, as white as snow, and owing to her celestial purity she was named 'Seraphita,' for Balzac's romance" (Singleton, 1895).

The first line of his work, *My Private Menagerie,* states, "I have often been caricatured in Turkish dress seated upon cushions, and surrounded by cats so familiar that they did not hesitate to climb upon my shoulders and even upon my head. The caricature is truth slightly exaggerated, and I must own that all my life I have been as fond of animals in general and of cats in particular as any Brahmin or old maid" (Gautier, 1902/2014, p. 4).

The French philosopher and writer Hippolyte-Adolphe Taine (1828-1893) was a proponent of positivism, a belief that all knowledge comes from sense perception. His senses obviously told him that cats were wise beings, as he is quoted as saying, "I have studied many philosophers and many cats. The wisdom of cats is infinitely superior."

The poet Rainer Maria Rilke (1875-1926) rose to become one of the most well-known Bohemian Austrian poets in the German language. Rilke was also a family friend to the artist Balthasar Klossowski (1908-2001), and eventually became his mother's lover and his surrogate father. Rilke inspired Balthus, as he later became known, to write and illustrate his first book, *Mitsou*, about a cat. Rilke's poetry is still popular today, and in his poem, *Black Cat* (1923), he portrays the cat as a mystical being engulfing insignificant man.

Black Cat

A ghost, though invisible, still is like a place
your sight can knock on, echoing; but here
within this thick black pelt, your strongest gaze
will be absorbed and utterly disappear:

just as a raving madman, when nothing else
can ease him, charges into his dark night
howling, pounds on the padded wall, and feels
the rage being taken in and pacified.

She seems to hide all looks that have ever fallen
into her, so that, like an audience,
she can look them over, menacing and sullen,
and curl to sleep with them. But all at once

as if awakened, she turns her face to yours;
and with a shock, you see yourself, tiny,
inside the golden amber of her eyeballs
suspended, like a prehistoric fly.

The Life and Opinions of the Tomcat Murr is an autobiography of a cat written (1819-1821) by the German writer and composer, E.T.A. Hoffmann (1776-1822). The story is about the very literate and precocious Tomcat Murr who decides to write his own autobiography. He feels he should write it because as a cat, he has been relegated to an inferior existence to humans, but in his own cat way, he doesn't care.

Of course Tomcat Murr believes himself superior to humans because he is feline. Murr is a well-read cat and looks down upon those who are not as educated as himself. Murr writes his autobiography on scraps of paper that he has found, which are the ripped apart fragments of the composer Johannes Kreisler's manuscript. Because of this, Murr intersperses his story with pieces of Kreisler's story and the two are merged. The two versions alternate side by side in a double narrative: the story of the intelligent confident lover and sometimes thug, Tomcat Murr, and the genius, albeit moody, hypochondriac Kreisler.

The Russian nobleman Alexander Pushkin (1799-1837), later known as the founder of modern Russian literature, was rather hot headed and prideful. Fighting in over 29 duels, in his last, provoked by an insult to his wife's honor, he died at the very young age of 37.

In Pushkin's epic fairy tale poem, *Ruslan and Ludmila* (1820) he mentions the cat a couple of times.

.

"A learned cat whiles away the hours
By walking slowly round and round.
To right he walks, and sings a ditty;
To left he walks, and tells a tale—"

A princess pines away in prison,
And a wolf serves her without treason;
A mortar, with a witch in it,
Walks as if having somewhat feet;
There's King Kashchey, o'er his gold withered;
There's Russian odour… Russian spirit!
And I there sat: I drank sweet mead,
Saw, near the sea, the green oak, growing,
Under it heard a cat, much-knowing,
Talking me its long stories' set.
Having recalled one of its stories,
I'll recite it to the world, glorious…"

Demon cat stories persisted in 19th century Japan, and the story *The Cat Witch of Okabe* was reenacted on stage. In order to terrify the young virgins at the local temple, the witch-cat disguised herself as an old woman. In Utagawa Kuniyoshi's depiction of a kabuki performance of about 1835, an evil woman with large cat ears and paws kneels in the center, with a huge, glaring cat, her protector, crouching behind her while two samurai on each side attempt to kill her *(figure 8.26).*

Next to each of the samurai is a cat with a cloth wrapped around its head dancing on its hind legs. The cloth on the cat's head represents the folk belief that a cat would steal a napkin to wear on its head and dance with other cats and howl at the top of their voices, "Neko ja! We are the cats!" This would be done in a temple hall or a place which was supposed to remain quiet (Rogers, 2006, p. 57).

Figure 8.26. Okabe The Cat Witch, Kuniyoshi Utagawa, c. 1844

Another Japanese story of menacing cat witches occurs when a samurai witnesses cats performing a crazed, violent dance when he enters a temple for the night. Instead of yelling "Neko ja!" the cats were screaming "Tell it not to Shippeitaro". The next day the samurai learned from the nearby villagers that once a year the cats forced them to imprison their most beautiful maiden in a cage and demanded that she be taken to the temple for sacrifice. The samurai then asked who or what Shippeitaro was. The villagers told him Shippeitaro was a courageous dog who belonged to the village's chief. The samurai decided he wanted to help the villagers, so he took the dog, and put him in the cage instead of the girl and he carried it to the temple. The ghost cats appeared at midnight with their leader, an extremely large and vicious tomcat. Growling with expectation, the tomcat jumped on to the cage and opened the door only to find

Shippeitaro waiting for him. Shippeitaro grabbed the great tom, and the samurai killed the surprised cat with his sword. The courageous dog then killed the rest of the cats and the village was freed from the curse.

The Boy Who Drew Cats, another Japanese fairy tale, published in 1898, revolves around a small, weak farmer's boy who was unable to perform his chores. Instead, he occupied himself by drawing cats. Because the boy was generally useless around the farm, they sent him to a temple to become a monk. This did not stop him from drawing cats. Exasperated with the boy, the older monk told him he could not be a monk at that temple and sent him away to a larger one. But the temple the monk had sent him to had been abandoned because of a large goblin-rat. Monks and warriors that had tried to fight the ferocious rat were eventually chased away by its strength and never seen again. When the boy arrived at the temple, a light was burning, so he went in. Inside he saw huge white screens, and he painted cats on them. Exhausted, he fell asleep in a small cabinet. During the night he heard fighting sounds, and in the morning he awoke to find the goblin-rat dead. All the cats he had painted had mouths wet with

Figure 8.27. Cat Dealer in Qing Dynasty China, 1843, George Newenham from 'China a Series of Views'

red blood. When the monks found out that his painted cats had slain the goblin-rat, he was hailed a hero and was allowed to become a famous cat artist.

The cat in 19th century China was not found so much in fairy tales, but instead as a delicacy to be enjoyed eaten. Cat merchants thrived on selling domestic cats caught in the streets of the towns. Some wildcats of Tartary were caught and consumed as well *(figure 8.27)*. The man in the drawing seems to be stroking a cat, but this is surely to see how much meat is on the poor animal's bones. The selling and eating of cat has not abated and around four million cats per year are brutally killed and consumed in China today.

The cat, a symbol of cleanliness, domesticity and independence became a welcome addition to bourgeoisie households. Captured in hundreds of anthropomorphized poses by several of the century's top photographers, the cat was afforded the opportunity to mingle even more intimately with its human providers. Now it was not just an animal, it was a member of the family, a child to be doted on. In addition, the cat established itself in the hearts of the artists and writers of the era who successfully publicized this bond by including it in paintings, stories, and poems. The cat had become the quintessential pet.

Chapter Nine

THE CAT IN THE 20TH CENTURY

By the beginning of the twentieth century, the cat had risen in popularity at a phenomenal rate. Now even less stigmatized by the evil mantra it had carried throughout history, as the 20th century proceeded, the cat would become even more ubiquitous. Its breakthrough into the literary and art world, which had started centuries ago, opened new doors, providing the cat with a continued spot as symbol and celebrity in the century's greatest works. From canvas, to TV and films, music, advertising, books, and even war, cats would continue to be the mascots of those independent thinkers who would make world history. Cat welfare organizations begun in the 19th century would flourish in the 20th , and expose incidents of animal cruelty like they had never done before. New laws and a sympathetic legal system would punish such abusers. The anthropomorphic photographs begun in the 19th century had allowed the cat to become not just a pet, but a true member of the family, an individual of its own merit to be cherished and looked after as if it were a child. The first cat shows in the 19th century paved the way for even more interest in cat breeds in the 20th, and The Cat Fanciers' Association (CFA), founded in 1906, now maintains the world's largest registry of pedigreed cats. In the wars of the 20th century, soldiers facing the grim reality of mankind's propensity for self-destruction found solace in the untainted and unconditional love of a kitten or cat. Cats kept men company in the damp and muddy trenches of WWI and became heroes in their own right in WWII. Plowing the seas as ships' mascots, just as they had been ordained to do thousands of years ago by their association with the Goddess Isis Pharia, courageous felines were decorated for their bravery and exemplary service. Much like the Romans who often carved images of cats into the bows of their ships, up until 1975, the British required their ships to carry black cats on board as good luck charms.

Likewise, it was a bad omen if a cat abandoned a ship. During the Titanic's sea trials in 1912, it is said that a cat with young kittens was aboard, but when the ship arrived in Southampton from Belfast, the cat quickly ran up and down the gangplank removing her kittens one at a time from the ship.

Cats in the Air

Cats accompanied man not only on ships but also in the air, and shared in the glory of setting new records in flight and in space. Kiddo, a stray hangar cat, was the first feline to attempt to cross the Atlantic in 1910. Taken aboard the dirigible *America* at Atlantic City, New Jersey, Kiddo was meant to serve as a good luck charm to enable the flight to achieve its goal of crossing the Atlantic to Europe. The airship *America* was the first aircraft to have radio equipment on board, and the chief navigator, F. Murray Simon, only twenty minutes into the flight noted in his log, "I am chiefly worried by our cat, which is rushing around the airship like a squirrel in a cage." Jack Irwin, the radio operator, complained that the cat was "raising hell" and "driving him mad" and suggested that perhaps they should leave it behind before they traveled too far. Simon disagreed, arguing, "We must keep the cat at all costs; we can never have luck without a cat aboard." Even so, the crew took a vote and decided to try to get rid of the unhappy feline by lowering it in a bag into a motorboat from the air, but the sea was too rough, and they ended up having to haul the now terribly disgruntled cat on board the airship again. In what was probably the first air-to-ground radio transmission, the upset chief engineer, Melvin Vaniman, sent a wireless message to the plane's owner back at base reading, "Roy, come and get this goddamn cat!" *(figure 9.1)*. Even though the *America* did not successfully cross the Atlantic, and the crew and cat had to abandon ship, the airship set other records such as the first air-to-ground transmission, time aloft and total distance traveled by air. The crew and the cat became celebrities. Kiddo, renamed Trent after the ship that rescued them, was proclaimed the mascot of the *America*. Kiddo even had a short stint at Gimbel's department store in New York City, where the recalcitrant grey tabby was displayed in a gilded cage filled with fluffy pillows on which he could lounge. Soon after, he retired from public view and spent the rest of his life with

Figure 9.1. M. Vaniman and Kiddo, Library of Congress Prints and Photographs Division, Washington, D.C.

Edith, the daughter of Walter Wellman (1858-1934), the owner of the airship.

Also in 1910, Captain Kitty, known as John Bevins Moisant, almost never flew without his tabby cat, Mademoiselle Fifi. Moisant was a showman and performed aerial maneuvers and also raced. Fifi accompanied him on at least 14 of his flights as well as his famous flight across the English Channel on August 23, 1910. To accommodate the illustrious feline, Moisant covered the seats with tape so that she would not scratch them and also secured her litter box to the floor on the passenger's seat side *(figure 9.2)*. A daring aviator, Moisant pre-deceased Fifi in an air crash, in which lucky Fifi did not accompany him *(figure 9.3)*.

Another airborne tabby was the kitten, Whoopsy, later known as Jazz who became the first cat to successfully cross the Atlantic from Britain to America. Smuggled on board by a stowaway, the kitten was

Figure 9.2. Mlle Fifi first cat to make flight across the English Channel and John Moisant, c. 1911, Library of Congress Prints and Photographs Division, Washington, D.C.

Figure 9.3. Moissant's Cat Fifi in Mourning, Bain News Service, 1900, Library of Congress Prints and Photographs Division, Washington, D.C.

a pleasant diversion for the crew and was soon announced to be the mascot of the airship until it crashed in 1921. Luckily, Whoopsy did not sustain any life threatening injuries.

Even though Charles Lindbergh was not accompanied by a cat on his famous trans-Atlantic flight in 1927, he did own Patsy who was his faithful pal during many of his other flights. When asked why he did not let Patsy come along on the transatlantic flight, he said, “It's too dangerous a journey to risk the cat's life.” A Spanish set of postage stamps featuring famous aviators of the period and dating to 1930 are the first to show a domestic cat. The one peseta stamp pictures Charles Lindbergh and The Spirit of St. Louis taking off as Patsy, Lindbergh’s black kitten, looks on in the right hand lower corner *(figure 9.4).*

Figure 9.4. Charles Lindbergh with Patsy the Cat on Stamp

Figure 9.5. Felicette on Stamp

Félicette, a lowly Parisian street cat, became the first cat sent into space on the 18th October 1963. The French feline survived the 15-minute flight which propelled her some 100 miles into space, only to be put to sleep two to three months after the voyage so that scientists could examine the electrodes they had implanted into her brain. Félicette, a martyr to space flight, was duly thanked by being commemorated for her brave service on several postage stamps *(figure 9.5)*.

Cats in Art

When not participating in dangerous flights and setting new records, the cat, just as it had done in previous centuries, played an integral part in art and photography. Enduring as a cultural and social icon, the cat symbolized femininity, sensuality, domesticity, lust, and evil. Artists such as Picasso, Félix Vallotton, Balthus, Leonor Fini, and many more used the cat's symbolic worth to great effect. However, the cat, not exclusive to Western art, could be found in Japanese and Chinese scrolls, paintings and porcelain works as well.

One of the most influential artists of the 20th century, Picasso was known to have loved cats and was photographed with kittens or cats throughout his lifetime. He also gave tribute to their symbolic importance in his many paintings. In one of his earliest works ascribed to his Blue Period, both figures in *Woman and Cat* seem to be inextricably united. Crazy cat ladies, already well documented, were not forgotten by Picasso who painted *Crazy Lady (Woman) with Cat.* However, from 1935 – 1945, the war years, Picasso produced many paintings with cats that focused on the dark side of feline nature as a reflection of man's own savagery. During those years, instead of fleeing France during the German occupation, Picasso stayed in Paris and continued to paint. Many of Picasso's works expressed symbolic references to the political situations of the time. *Cat Seizing a Bird,* April 1939, depicts a self–satisfied cat triumphantly gripping a defenseless bird, its flesh torn to reveal a gaping wound. Here the cat represents the Fascist General Franco defeating Madrid the preceding March. In 1941, while living with his mistress Dora Maar, he painted *Dora Maar au chat,* now one of the world's most expensive paintings, sold in 2006 for over 95 million dollars. The painting shows Picasso's mistress seated with a small black cat (kitten) behind her shoulder, seemingly balancing on the chair back. Picasso uses the cat and all its symbolism to express Dora Maar's predatory cat-likeness. Maar's long fingers and sharpened nails remind one of the savageness of feline claws. Dora Maar was a pivotal force in Picasso's life, perhaps the only mistress that was his intellectual equal, and he likened her to an "Afghan cat".

In the 1960s, Picasso painted his wife Jacqueline Roque with cats as well. In one painting, Jacqueline sits with a small black cat on her lap. The cat's eyes are so round and large that they reflect an innocence and beauty that matches Jacqueline's. Picasso perhaps hints that even though she is a cat, she is a kind one. Jacqueline's hands are placed on the arms of the chair just as Dora Maar's are. However, her hands, short, stubby and almost mannish are much different from Maar's; they are not predatory.

In addition to his portraits, Picasso did a series of paintings of cats and lobsters and cats on the beach. *Lobster and Cat* (1965) could just be a humorous study of a cat surprised by a lobster, but it could also symbolize the conflict of the time, the Cuban missile crisis.

Greatly influenced by Holbein, Dürer and Ingres, and later by Japanese print art, the Swiss painter Félix Vallotton (1865-1925*)* produced both woodcuts and paintings in which he sometimes included cats. His woodcuts consist of a black background with only a few white lines to outline his images. In a series of six woodcuts called *Instruments de musique*, one of the woodcuts features a cat standing on a chest of drawers with its tail up next to a solitary man playing a flute. The cat playfully seeks attention and brings lightness to the composition. In another black and white woodcut, *La Paresse (Laziness)*, dated 1896, a nude woman lies across a patterned bedspread and reaches for a white cat. Both woman and cat connect fluidly as one in their whiteness, the color invoking the idea of purity, hinting of an emotionless sensuality *(figure 9.6)*. Painted in the same year, *Women with Cats* is almost reminiscent of Paul Gauguin's composition of Tahitian women seated on the floor. Here the cat is indisputably a symbol of fertility *(figure 9.7)*. Vallotton cannot be categorized as either an impressionist or a post-impressionist. Part of the *Les Nabi* group of Parisian painters, he was mainly interested in depicting a specific moment in time using color, space and abstraction. Vallotton's work is very different from his friends Pierre Bonnard and Edouard Vuillard who also included cats in their works.

Figure 9.6. Laziness (La Paresse), Félix Vallotton, Woodcut,1896, Museum of Fine Arts, Houston

Even though they too were part of the *Les Nabis*, their works are not quite as abstract as Vallotton's.

Born in Paris, Balthasar Klossowski (1908-2001), later known as Balthus, grew up in a family of painters and intellectuals. When he was eight years old, his mother painted him with the family cat. Thus began his long relationship with cats and art. Three years later, at just age eleven, he produced a book entitled *Mitsou* with 40 pen and ink drawings illustrating the story of a young boy who rescues a stray cat. As part of the story, we see Mitsou giving Balthus a dead mouse and the two playing under a table. Then, in the final scene, we see Balthus hunting for the missing cat and crying inconsolably.

The Austrian-German poet Rainer Maria Rilke (1875-1926), mentioned earlier, was a family friend and eventually the lover of Balthus's mother Baladine. Rilke encouraged the publication of the short book in 1921 even writing the preface. Rilke was an important creative influence in Balthus' life, sometimes even acting as a surrogate father after Balthus' mother and father had separated. Balthus's love of cats continued throughout his life as mirrored in his art. The epitome of this love is seen in the full length self-portrait of

Figure 9.7. Women and Cats, Félix Vallotton, 1897-1898, Van Gogh Museum, Amsterdam

Balthus standing next to a big tabby cat which leans lovingly against his leg. The painting is called: *H.M. The King of Cats Painted by Himself,* completed in 1935 when he was 27 years old. Later on, he would paint *The Cat of La Méditerranée* (1949), again a self-portrait, but this time he is the happy cat with a rainbow of fish on his plate. However, perhaps more controversial are his languorously seductive paintings of young adolescent girls and cats which would span two decades beginning in the 1930s. In these paintings, young girls are erotically posed with a seemingly disinterested cat somewhere on the canvas. Sacred and profane are balanced with the cat being representative of the artist himself. Many of these paintings were of his neighbor in Paris, Thérèse Blanchard (1925-1950).

The Argentine artist Leonor Fini (1907-1996) moved in the same circles as Picasso, Max Ernst, and the photographer Henri Cartier Bresson and was later even associated with Andy Warhol, all of whom valued the cat's presence in their art. Fini was a true cat lover. Not only did she paint cats, but she also kept as many as 23, mostly Persians, as her pets. Like any cat lover, she let them sleep with her and share her meals, generously allowing them to walk over the dining room table in search of tasty tidbits. Her guests never dared complain. A friend recalled, "…the cats would come all around her;

on the easel, on the bed, on the palate" whenever she painted. Some of her works were even identified by the stray cat hairs attached to the paint or the odd cat scratched canvas. Whenever she traveled to the Loire Valley for the summer, her cats accompanied her in their own car. A good friend of Brigitte Bardot, Fini was active in the French SPA and contributed some of her works to draw attention to the plight of strays. Fini owned over 50 cats during her lifetime and became distraught whenever one would get sick, and never got used to losing one. She is known to have said, "In every way cats are the most perfect creatures on the face of the earth, except that their lives are too short."

Perhaps the most prolific Japanese-French cat painter of the period was Leonard Tsugouharu Foujita (1886-1968). Born in Tokyo, Japan, Tsugouharu[†] Foujita (1886-1968), became a well-known painter and print maker who adeptly blended traditional Japanese art with European Modernism. He is best known for his paintings of cats and nudes. In Japanese his name means "field of Wisteria and Peace". Foujita was a cat-loving eccentric. His hairstyle resembled that of a skull cap, and he wore earrings, dressed in tunics and had a tattoo around his wrist.

After graduating high school, Foujita began to study western art and graduated from Tokyo National University of Fine Arts and Music in 1910. Following his interest in western art, three years later he arrived in Paris knowing no one. Soon, however, he met the great artists Picasso, Modigliani and Matisse and even took dance lessons from Isadora Duncan. Man Ray's lover, Kiki, even posed for him for *Reclining Nude with Toile de Jouy* which became quite a success, selling for 8,000 francs in 1922. He shared an interest in cats with Jean Cocteau, and they attended cat shows together. Foujita firmly equated women with cats; in an interview with the Milwaukee Journal in 1930 he stated, "Ladies who would be alluring to men should surround themselves with cats….I never look at men, only at women—they have, each one, such marvelous possibilities of beauty. But unfortunately most of them have not developed these possibilities because they have not learned the lessons cats can teach." He went on to say, "The good and bad qualities of cats closely resemble the attributes of women... Cats never give anything

[†] He later changed his name to Leonard.

away. They are out for what they can get. They have tigerish passions when aroused. They have grace, beauty of movement, intriguing languor. Cats are never in a hurry, never angular. They move softly, gently, insinuatingly...Clever women live with cats. They study the animal's movements, habits and emotional reactions—" (Women, 1930 p. 19). Foujita known for his paintings of nudes and cats was one of the few artists to be financially successful so early in his career. By 1925, he had received state honors from both Belgium and France.

Cats in Film

From canvases, the cat first entered the new dynamic art form of silent films to eventually share the screen with such stars as Rudolph Valentino, Lillian Gish, Greta Garbo, Douglas Fairbanks and Charlie Chaplin. A Maltese cat named Pepper *(figure 9.8)* became the first feline film star. Born under a sound stage at Keystone Studios in 1912, Pepper was discovered by Mack Sennett who introduced her to

Figure 9.8. Pepper, Photographed before 1920

the silver screen in 1913 in *A Little Hero*. In that film she was paired with her lifelong partner Teddy the Dog. Pepper appeared in 17 films throughout her career, and in one of her more demanding roles she played checkers with the comedian Ben Turpin. The cross eyed Turpin and Pepper appeared together in *Are Waitresses Safe?* (1917),

Whose Little Wife are You (1918), *When Love is Blind* (1919), *Trying to Get Along* (1919) and *The Quack Doctor* (1920). The cat also frequently appeared with Marie Prevost in *His Hidden Purpose* (1918), *Never Too Old* (1919), *When Love is Blind* (1919), and *The Dentist* (1919). Sennett thought highly of Pepper, insuring her for a record $5,000.00. Pepper remained at the studio for 16 years until her death in 1928.

The cat we have all come to know as Felix first made his appearance as Master Tom in *Feline Follies*. Released just after WWI in 1919, and directed by Otto Messmer, the 4-minute short features the original Felix the Cat, here called Master Tom. Our hero cat is lured away from his duties of protecting his house from mice by the seductive charms of Miss Kitty *(figure 9.9)*. While he is away, the mice take over and destroy the house. The house owner comes home to find the place a mess and blames Master Tom and throws him out. Master Tom goes to find his love, Miss Kitty, but she is surrounded by so many other male cats that he flees and decides to commit suicide by breathing in gas. In subsequent films, Master Tom becomes Felix the Cat, and in the 1920-29 *Arabiantics* Felix whisks away on a magic carpet and lands in Arabia where he trades the carpet for a bag of jewels. An evil Arab unleashes an army of mice to take the bag. After beating up an Arab guard, Felix finds the hooka-smoking Arab who had stolen his jewels for his many wives. The mice again defeat Felix and throw him out of the house. The devious Felix then schemes to play music for the Arab's wives to dance to and while they are dancing, all the jewels fall from their bodies into Felix's bag. Felix's cunning wins the day. In the short, *Eats are West* a hungry Felix steals Mammy's flap jacks and flies away using the flap jacks as a make shift plane. Mammy shakes her fist at him in her anger. Felix then parachutes down to steal food from a pony express rider. A fight ensues with Felix defeating them all. Then he goes on to have a fight with some Indians and completely destroys the cigar store Indian. In *Felix the Cat Ducks His Duty* all the mice declare war, and he is forced to enlist to aid his cat brethren. Wearing a WWI helmet at the front, Felix tries to desert but is forced again to stay and fight. He faces gassing by the mice with old cheese and then he is sentenced to be shot. However, the clever Felix escapes and tries to get married but returns to the front because of the constant nagging of his wife.

The ingenious Felix entered the psyches of a whole generation as a courageous feline who would never give up. So pervasive was the Felix persona that even the great aviator Charles Lindbergh chose a Felix doll to be his lucky mascot on his historic 1927 transatlantic flight. The children that had grown up watching Felix cartoons would eventually fight in WWII. Bomber pilots proudly adorned their

Figure 9.9. Felix the Cat, 1919, from Feline Follies

Figure 9.10. Felix-Anarchist Cat - a WWII Patriotic Stamp

planes with images of the undefeatable Felix, while his image appeared on battalion and regimental insignia *(figure 9.10)*. Felix the Cat had become a cultural icon representing the clever overcoming of all odds. Because of Felix's iconic notoriety, NBC television used his image, a Felix doll rotating on a record, for its first test broadcast in 1929.

Early films, sometimes based on 19th century novels, featured vicious felines that were latent killers. Edgar Allan Poe's *Black Cat*, which was discussed in the last chapter, became a popular horror film starring Boris Karloff and Bela Lugosi in the 1934 version. The 1965 film *The Tomb of Ligeia*, based on another of Poe's short stories, revolves around the main character, Ligeia's, desire to be immortal. At the beginning of the film, a black cat jumps on Ligeia's coffin and Ligeia opens her eyes, a foreshadowing of her soul going into the cat. Shortly thereafter, the cat leaps to Ligeia's gravestone and looks down. Verden, Ligeia's husband, later falls in love with Lady Rowena. Ligeia, in the cat body, is jealous of Lady Rowena, and tries to frighten and even kill her. Meanwhile, references to ancient Egypt abound, as a pharaoh's head and statues of Bast appear as background props. In the end, the black cat, the vessel for Ligiea's soul, and Ligiea herself are both consumed by fire. The theme of cats as mysteriously evil beings bound to women, based on Egyptian and Greek goddesses, is amazingly still evident centuries later.

In the 1942 film *Cat People,* the duality of woman and cat plays a central role. Based on the 1930 short story, *The Bagheeta,* written by Val Lewton and starring Simone Simon, the film tells the story of Irena, a Serbian, who believes that she is the descendant of a line of people who can turn into cats when emotionally provoked. Because of her jealousy, Irena turns into a black panther in order to kill her husband's colleague and new love, Alice. At the beginning of the film, a statue of King John of Serbia with a cat impaled upon his sword foreshadows the ending of the film when the main character commits suicide by allowing herself to be attacked and killed by a black panther caged at the zoo. Her demise is brought about when her psychologist tries to molest her, and she turns into a vicious cat and kills him. With nowhere to turn, after changing back into her human form, she allows the caged panther to kill her.

In a somewhat similar vein, the 1957 British film *Cat Girl* is based on the same premise of a woman being able to turn into a cat. The main character, Leonora, is unhappily married and suffers from the family curse, that of turning into a leopard. After taking revenge on her cheating husband by tearing him to shreds as her leopard alter ego, she comes to a tragic end when she, as the cat, is struck by a car and dies. Both films end with the deaths of the women and cats. Their power and savagery must be extinguished.

Released in the same year as *Cat Girl*, Alfred Hitchcock's *Miss Paisley's Cat* features Stanley, the stray cat, who gives Miss Paisley the courage to stand up against a vulgar world and commit murder on his behalf. Originally written in 1953 by Roy Vickers, the story revolves around a lonely spinster's love for a stray cat, Stanley. Stanley, the ugly cat, teaches Miss Paisley how to stand up against others by defeating the vicious attack of a dog. And from Stanley, she finds the courage to stand up against her brutish neighbor.

In the 1961 film *Shadow of the Cat,* Tabitha the loyal cat whose mistress has been brutally killed plots her cat's revenge on the murderers. Both *Miss Paisley's Cat* and *Shadow of the Cat* portray the animals as loyal companions willing to give their love, support and even their lives to aid their mistresses as their devoted familiars.

Not all films, of course, depicted the cat as a loyal companion. The 1972 low budget Mexican film, *Night of a 1000 Cats,* also known as *Blood Feast,* features a serial killer Hugo Stiglitz who feeds the bodies of his victims to caged cats in some sort of demonic ritual. However, justice prevails at the end of the film when the cats escape their cages and devour Stiglitz himself. The film has been rated the worst feline horror film and includes questionable behavior towards the cats especially when Stiglitz grabs a white cat by its neck and hurls it over a fence.

On the other hand, a revival of the Victorian belief in the cat's importance to motherhood and the raising of children gave rise to a number of children's films starring adorable cats and kittens that melted the hearts of both young and old. The 1964 Walt Disney movie *The Three Lives of Thomasina*, tells the story of a Scottish girl whose cat dies at the hands of her widowed veterinarian father. The relationship between father and daughter is repaired when Thomasina returns to life with the help of a beautiful, kind witch who heals animals.

Aristocats (1970) was the last film to be approved by Walt Disney before his death, and was also the last film in which Maurice

Chevalier would sing before he too died in 1972. The animated film takes place in 1910 Paris and tells the story of Duchess and her three kittens. Owned by a rich socialite, Madame Adelaide Bonfamille, the cat family enjoys a very comfortable life. The aging Madame decides to leave all her possessions to her cats, and the butler becomes jealous and seeks to remove the cats from the villa so that he can become the beneficiary of her will. After being dumped in the countryside and left to fend for themselves, they come across a clever stray tomcat Thomas O'Malley who helps them return home and live happily ever after.

In the 1951 film *Rhubarb,* a millionaire baseball team owner takes a liking to a dog-chasing cat[†] who is named *Rhubarb* after the slang term for an on field fight or argument. The eccentric owner then dies and leaves the team to the cat. His daughter files a lawsuit against the cat's inheritance, and the team protests the insult of being owned by a cat. Soon the cat is kidnapped and held for ransom, but cleverly escapes and runs to the ballpark where it inspires the team to win and captures the hearts of all.

Another Disney film, *That Darn Cat* (1965), tells the story of DC (Darn Cat)[†] a beautiful recalcitrant Siamese who just happens to come upon a hostage in a bank robbery while looking for food. The desperate woman scratches a partial message for help on the cat's collar. From there, the FBI try following DC to find the woman. The film focuses on the antics of a typically self-obsessed, hungry cat. Bosley Crowther of *The New York Times* wrote, "The feline that plays the informant, as the F.B.I. puts it, is superb. Clark Gable at the peak of his performing never played a tom cat more winningly. This elegant, blue-eyed creature is a paragon of suavity and grace", and concluded, "...it's an entertaining picture. Even a king might profitably look at That Darn Cat." Syn Cat, the cat actor, won a Patsy award for his performance.

Depicted primarily as metaphors for women, cats acted as trusted familiars and/or as sweet companions to young girls. However, soon men, too, began to be cast with cats in films. In the 1974 road film *Harry and Tonto,* a cat is the co-star and companion to an aging man

---

[†] Orangey, who also starred in *Breakfast at Tiffany's*, won a PATSY award (Picture Animal Top Star of the Year) for both his performances. Orangey has so far been the only cat to win the award twice.

[†] Syn Cat, the cat actor, won a PATSY award for his performance.

who sets off on his last journey. Art Carney noted that prior to his work in *Harry and Tonto*, he "never liked cats" but said he wound up getting along well with the cat† in the film.

The rough and indisputably masculine Rooster Cogburn, played by John Wayne in the original *True Grit* (1969), even had an orange tabby cat named General Sterling Price whom he introduces to Mattie Ross as his nephew.

In the TV series *Early Edition* (1996-2000), again it is a friendly orange tabby cat played by three cats, Panther, Pella and Carl, who act as Gary's familiars.

Cats sometimes served as the companions of maniacal deviants and gangsters such as the character Ernst Stravo Blofeld in the James Bond films, who was always accompanied by his nameless white Persian. The *Austin Powers* satirical spinoff doesn't forget the cat either, and features a hairless Sphynx as Mr. Bigglesworth, a complete opposite to the white fluffy Persian.

Marlon Brando as *The Godfather* affectionately holds and strokes his cat while he is making an offer that cannot be refused. The cool superiority of man and cat typifies the power of the mobster. Brando, a well-known cat lover, had found the stray cat on the set just before shooting started on *The Godfather*. When Brando held the cat in his arms, it purred so loudly that Brando and the other actor's lines had to be dubbed.

Cats and Music

As poetry moved to music, so did the cat. Early on cats exerted their influence on music. Songs such as the 1891 *Johnny Doolan's Cat* sung by Burl Ives, and *The Cat Came Back* (1893) by Harry S. Miller recount how it is impossible to get rid of a cat. Both eventually became children's songs. *Has Anyone seen our Cat*—1897*(figure 9.11)* became another popular ditty bemoaning the loss of a cat. Aaron Copeland's composition, *Cat and Mouse* (1921) is based on the fable written by Jean Le Fontaine, *The Old Cat and the Young Mouse.*

Black cats historically considered demonic and evil were now hip and cool in the music of the 20th century. Jethro Tull recounts the loss of his cat in this 1967 song, *Old Black Cat.*

† Tonto also won a PATSY award for his performance.

Figure 9.11. Has Anyone Seen our Cat, Sheet Music, 1897

Old Black Cat

by Jethro Tull Band 1967

My old black cat passed away this morning
He never knew what a hard day was.
Woke up late and danced on tin roofs.
If questioned "Why?"—answered, "Just because."

He never spoke much, preferring silence:
eight lost lives was all he had.

Occasionally sneaked some Sunday dinner.
He wasn't good and he wasn't bad.
My old black cat wasn't much of a looker.
You could pass him by – just a quiet shadow.
Got pushed around by all the other little guys.
Didn't seem to mind much – just the way life goes.

Padded about in furry slippers.
Didn't make any special friends.
He played it cool with wide-eyed innocence.
Receiving gladly what the good Lord sends.
Forgot to give his Christmas present.
Black cat collar, nice and new.

Thought he'd make it through New Year.

I guess this song will have to do.
My old black cat…
Old black cat.

In Janet Jackson's song *Black Cat,* the chorus sings lyrics threatening vengeance on a lost love: "*Black cat, nine lives, short days, long nights, Livin on the edge not afraid to die, Heart beat real strong, but not, for long, Better watch your step, or you're gonna die,..*"

Year of the Cat by Al Stewart (1976) equates the cat once again to woman: *"She'll just tell you that she came in the year of the cat." "Her eyes shine like the moon in the sea…"*

Andrew Lloyd Webber's opera *Cats,* based on the T.S. Eliot's collection of poems, *Old Possum's Book of Practical Cats,* opened in the West End in 1981, and ran for 21 years in London, winning numerous awards.

Ever popular, the cat found its way into the more contemporary songs of Bob Dylan, David Bowie and many other famous artists. Johnny Cash's *Mean Eyed Cat* can only make a cat lady smile:

"I give my woman half my money at the general store
I said, 'Now buy a little groceries, and don't spend no more.'
But she gave ten dollars for a ten cent hat
And bought some store bought cat food for a mean eyed cat."

Cats in Literature

The cat naturally came to the pages of 20th century literary works as the usual symbol of feminine sexuality, lust and desire. However, writers loved cats not because they could use them in their literary works as symbol and metaphor, but because they, just like the independent thinkers of the 17th 18th, and 19th centuries, admired the cat's natural aloofness and haughty superiority. Long since glorified by the ancient Romans as the goddess of freedom, the cat could not be tamed, an attribute that writers chose to emulate.

The French writer Colette (1873-1953), *(figure 9.12)* who epitomized the bohemian lifestyle of the period by living with both female and male lovers, and writing scandalous novels, had a special love of cats. Her devotion to her pets caused her second husband to complain, "When I enter a room where you're alone with animals, I feel I'm being indiscreet." One of the French novelist's books is even entitled *La Chatte (Cat)* and focuses on a love triangle between a man, woman and cat. Oddly enough it is the man who is in love with the cat and cannot give her up, summarized in brief from a 1936 New York Times Review:

"***The Cat La Chatte*** *is a French novel by Sidonie-Gabrielle Colette. Released in 1933, the book tells of a love triangle involving Camille Malmert, her husband Alain Amparat and his Chartreux cat Saha. Camille loves Alain, but Alain loves his cat, whom he has had from childhood, more than he could love any woman. The book mainly focuses on Alain and his refusal to grow up; his cat is the embodiment of his childhood.*

In the story, Camille and Alain get married and temporarily move into one of Camille's friend's flats. Alain does not like this, as he is away from his childhood home and his cat. Eventually, Camille becomes so annoyed at Alain's obsession with the cat that she pushes Saha from the balcony of the flat, to what she hopes is her death. The cat survives and Alain, furious, leaves Camille to move back in with his mother and his cat.

Alain is rumored to be based upon Colette's own brother. Saha is based upon a Chartreux cat that Colette once owned called "la chatte".

There is some writing in this novel which would be hard to match for delicacy and exactness, and there are dozens of delightful pictures of Saha. No one who is fond of cats can afford to miss the acquaintance of this one" (Wallace, 1936).

Another famous cat lover was the writer, poet and filmmaker Jean Cocteau (1889-1963). Cocteau, a thorough cat enthusiast, founded a club in Paris called the "Cat Friends Club" *Club des amis des chats* that sponsored cat shows. He is also famous for the quote "I love cats because I enjoy my home: and little by little, they become its visible soul.", as well as "A meow massages the heart." Famous artists such

Figure 9.12. Colette and Cat, c. 1932, Library of Congress Prints and Photographs Division, Washington, D.C.

as Léonard Tsugouharu Foujita, mentioned earlier, joined the club as well.

Tove Jansson (1914-2001) was a Finish author and cat enthusiast. An excerpt from a chapter entitled *Cat* from *The Summer Book* recounts the story of a small kitten. *'It was a tiny kitten when it came and could drink its milk only from a nipple. Fortunately, they still had Sophia's baby bottle in the attic. In the beginning, the kitten slept in a tea cozy to keep warm but when it found its legs they let it sleep in the cottage in Sophia's bed. It had its own pillow, next to hers. It was a gray fisherman's cat and it grew fast. One day, it left the cottage and moved into the house, where it spent its nights under the bed in the box where they kept the dirty dishes. It had odd ideas of its own even then. Sophia carried the cat back to the cottage and tried as hard as she could to ingratiate herself, but the more love she gave it, the quicker it fled back to the dish box. When the box got too full, the cat would howl and someone would have to wash the dishes. Its name was Ma Petite, but they called it Moppy. 'It's funny about love,' Sophia said, 'The more you love someone, the less he likes you back.' 'That's very true,' Grandmother observed. 'And so what do you do?' 'You go on loving,' said Sophia threateningly. 'You love harder and harder'* (Jansson, 2003).

The author of *The Big Sleep*, Raymond Chandler, started his writing career at age 44, and wrote letters as his cat Taki. "Come around sometime when your face is clean (he wrote to a friend) and we shall discuss the state of the world, the foolishness of humans, the prevalence of horsemeat, although we prefer the tenderloin side of a porterhouse, and our common difficulty in getting doors opened at the right time and meals served at more frequent intervals. I have got my staff up to five a day, but there is still room for improvement." Chandler's literary agent, H.N. Swanson, said that Chandler's cat "knew more about him than anybody else." Chandler was quoted as saying, "I said something which gave you to think I hated cats. But gad, sir, I am one of the most fanatical cat lovers in the business. If you hate them, I may learn to hate you."

The American author, Truman Capote, (1924-1984) gave the nameless orange cat in his novel *Breakfast at Tiffany's* a major role as a reflection of the main character, Holly. "(Holly) She was still hugging the cat. 'Poor slob,' she said, tickling his head, 'poor slob without a name. It's a little inconvenient, his not having a name. But I haven't any right to give him one: He'll have to wait until he belongs to somebody. We just sort of hooked up by the river one day, we don't belong to each other. He's an independent, and so am I. I don't want to own anything until I know I've found a place where me and things belong together…If I could find a real-life place that made me feel like Tiffany's, then I'd buy some furniture and give the cat a name" (Capote, 1958/1993).

T.S. Eliot (1888-1965) one of the 20th century's greatest poets, found the cat an inspiration for *The Naming of Cats*, a lengthy poem about the importance of cats' names, which was the basis for the long running Broadway hit *Cats* previously mentioned. His book *Old Possum's Book of Practical Cats* might have been a tribute to Ezra Pound's love of cats, as Pound was known by the nickname Old Possum.

The Naming of Cats

The Naming of Cats is a difficult matter,
It isn't just one of your holiday games;

You may think at first I'm mad as a hatter
When I tell you, a cat must have THREE DIFFERENT NAMES.
First of all, there's the name that the family use daily,
Such as Peter, Augustus, Alonzo or James,
Such as Victor or Jonathan, George or Bill Bailey—
All of them sensible every-day names.
There are fancier names if you think they sound sweeter,
Some for the gentlemen, some for the dames:
Such as Plato, Admetus, Electra, Demeter—
But all of them sensible everyday names.
But I tell you, a cat needs a name that's particular,
A name that's peculiar, and more dignified,
Else how can he keep up his tail perpendicular,
Or spread out his whiskers, or cherish his pride?
Of names of this kind, I can give you a quorum,
Such as Mukustrap, Quaxo, or Coricopat,
Such as Bombalurina, or else Jellylorum—
Names that never belong to more than one cat.
But above and beyond there's still one name left over,
And that is the name that you never will guess;
The name that no human research can discover—
But THE CAT HIMSELF KNOWS, and will never confess.
When you notice a cat in profound meditation,
The reason, I tell you, is always the same:
His mind is engaged in a rapt contemplation
Of the thought, of the thought, of the thought of his name:
His ineffable effable
Effanineffable
Deep and inscrutable singular Name.

Best known for authoring *The Jungle Book*, Rudyard Kipling (1865-1936) was the first English language writer to win the Nobel Prize for Literature. In his children's story *The Cat that Walked by Himself*, he describes a time when Man and Woman lived in caves and animals had not yet been tamed. The superior, independent Cat vows that he will always walk alone and go wherever, whenever, he pleases. Unlike the other animals that eventually let themselves be easily tamed, the cat makes a deal with the Woman that if she praises him three times, the cat will be able to come into the cave and warm himself by the fire and enjoy a drink of milk. She does so, and the cat is free to enjoy his new privileges without having been tamed; thus proving the intelligence and independence of the cat.

Cats played an important part in the short stories and novels of the American science fiction writer H.P. Lovecraft (1890-1937). Lovecraft's *The Cats of Ulthar* (1920) is a short story that focuses on the dreadful fate that befalls those who kill cats. A defenseless black kitten is stolen in the town by a couple who kill cats. The cat Menes then chants a curse that causes all the town's cats to gather and attack and devour the couple in revenge. The town then passes a law against the killing of cats.

In the story *Rats in the Walls* (1924) the narrator moves to his ancestral home with his seven cats, but it is his black cat, Nigger-man, that becomes anxious, roving around the gothic house sniffing and scratching at the ancient walls. Once both narrator and cat find out the truth of the priory, the cat remains unfazed by the diabolical happenings, but his owner, on the other hand, goes mad.

In *The Dream-Quest of Unknown Kadath* (1943) the protagonist wanders the moon until he is saved by howling cats that take him back to earth.

"Carter now spoke with the leaders in the soft language of cats, and learned that his ancient friendship with the species was well known and often spoken of in the places where cats congregate. He had not been unmarked in Ulthar when he passed through, and the sleek old cats had remembered how he patted them after they had attended to the hungry Zoogs who looked evilly at a small black kitten. And they recalled, too, how he had welcomed the very little kitten who came to see him at the inn, and how he had given it a saucer of rich cream in the morning before he left. The grandfather of that very little kitten was the leader of the army now assembled, for he had seen the evil procession from a far hill and recognized the prisoner as a sworn friend of his kind on earth and in the land of dream."

In the collection of short stories, *Something About Cats*, Lovecraft contends that the cat lover is devoid of the need for society by turning away from "pointless sociability and friendliness, or slavering devotion and obedience." The cat lover is, like his cat companion, a 'free soul' (Lovecraft, 1949, pp. 4, 8).

The Irish poet William Butler Yeats (1865-1939) equates himself with the cat in his poem *The Cat and the Moon*, and his lost love Maud Gonne with the moon. By using several opposites such as the cat's black color and the moon's whiteness, he metaphorically contrasts his feelings with Gonne's. Minnaloushe was the cat of Maude Gonne's daughter. There are 28 lines in the poem representative of the 28 phases of the moon.

THE CAT AND THE MOON

THE cat went here and there
And the moon spun round like a top,
And the nearest kin of the moon,
The creeping cat, looked up.
Black Minnaloushe stared at the moon,
For, wander and wail as he would,
The pure cold light in the sky
Troubled his animal blood.
Minnaloushe runs in the grass
Lifting his delicate feet.
Do you dance, Minnaloushe, do you dance?
When two close kindred meet,
What better than call a dance?
Maybe the moon may learn,
Tired of that courtly fashion,
A new dance turn.
Minnaloushe creeps through the grass
From moonlit place to place,
The sacred moon overhead
Has taken a new phase.
Does Minnaloushe know that his pupils
Will pass from change to change,
And that from round to crescent,
From crescent to round they range?
Minnaloushe creeps through the grass
Alone, important and wise,
And lifts to the changing moon
His changing eyes (Yeats, 1912/2013, p. 53).

The masculine hunter, fisherman, bullfight enthusiast and 1954 Noble prize winner for literature, Ernest Hemingway, doted on his cats. After being given "Snowball" a white six-toed cat by a ship's captain, Hemingway let nature take its course until by 1945 he had 23 felines. A whole tribe of polydactyl cats have inhabited his Key West, Florida estate ever since, and The Hemingway House and Museum still care for them today. The book *Hemingway's Cats: An Illustrated Biography,* with a forward by his niece, provides some insight into his relationship with his cats. Uncle Willie, one of Hemingway's cats was found after being hit by a car on February 22, 1953. Afterwards, Hemingway wrote a heartfelt letter to his close friend Gianfranco Ivancich.

Dear Gianfranco:

Just after I finished writing you and was putting the letter in the envelope Mary came down from the Torre and said, 'Something terrible has happened to Willie.' I went out and found Willie with both his right legs broken: one at the hip, the other below the knee. A car must have run over him or somebody hit him with a club. He had come all the way home on the two feet of one side. It was a multiple compound fracture with much dirt in the wound and fragments protruding. But he purred and seemed sure that I could fix it.

I had René get a bowl of milk for him and René held him and caressed him and Willie was drinking the milk while I shot him through the head. I don't think he could have suffered and the nerves had been crushed so his legs had not begun to really hurt. Monstruo wished to shoot him for me, but I could not delegate the responsibility or leave a chance of Will knowing anybody was killing him…

Have had to shoot people but never anyone I knew and loved for eleven years. Nor anyone that purred with two broken legs (Brennen, 2006).

Norman Mailer said of William S. Burroughs that he was "The only American novelist living today who may conceivably be possessed by genius." Penguin Books described him as "one of the most politically trenchant, culturally influential, and innovative artists of the 20th century." Even so, the cranky Burroughs had a special affinity for his cats, and in his *Last Words: 7/30/97* he wrote, "There is no final enough wisdom, experience –any fucking thing. No Holy Grail, No Final Satori, no solution. Just Conflict. Only thing that can resolve conflict is love, like I felt for Fletch and Ruski, Spooner, and Calico. Pure love. What I feel for my cats past and present."

In an interview with Victor Bockris, Burroughs responded to his question. "Do you think you've learned a lot from living with your cats?"

"Oh heavens! I've learned immeasurably. I've learned compassion. I remember when I was out at the stone house Ruski sort of attacked one of the kittens. I gave him a light slap and then he disappeared. He was so hurt. And I knew where he was. I went out into the barn and found him sulking there, picked him up and carried him back. Just the slightest slap like that. This is his human, his human had betrayed him. Oh heavens, yes, I've learned from my cats. They reflect you in a very deep way. They just opened up a whole area of compassion in me. I remember lying in my bed and weeping and weeping to think that a nuclear catastrophe would destroy them. I could see people driving by saying: "Kill your dogs and cat." I spent hours just crying. Oh, my God. Then there is constantly the feeling that there could be some relationship between me and the cats and that I might have missed it. Some of this is in The Cat Inside. Some of it is so extreme that I couldn't write. People think of me as being cold – some woman wrote that I could not admit any feeling at all. My God, I am so emotional that sometimes I can't stand the intensity. Oh, my God. Then they ask me if I ever cry? I say, 'Holy shit, probably two days ago.' I'm very subject to these violent fits of weeping, for very good reason" (Bockris, 1996, pp. 247-248).

The Noble Prize winning author Doris Lessing was influenced by her deep relationships with cats. In *An Old Woman and Her Cat* (1972) the main character Hetty, poor, widowed and abandoned by her children, finds her only comfort in her faithful tomcat. Both outcasts of society, Hetty dies of exposure while trying to hide from the authorities that want to commit her to an old folk's home. Her cat is caught and put to sleep. A neat society has disposed of its non-conformists. Lessing not only used cats in her fiction, but she also documented the lives of her own. *On Cats* (2002) consists of a collection of stories, *Particularly Cats and Rufus the Survivor*, and the memoir, *The Old Age of El Magnifico* wherein Lessing observes and offers her adept insights into the actions of her felines. Sometimes ruthless in her telling of the fates of unlucky cats, the book is likewise filled with emotion at their eternal beauty. In an interview with the *Wall Street Journal*, she stated, "The cat I communicated with best was El Magnifico. He was such a clever cat. We used to have sessions when we tried to be on each other's level—" (Crossen, 2008).

Jack Kerouac (1922-1969) author of *On the Road* (1957) wrote about the death of one of his favorite cats, Tyke, in his memoir *Big*

Sur (1962). Tyke was Kerouac's calico Persian whose death he strangely equated with his little brother Gerard's. Jack writes that it was Gerard "who'd taught me to love cats when I was 3 and 4 and we used to lie on the floor on our bellies and watch them lap up milk." Knowing how important the cat was to Jack, his mother made sure that Tyke had a proper burial, "under the Honeysuckle vines, at the corner of the fence". She told Jack that the black birds in the garden must have realized what was going on. "There was lots and lots of 'em flying over my head and chirping, and settling on the fence, for a whole hour after Tyke was laid to rest — that's something I'll never forget — I wish I had a camera at the time but God and Me knows it and saw it," she told Kerouac. (Kerouac, 1992)

"When we're alone he says, 'Your mother wrote and said your cat is dead.' Ordinarily the death of a cat means little to most men, a lot to fewer men, but to me, and that cat, it was exactly and no lie and sincerely like the death of my little brother—I loved Tyke with all my heart, he was my baby who as a kitten just slept in the palm of my hand and with his little head hanging down, or just purring for hours, just as long as I held him that way, walking or sitting—He was like a floppy fur wrap around my wrist, I just twist him around my wrist or drape him and he just purred and purred and even when he got big I still held him that way, I could even hold that big cat in both hands with my arms outstretched right over my head and he'd just purr, he had complete confidence in me—and when I'd left New York to come to my retreat in the woods I'd carefully kissed him and instructed him to wait for me 'Attends pour mue kitigingoo'—But my mother said in the letter he had died the NIGHT AFTER I HAD LEFT" (Kerouac, 1992 p. 11).

"Holding up my

Purring cat to the moon

I sighed"
(Kerouac, American Haiku, 1959).

The Japanese author Haruki Murakami, known for liking and having cats has included them in many of his works. In *The Wind-Up Bird Chronicle* the story revolves around Toru Okada's missing cat that he loves more than any of the women with whom he has encounters. The cat also serves as an omen for the eventual disappearance of his wife. In *Kafka on the Shore,* the protagonist, Kafka Tamura, cannot pass a cat without petting it. Nakata, is an old man who, after having lost the ability to read, gains the ability to converse with cats. Because he can talk with the cats, he becomes a finder of lost cats. Nakata finds a Siamese cat named Mimi particularly impressive, as she can quote from Puccini operas and hold conversations.

Murakami has also written several essays. One of these, *On the Death of My Cat,* discusses the death of one of his many cats.

"On the Death of My Cat

My cat died the other day. It was an Abyssinian I got from Ryu Murakami and her name was Kirin. Because she was Ryu Murakami's cat, the name "Kirin" comes from the mythical Chinese unicorn- no relation to the beer.

She was four years old, which in human years would have put her in her late twenties, maybe 30, so it was an early death. She was prone to getting kidney stones in her urinary tract, had had surgery already, her meal regimen comprised solely of diet cat food (which is something that exists in this wide world), but in the end, it was complications in her urinary tract that took her life. We had her cremated, put her tiny bones in an urn, and placed her in our household shrine. The house I live in now is an old Japanese style house, so it's very convenient to have a household shrine at times like these. It seems to me that it would be hard to find a place to put your cat's bones in a brand new two bedroom apartment. It just doesn't seem right to put it on top of the refrigerator, you know?

Besides Kirin I also have an eleven year old female Siamese cat named Muse. The name comes from a character from the famous shoujou manga Glass Castle. Before that I had two male cats named Butch and Sundance, the classic duo from Butch Cassidy and the Sundance Kid. When you have a lot of cats it gets annoying coming up with name after name after name, so I do some extremely easy naming. I've had a mackerel cat named Mackerel, and a calico cat named Calico. When I had a Scottish fold I named him "Scotty". I'm sure you can derive from this pattern that I've also had a black cat named "Black" before too.

If we organize the fates of the various cats that have come and gone in the fifteen years I've lived in this house, we get:

A) Dead cats: 1) Kirin 2) Butch 3) Sundance 4) Mackerel 5) Scotty

B) Cats I've given away: 1) Calico 2) Peter

C) Cats who suddenly disappeared: 1) Black 2) Tobimaru

D) Cats I still have left: 1) Muse

Thinking about it, there's only been a two month period in these last fifteen years when there wasn't a single cat in my house.

This is kind of an obvious statement, but cats have lots of different personalities, and their behavioral patterns, as well as the way they think, differ from cat to cat. The Siamese I have now is that kind of unusual cat that can't give birth unless I hold her hand. When the labor pains start up, this cat immediately jumps up from my lap onto the floor and sets herself down heavily, grunting like an old lady, onto a floor cushion. I take both of her hands tightly, and out comes one kitten after another. It's pretty fun, watching this cat give birth.

For whatever reason, Kirin loved the rustling noise that plastic wrap makes when she rolled around in it, and if someone crumpled up an empty cigarette box, she'd burst out of nowhere to pull it out of the garbage and play with it by herself for fifteen minutes or so. As to what circumstances led to this one cat's habits, vices, and tastes to be formed is a total mystery to me. This cat - this strange, energetic, solidly built, vigorous appetite-having cat - is the complete opposite of Ryu Murakami. She was a real free spirit, and was popular with anyone who came over to my house. When her urinary tract got worse she became less energetic, but even until the day before her death, it didn't seem like she was going to die like she did. I brought her to the nearby vet, who let out all the blocked-up urine and gave her medicine to dissolve the kidney stones, but as the night came to an end, she crouched down onto the kitchen floor, her eyes opened wide, and grew cold. Cats are creatures that always die rather easily. Her face was too pretty in death–you might've thought that if you placed her out in the sun, she would thaw out and come back to life.

In the afternoon pet specialists from a burial service company came in a minivan to pick her up. They were dressed just like the people in the movie The Funeral, and they even said their condolences like they were supposed to, but, you can just think of their remarks as a suitably simplified version of the condolences you would say for humans. Then it became a matter of money. The course from cremation to urn, along with the urn itself, came to 23000 yen. In the trunk of the van we could also see the figure of a German shepherd in a plastic storage bin. Maybe Kirin's going to be cremated along with that German shepherd.

After Kirin was carried off in that minivan, my house quickly started to feel empty, and neither me, nor my wife, nor Muse could settle down. Family – even if that includes cats too – is a living thing that has a certain balance, and when one corner of it falls apart, it doesn't take long before everything subtly breaks down. Unable to go about my work at home, I thought I'd go hang out in Yokohama, so I walked to the train station in a soft, drizzling rain. But even that somehow didn't seem worth the trouble, and halfway there I turned back and went home" (Murakami, 1985).

In another essay, *Murakami Harukido wa ikanishite kitaeraretaka,* Murakami tells the story of an aged cat that he once owned. In a piece entitled *Choju Neko no Himitsu* he tells the story of how he asked an executive at Kodansha Ltd., a publishing company, to take care of his cat while he was away. In return for the favor, Murakami promises to write a novel for the company which turned out to be *Norwegian Wood*, a bestseller. Murakami writes that when he was writing his first novel *Hear the Wind Sing*, "I still remember well the days when I was writing my first novel at night, with the cat on my lap and sipping beer. The cat apparently didn't like me writing a novel and would often play havoc with my manuscript on the desk."

Town of Cats, recently published in the New Yorker, is a tale included in Murakami's novel *1Q84*, which is about a man who becomes lost in a town where only cats reside. Murakami said the following about the story, "*Town of Cats* is a story that I made up. I think I probably read something like it a long time ago, but I don't have a very precise recollection of whatever it was that I read. In any case, this episode performs a symbolic function in the novel in many different senses—the way a person wanders into a world from which he can never escape, the question of who it is that fills up the empty spaces, the inevitability with which night follows day. Perhaps each of us has his or her own 'town of cats' somewhere deep inside—or so I feel" (Treisman, 2011).

Murakami has admitted to being influenced by Natsume Soseki who wrote *I am a Cat,* an early 20th century novel, in which the narrator is a domestic house cat.

Not all authors, however, adored the cat. Several books were published in the 80's and 90's by cat, and essentially woman haters. *101 Uses for a Dead Cat* (1981) written by Simon Bond illustrates this hostility by giving an example of a dead cat as a pencil sharpener. The pencil is inserted into its anus, a symbolic rape. In yet another book,

How to Kill your Girlfriend's Cat, Dr. Robert Daphne writes out of his own frustration at his girlfriend's fondness for her cat. He instructs those in a similar position on how killing the cat will free a girlfriend so that she can give her individual attention to a boyfriend or husband. One such book was not enough, and he published yet another, *How to Kill your Girlfriend's Cat Again* (1990) which describes 40 more ways to kill a cat. Both his books appeal to misogynists and cat haters simply because women and cats cannot be controlled, are independent and untrainable.

Joyce Carole Oates, herself a cat lover, paints a picture of this controlling, cat jealous, male mentality in *The White Cat.* An aging Julius Muir gives his younger wife a cat, Miranda. The cat, sensing hostility in Julius, refuses to give him any attention or affection in the way only a cat can. Julius is furious at what he sees as the cat's ingratitude, since he bought her and provides for her. Miranda becomes a metaphor for Julius' wife.

Cats and Politicians

From presidents to prime ministers, to adventurers, the cat served as a wise mascot. Beginning with President Theodore Roosevelt (1858-1919) who had two cats: Tom Quartz and Slippers, almost every 20th century president has had a cat or cats to accompany him and his family in the White House.

Cats have even been long standing residents of 10 Downing Street, brought to the address by Prime Ministers and other staff as mousers or just pets. However, perhaps the most famous cat lover and resident of 10 Downing Street was Sir Winston Churchill, who served as Britain's Prime Minister from 1940-1945 and 1951-1955. Churchill formed attachments to several cats throughout his lifetime, whom he kept by his side at both his official and private residences. Sir John Colville wrote about a meeting he had with Churchill.

Churchill kept his wife informed of the goings on of the cats while she was on a cruise in the South Pacific. In a letter dated March 2nd 1935 he writes, "The cat (Tango) treats me well very graciously and always wishes to sleep on my bed (which I resent). When I dine alone, and only then, she (Tango was actually a male) awaits me on the table" (Soames, 1999).

During a particularly bad time in the war, on June 3rd, 1941, Sir

John Colville noted what transpired during the lunch which he had with Churchill that day.

"I had lunch with the P.M. and the Yellow Cat, which sat in a chair on his right-hand side and attracted most of his attention. He was meditating deeply on the Middle East, where he is intent on reorganizing the rearward services, and on Lord Beaverbrook who is proving particularly troublesome...While he brooded on these matters, he kept up a running conversation with the cat, cleaning its eyes with his napkin, offering it mutton and expressing regret that it could not have cream in war-time" (Coleville, 1986).

Grace Hamblin, who was Churchill's secretary as well as his wife's from 1932-1965, commented on Churchill's love of animals, in particular cats, at the 1987 International Churchill conference.

"He loved cats. So do I and he knew it. He always had a cat, if not two. I must tell you one lovely cat story. It was way, way back in the Thirties. He came to his door one morning with some papers in his hand and a cat was sitting in the passage: "Good morning, Cat." But the cat didn't answer. It was one of those horrible snooty things. So he said again, "Good morning, Cat." The cat made no effort to be near him. He slashed at it with his papers and the cat ran from the house. Cat didn't return the next day or the next or the next. Finally he said, "Do you think it's because I hit him?" Of course I said, "Yes, definitely."

That evening I was whiling away my time while the family had dinner downstairs, when Sarah came up and said, 'Hambone, I have a message for you from Papa. He said if you like you may go home, and if you wish before you go, you may put a card in the window to say that if Cat cares to come home, all is forgiven.' Cat did come home several days later with a wire round his neck. Given cream and the best salmon and so on, he did recover, I'm glad to say" (Hamblin, 1989).

Two resident cats of Chartwell were Mickey, a large tabby, and the orange tabby Tango. William Manchester, Churchill's biographer, recalled an amusing incident while Churchill was speaking on the phone with the Lord Chancellor. His cat Mickey started to play with the telephone cord and Churchill shouted, "Get off the line, you fool!" Quickly afterwards he realized the misinterpretation and said to the Lord Chancellor, "Not You!" Manchester wrote, "He offered the cat his apologies, which he never extends to human beings, cajoling the pet, cooing, 'Don't you love me anymore?' and proudly telling his valet at breakfast next day, 'My Mickey came to see me this morning. All is forgiven'"(Manchester, 1988).

Even though quite a bit has been written about Churchill's cat Tango, a grey cat named Nelson was the most well-known during the war years. Churchill commented about Nelson stating, "Nelson is the bravest cat I ever knew. I once saw him chase a huge dog out of the Admiralty. I decided to adopt him and name him after our great Admiral…" While speaking, Churchill sneaked pieces of salmon to Nelson under the table (Reynolds, 1964). When Churchill had been elected prime minister, and it was inevitable that he would move to 10 Downing Street, the press commented that "Nelson will follow his master shortly to Downing Street and make a problem of protocol. How, it is asked will the Munich cat (a mouser that was already living at the residence brought in by Neville Chamberlain's administration) react to Nelson? Will he follow Chamberlain next door to his new home at No. 11 leaving the field at No. 10 to Nelson? Or will he refuse to abdicate and call for a show-down in His Majesty's court of justice?" (Downing St. Cats, 1940, p. 6). Soon afterwards, Nelson chased Munich Mouser out of the residence.

Another cat who took up residence at No. 10 was another grey cat, Smoky. In January 1943, while Churchill was traveling to meet President Roosevelt in Casablanca, Mrs. Churchill wrote, "The "Annexe" & No 10 are dead and empty without you—Smoky wanders about disconsolate—I invite him into my room & he relieves his feelings by clawing my brocade bed-cover and when gently rebuked, biting my toe through it" (Soames, 1999, p. 471).

While meeting with President Roosevelt in August 1941 aboard the HMS Prince of Wales *(figure 9.13)*, the ship's cat Blackie came up to Churchill who bent down and patted his head. The moment was caught in a photograph which was widely published. Shockingly though, the Prime Minister's behavior toward the cat was criticized by the Cats' Protective League, which stated, "He should have conformed to the etiquette demanded by the occasion, offering his hand and then awaiting a sign of approval before taking liberties" (Churchill Should Pet Cat, 1941). The crew of the ship renamed Blackie, Churchill in honor of the meeting.

Throughout the years Churchill enjoyed the company of many cats and kittens. His last cat was given to him for his 88th birthday in 1964 by Sir John Colville. Churchill named the ginger cat with white chest and paws Jock after Sir John Colville. Later he even commissioned a painting be done of Jock. When Churchill died at age 90 with Jock at his bedside, he made sure that provision was made to keep the beloved cat on at Chartwell, which became a National Trust. He also requested that there always be a cat named Jock at Chartwell. The original Jock died in 1975 at age 13 and was replaced by a new ginger cat called Jock II. The tradition lives on today, and Jock VI now inhabits Chartwell.

Figure 9.13. Blackie the cat meets Churchill aboard the HMS Prince of Wales, 1941, Imperial War Museums

Adventurous Cats

Adventurous cats traveled the world on sometimes dangerous expeditions. An unlucky black tomcat named Nigger *(figure 9.14)* accompanied Robert Scott's (1868-1912) team on the Terre Nova Expedition (1910-1912) to the South Pole, but was swept overboard and lost. The kitten had boarded the ill-fated ship in 1910 while docked in London. The loss of their good luck charm, turned out to be a bad omen, as their expedition was doomed with all of Scott's party eventually suffering a lonely death in the Antarctic.

As WWI was just beginning, another adventurous cat, Mrs. Chippy, accompanied Sir Ernest Shackleton's Antarctic voyage of 1914-1915. Mrs. Chippy, a grey tabby tomcat, acquired his name because he constantly followed the ship's carpenter and master shipwright Henry (Harry) McNeish around. "Chippy" is a British nickname for a carpenter, and even though the cat was male, he was called Mrs. because of his attachment to McNeish. Even so, the only photograph of Mrs. Chippy is one with him perched on the shoulder

Figure 9.14. Nigger in hammock, before 1920

Figure 9.15. Blackborow with Mrs. Chippy, before 1920

Figure 9.16. Mrs. Chippy Postage Stamp

of the stowaway Blackborow, who also took a liking to the cat *(figure 9.15)*.

The ill-fated expedition ended when the Endurance became trapped in ice and was eventually crushed. It was Shackleton's decision to shoot all the dogs and the lone cat Mrs. Chippy on October 29th, 1915 before they started out on their 350 mile trek over the ice to the nearest land in order to bring back help for the remaining men. Shackleton recorded in his diary, "This afternoon Sallie's three youngest pups, Sue's Sirius, and Mrs. Chippy, the carpenter's cat, have to be shot. We could not undertake the maintenance of weaklings under the new conditions" (Shackleton, 1919). Macklin, Crean, and the carpenter were particularly upset. The ship's crew doted over Mrs. Chippy in his last hours giving him hugs and feeding him his favorite food, sardines, perhaps laced with a sleeping drug. McNeish never forgave Shackleton for killing his cat, and the two were on such bad terms that Shackleton refused to recommend him for the Polar Medal that the rest of the crew received. In 1925, McNeish went to live in Wellington, New Zealand, where he died in destitution in 1930. Even though buried with full military honors in Karori cemetery, he was interred in an unmarked grave until 1959 when a headstone was finally erected. In 2004, a life sized bronze replica of Mrs. Chippy was created and now sits atop of McNeish's grave in honor of his never ending love of his cat. McNeish's grandson, Tom McNeish, 76, from Norwich, said: "If it wasn't for him they would all have perished. His skills got them to safety. But all you hear about the expedition is Shackleton. I think he would be over the moon about the statue. The cat was more important to him than the Polar Medal" (Chapman, 2004). In 1998, an Island near South Georgia was named after McNeish, and in February 2011, Mrs. Chippy was featured on a postage stamp issued by South Georgia and the South Sandwich Islands *(figure 9.16).*

Cats in War

Throughout both World War I and World War II the cat exhibited its bravery in extreme situations. Serving on battleships and in the trenches, cats proved their heroism in dire circumstances by doing what they were best at: being mousers, mascots, and affectionate companions. During WWI, the British employed more than 500,000 cats to clear the often treacherous trenches of mice and rats. Cats also alerted troops to drifting poisonous gas clouds, saving thousands of lives. Both cats and dogs were even accused of spying for the Germans. When they were observed crossing back and forth across British trenches by the 36th brigade of the 12th Division in July

Figure 9.17. A French soldier with his kittens on the Western Front, Argonne, 1916

1915, officers believed that they might have been delivering German messages across the lines (Copping, 2014) *(figure 9.17).*

During WWII, cats protected valuable food stores from vermin and were considered so important that they each received an extra powdered milk ration for their service. The United States even sent thousands of American cats to France in its "Cats for Europe" campaign.

Most pictures of cats during WWII show them as affectionate companions or mascots. Images of Felix the Cat, already so important to American history, were used, as mentioned earlier, as battalion and regimental emblems in WWI and WWII, and fighter pilots often drew pictures of cats on the sides of their planes. Felix type emblems were also worn as company insignia.

Pooli, short for Princess Papule, born on July 4th, 1944 in the Navy Yard at Pearl Harbor, became the ship's mascot on the USS Fremont (APA-44). Pooli earned three service ribbons and four battle stars for her courage in the face of battle during WWII and the Korean War *(figure 9.18).*

Figure 9.18. WWII hero Pooli, July 4, 1959, © Los Angeles Times Staff Photographer, Reprinted with Permission

The black and white cat Oscar, or as he later became known, Unsinkable Sam, was ship's mascot on the German battleship, Bismarck. Out of a crew of 2,200, only a 118 and Oscar survived the sinking on May 27th, 1941. Rescued by the HMS Cossack, Oscar again survived another sinking on October 24th when the Cossack was torpedoed and 159 of her crew were killed. Rescued again, the lucky feline was taken to Gibraltar where he became the ship's cat on the HMS Ark Royal that was ironically instrumental in sinking the Bismarck, but like the Cossack was torpedoed and sunk. Clinging to a floating plank, Sam along with the survivors were found. Rescuers described Sam as "angry but quite unharmed" (Jameson, 2004, p. 372). After being rescued yet again, Oscar was then transferred to a job on land hunting mice at the office buildings of the Governor General of Gibraltar. Eventually Unsinkable Sam returned to the UK where he remained for the rest of his life at a "Home for Sailors" in Belfast where he died in 1955.

Even though Unsinkable Sam never earned an award for his bravery, several cats earned awards and medals for their distinguished service during wartime. Created in 1943, the Dickin Medal, also known as the Animals Victory Cross, is awarded to animals for "conspicuous gallantry and devotion to duty" while serving in Britian's military or civil service. The only cat to have gotten this award to date is Simon, the mascot of the British frigate HMSA Amethyst during the Yangtze Incident in 1949. Simon was badly wounded by a blast from a Communist shell, but stayed at his post to kill rats throughout the ship's 101 day ordeal. Simon survived even though 23 of the crew and the captain were killed. He lived to return to Britain, only to eventually die of his wounds a month later. Simon's Dickin Medal was auctioned for more than $42,000 in 1993.

Faith, the church cat, was awarded a Silver medal for her bravery during the London Blitz. In 1936, Faith came to live at St. Augustine's church, and as perhaps part of her gratefulness she regularly attended Sunday services and many parishioners came to adore her. Not long after her residency in the church, Faith gave birth to a tiny black and white kitten which looked like a panda bear, and so the kitten was named Panda. A picture of Faith hangs in the church today and underneath it on the Chapel wall are these words:

"Faith"

Our dear little church cat of St. Augustine and St. Faith.
The bravest cat in the world.
On Monday, September 9th, 1940, she endured horrors and perils beyond the power of words to tell.
Shielding her kitten in a sort of recess in the house (a spot
she selected three days before the tragedy occurred), she
sat the whole frightful night of bombing and fire, guarding her little kitten.
The roofs and masonry exploded. The whole house blazed. Four
floors fell through in front of her. Fire and water and ruin
all round her.
Yet she stayed calm and steadfast and waited for help.
We rescued her in the early morning while the place was still burning, and
By the mercy of Almighty God, she and
her kitten were not only saved, but unhurt.
God be praised and thanked for His goodness
and mercy to our dear little pet.

Cats as Inspiration

Finally, the cat would serve as an inspiration for the life-long work of the noted scientist Nikola Tesla (1856-1943). In Tesla's memoir, *A Story of Youth Told by Age (1939),* dedicated to Miss Pola Fotitch, he describes his relationship with his cat Macak, "*the finest of all cats in the world. I wish I could give you an adequate idea of the affection that existed between us. We lived for one another. Wherever I went, Macak followed, because of our mutual love and the desire to protect me.*" Tesla ends his story stating that it was Macak who awakened his lifetime interest in electricity.

"In the dusk of the evening, as I stroked Macak's back, I saw a miracle that made me speechless with amazement. Macak's back was a sheet of light and my hand produced a shower of sparks loud enough to be heard all over the house. My father was a very learned man; he had an answer for every question. But this phenomenon was new even to him. 'Well,' he finally remarked, 'this is nothing but electricity, the same thing you see through the trees in a storm.' My mother seemed charmed. 'Stop playing with this cat,' she said. 'He might start a fire.' But I was thinking abstractedly. Is nature a gigantic cat? If so, who strokes its back?

It can only be God, I concluded. .....I cannot exaggerate the effect of this marvelous night on my childish imagination. Day after day I have asked myself 'what is electricity?' and found no answer. Eighty years have gone by since that time and I still ask the same question, unable to answer it."

The 20th century cat had ventured into every aspect of man's life, and its importance had expanded not through its ability to be tamed and controlled, but instead, by its insistence on respect for its independence and love of freedom. In good times and in bad, the cat has been at man's side, perhaps even more so than the dog. Abiding, unobtrusive, quiet yet pervasive, the cat continues to endure as both an important cultural icon and a loving companion.

Chapter Ten

Epilogue

THE CAT TODAY

Today the cat is a goddess risen. The bond between cats and man, begun over two thousand years ago, has steadily grown stronger throughout time producing the greatest number of cat lovers in history. Cat appreciation days such as Hug Your Cat Day, Black Cat Appreciation Day, and National Cat Day are celebrated with much fanfare. Cats in the media amuse us with their cute cat antics and irreverent behavior and have given rise to social media cat stars such as Grumpy Cat and Lil Bub who have become America's sweethearts, ubiquitously appearing on the news, in magazines and in advertisements. Social media giants such as Facebook, Twitter, Instagram and Pinterest are overflowing with photos of every sort of cat and provide a platform for thousands of cat owners who devotedly post daily accounts of their cats' activities. Sushi cats, cats in space, existential cats, and cats dressed in cute costumes have formed a feline invasion into our hearts and psyches because they simply make us feel good. Even though these activities attempt to anthropomorphize the cat, they can never diminish its innate untamable nature, as there will always be a part of every cat that remains aloof, regal and forever godly. Its haughty independence demands respect, for it cherishes and values freedom, individualism, and exudes a healthy dose of disdain, attributes that arouse love and adoration as well as fear and loathing.

With this increased interest in cats, stories of cat heroes have been reported and gone viral in social media circles. Cats saving their owners from certain death surprise and bewilder, as this behavior from seemingly detached felines is totally unexpected. Several centuries ago, such behavior might have been thought the product of witchcraft. Because of the cat's aloof moodiness, we assume that cats do not love us at least as much as dogs because they do not fawn over us in slobbering loyalty. But this is not so. The cat, even though snobbish and inscrutable, is a loving and devoted pet, but only if its human is deemed worthy of its affections. Due to increased communications and more people owning cats, cats have been recognized as loyal pets that will in some circumstances go above and beyond to protect those that they love. The most recent evidence of such devotion was captured on a surveillance camera and went viral on You Tube. Tara the cat saved a Bakersfield family's little boy, Jeremy Triantafilo, aged 4, from a potentially fatal dog attack by running at the dog and scaring it away. Such aggressive behavior in a cat was miraculous and confirmed cat lovers' beliefs that cats could in fact be altruistic, loyal and protective. Cat heroes have alerted their owners to imminent danger such as fire and gas leaks. This was the case with the kitten Schnautzie who in October 2007 persistently tried to wake her owners up to warn them of a hazardous gas leak which could have led to their house exploding. In another incident, Josh Ornberg and Letitia Kovalovsky—who was seven months pregnant with twins— were saved by their 13 year old tabby, Baby, from a fire in 2010. The cat warned Letitia by jumping up and down in her lap. These are but a few of the many examples of cats helping their owners.

Perhaps because of this booming popularity of cats, a new concept in coffee houses, the cat café, was first started in Taiwan in 1998 and quickly caught on in Japan with the first café opening there in 2004. These cafes have now begun to spread across the world offering serious competition to mainstream coffee and tea houses in the world's largest cities. Lonely "catless" ailurophiles in particular would definitely choose a cat café over a Starbucks or Costa. Caressing and playing with sleek amiable felines over a cup of java while contributing to their welfare, rescue and adoption, through purchases in the café, meet a deep need to make a difference in a cat's life.

A booming cat product business exists both online and in brick and mortar stores. Entrepreneurs that love cats (and those who do not), produce a myriad of products all with cat pictures or cat themes that support a 58.51 billion dollar a year business within the U.S. market alone according to the American Pet Products Association. Americans certainly love their cats.

It is hard to believe that just a few centuries ago the cat was being equated with witchcraft, burned at the stake, and believed to be a demonic beast with fearful powers. Even though the cat is still identified with the ancient pagan ritual of Halloween, and black cats are discriminated against, overall the cat is much better off than it has ever been in history. The cat's reflective mysterious eyes that Plato commented on centuries ago still make us wonder if there is in fact something other-worldly about this untamable beast. Perhaps the ancient Egyptians' laws against the killing and export of cats showed a wisdom that the world had lost for many centuries. However, today those that dare to try and abuse our much-loved felines find themselves prosecuted and put in jail.

Travelling with the cat through history, we have witnessed its height as the goddess Bast and learned of its persecution as an animal reviled. So close to us, but yet so detached, cats give pause to thought, creativity. Rarely deferential or obsequious, cats maintain their regal presences and encourage artists, writers and even statesmen and politicians to aspire to more. At last the cat has reclaimed its rightful place as a goddess to be worshipped and adored. Today the cat is undeniably a goddess reborn.

TIMELINE OF THE CAT IN HISTORY

20 Million Years Ago	Pseudaelurus ancestor of all cats appears.
5 Million Years Ago	Cat family Panthera and Acinonyx appear.
2 Million Years Ago	Felis sylvestris, ancestor of all domestic cats appears.
1 Million Years Ago	Lynx, Puma/Cougar, Clouded Leopard as well as small cats appear.
8,000 BC	First evidence of cat domestication on Cyprus.
3700 BC	Domesticated cat found in Egyptian Pre-Dynastic grave at Hierakonpolis.
3000 BC	Cats mentioned in Sanskrit writings.
2000-1900 BC	Evidence of domesticated cats in Egypt.
1700 BC	Pictographs of domesticated cats appear in Israel.
1785-1557 BC	Ancient Egyptians worship the cat.
1400 BC	First evidence of cats in Greece.
950 BC	Mummified cats appear in Egypt.
5th Century BC	Herodotus mentions the cat goddess Bast.
4th century BC	Aristotle comments on the lustfulness of female cats.

525 BC	Battle of Pelusium, Persians defeat Egyptians using cats.
500 BC	Domesticated cats appear in southern Europe.
200 BC	Cats enter China. (New research states that cat domestication in China began at 3500 BC but with P. Bengalansis, not Felis sylvestris libyca).
200 BC-AD 1400	Cats continue to spread throughout Europe.
AD 350	Palladius uses the word *cattus* to refer to cats.
4th century AD	Evidence of domesticated cats found at Caesaromagus (Chelmsford, Essex).
AD 500	Indian *Panchatantra* fables mention the cat.
AD 570-662	Prophet Mohammed has cat named Muezza.
AD 600	Buddhist monks introduce the cat to Japan.
AD 700	First illustration of cats found in *The Lindisfarne Gospels* in Ireland.
9th century	*Pangur Ban*, first recorded poem about a cat.
10th century	The Welsh King Hywel Dda is the first to write laws to protect the cat.

AD 1,000	Royal Japanese cats are considered sacred.
11th century	Norse mythology depicts the goddess Freya in a cat driven chariot.
1227-1241	Pope Gregory IX equated the cat to the devil.
1230-1700	Millions of cats slaughtered.
1307	Bishop of Covenry and Cathars accused of worshipping cats.
1492	Cats make their way to the New World with Columbus.
1510	Leonardo da Vinci sketches cats.
1570	First novel in English is written, *Beware the Cat* by William Baldwin.
1603-1867	Edo Period Japan legend of Maneki-Neko.
1620	Pilgrims bring first cat to the new world.
1660-1685	Pope's effigy traditionally stuffed with live cats and then burned.
1692-1693	Salem witch trials.
1661-1715	Louis XIV bans the burning of live cats.
1713	Alexander Pope protests cruelty to cats in Guardian essay.

1727	First book on cats written by Paradis de Moncrif.
1733	Last cat sacrifices performed in France.
17th century	Scotland Ritual of Taigheirm where cats were impaled.
1788	Cats first evident in Australia.
1817	Last cat massacre in Ypres, Flanders, Belgium.
1871	First cat show held at Crystal Palace, U.K.
1895	First cat show held at Madison Square Garden, U.S.A.
1906	Cat Fanciers' Association founded.
1910	Kiddo is the first cat to fly in a dirigible.
1910	Fifi is first cat to fly across the English Channel.
1913	Pepper is the first cat to be in films.
1919	First *Felix the Cat* cartoon is produced.
1927	Charles Lindbergh takes a Felix the Cat doll with him on the first trans-Atlantic flight.

1963	Félicette is first cat in space.
1981	Musical play *Cats* performed based on T.S. Eliot's *Old Possum's Book of Practical Cats.*
1998	First Cat Café opened in Taiwan.

LIST OF THEBAN TOMBS WITH CATS

TOMB #	PERSON'S TOMB	LOCATION	REIGNING PHARAOH	DEPICTION
TT 10	Penbuy and Kasa Royal Craftsmen	Deir el-Medina	Ramesses II	Cat and goose
TT A24	Simut Second prophet Of Amun	Dra Abu El Naga	Amenhotep III 18th Dynasty	Cat clinging to owner's robes
TT 39	Puimre Second prophet of Amun	El Khokha	Hatshepsut Thutmosis III	Cat named The Pleasant One
TT 50	Neferhotep Priest of Amun-Ra	Sheikh Abd el-Qurna	Horemheb	Cat and monkey
TT 52	Nakht Astronomer of Amun	Sheikh Abd el- Qurna	Tuthmosis IV	Cat and goose
TT 53	Amenemhat Administrator of Amun temple	Sheikh Abd el- Qurna	Tuthmosis III	Cat with fish and fowl (M)
TT 55	Ramose Govenor of Thebes-Vizier	Sheikh Abd el- Qurna	Amenhotep III Akhenaten	Cat and goose
TT 56	Usernat Royal Scribe	Sheikh Abd el- Qurna	Amenhotep III	Cat on lap
TT 69	Menna Scribe	Sheikh Abd el- Qurna	Tuthmosis IV Amenhotep III	Hunting and fowling scenes with cat
TT 96	Sennufer Mayor of Thebes	Sheikh Abd el- Qurna	Amenhotep II	Cat and haunch
TT 120	Anen Second priest of Amun	Sheikh Abd el- Qurna	Amenhotep III	Cat, monkey and goose

TOMB #	PERSON'S TOMB	LOCATION	REIGNING PHARAOH	DEPICTION
TT 159	Raya Fourth priest of Amun	Dra Abu el-Naga	19th Dynasty	Cat and monkey
TT 168	Ani	Dra Abu el-Naga	11th Dynasty Ramesses II	Book of the Dead Ra as Cat papyrus
TT 178	Neferrenpet Kenar Scribe of the Treasury	El Khokha	Ramesses II	Cat gnawing on bone
TT 181	Nebamun Accountant of the granary of Amun	El Khokha	Amenhotep III and Akhenaten	Long tailed cat Fowling, under chair in marshes
TT 217	Ipuy Sculptor	Deir el Medina	Ramesses II	Mother cat, kitten, bird, and cat
TT 219	Nebenamet Servant in the Place of Truth	Deir el Medina	Ramesside	Cat and monkey
TT 299	Inherkhau Chief of Works	Deir el Medina	Ramesses IV 20th Dynasty	Cat as Ra cutting the head off Apophis
TT 331	Penna/Sunero High priest of Mont	Sheikh Abd el- Qurna	Ramesside	Cat and monkey
TT 342	Thutmosis III	Shieikh Abd el-Qurna	18th Dynasty	Cat Sarcophagus
TT 357	Thuthermeketef Servant in the Place of Truth	Deir el Medina	19th Dynasty	Cat and monkey

LIST OF CAT CEMETERIES IN EGYPT

Abusir Al Malik
Abydos
Akhmim Al Hawawish
Armant
Asyut
Badari
Beni Hasan (Speos Artemidos)
Dakhla
Dendera
Gebel Abu Feda
Ghoran
Hu
Koptos
Manfalut es Samun Al Maaba
Qaw
Saqqara
Sharuna
Tanis
Bubastis
Thebes
Umm al Burigat Tetynis
Zawiyet Al Aryan Giza

REFERENCES

CHAPTER 1

American Genetic Association, (1917, September). Ancestry of the cat. *Journal of Heredity, 8(9),* 397-399

Driscoll, C. A., Menotti-Raymond, M., Roca, A.L., Hupe, K., Johnson, W.E., Geffen, E. Macdonald, D.W. (2007, July 27). The Near Eastern origin of cat domestication. *Science 317*(5837), 519. doi: 10.1126/science.1139518.

Ewer, R. F. (1997). *The carnivores.* Ithaca, NY: Cornell University Press.

Hubbell, S. (2002). *Shrinking the cat: genetic engineering before we knew about genes.* New York, NY: Houghton Mifflin Harcourt.

Linseele, V., Van Neer, W., Hendrickx, S. (2007). Evidence for early cat taming in Egypt. *Journal of Archeological Science, 34,* 2081-2090.

Mott, M. (2006, January 11). Cats climb new family tree. *National Geographic News.* Retrieved from http://news.nationalgeographic.com/news/2006/01/0111_060111_cat_evolution.html.

Rincon, P. (2004, April 8). *Dig discovery is oldest 'pet cat'. BBC News.* Retrieved from http://news.bbc.co.uk/2/hi/science/nature/3611453.stm.

Vigne, J.D., Guilaine, J., Debue, K., Haye, L., & Gerard, P. (2004, April 9). Early Taming of the Cat in Cyprus. *Science*, 304, (5668), 259. doi:10.1126/science.1095335.

Wade, N. (2007, June 29). Study traces cat's ancestry to Middle East. *New York Times* Retrieved from http://www.nytimes.com/2007/06/29/science/29cat.html?_r=2&ex=1187236800&en=2b553cb12899e818&ei=5070.

Yurco, F.J. (1990, January/February).The cat and ancient Egypt. *Field Museum of Natural History, 61*, (1). 46-54.

CHAPTER 2

Bard, K. A. & Shubert, S. B. (1999). *Encyclopedia of the archeology of ancient Egypt.* New York, NY: Routledge.

Belzoni, G. (1890). *Narrative of the operations and recent discoveries with in the pyramids, temples, tombs and excavations in Egypt and Nubia.* London, England: John Murray.

Breasted, J. H. (1906). *Ancient records of Egypt historical documents* (Vol. 1-4). Chicago, IL: University of Chicago Press.

Breasted, J. H. (1908). *A history of the ancient Egyptians.* New York, NY: Charles Scribner's and Sons.

Breasted, J. H. (1909). *A history of Egypt from the earliest times to the Persian conquest.* New York, NY: Charles Scribner's and Sons.

Budge, W. E.A. (1895). *The papyrus of Ani, the Egyptian book of the dead.* London, England: The British Museum Press.

Budge, W. E.A. (1929). *The Rosetta stone in the British museum.* Mineola, NY: Dover Publication.

Clarysse, W. (1998). *Egyptian religion: The last thousand years: Part 1.* Leuven, Belgium: Peeters Publishers.

Dodson, A. (2009). *Rituals related to animal cults.* In J. Dieleman & W. Wnedrich (Eds.) *UCLA Encyclopedia of Egyptology.* Los Angeles, CA: UCLA: Department of Near Eastern Languages and Cultures. Retrieved from http://escholarship.org/uc/item/6wk541n0.

Erman, A. (1907). *A handbook of Egyptian religion.* London, England: Archibald Constable and Co. Ltd.

Ikram, S. (Ed.). (2005). *Divine creatures: Animal mummies in ancient Egypt.* Cairo, Egypt: American University of Cairo Press.

Lesko, B. S. (1999). *The great goddesses of Egypt.* Norman, OK: University of Oklahoma Press.

Macaulay, G. (1890). *The history of Herodotus*, Book 2, Euterpe. New York, NY: MacMillan.

Malek, J. (1993). *The cat in ancient Egypt.* London, England: The British Museum Press.

Maspero, G., Rappopoport, A.S., King, L.W., Hall, H. R. (1903). *History of Egypt, Chaldea, Syria, Babylonia and Assyria* (Vol. 12). London, England: The Grolier Society.

Maspero, G. (1914). *Manual of Egyptian archeology and guide to the study of antiquities in Egypt.* London, England: H. Grevel & Co.

Mercer, S. A. B. (1952). *The pyramid texts translation.* New York, NY: Longmans, Green & Co.

Mery, F. (2006). *Just cats.* Alcester, England: Hesperides Press.

Naville, E. (1891). *Bubastis.* London, England: K. Paul, Trench, Trübner.
Oldfield, H. M. (2003). *The cat in magic and myth.* Mineola, NY: Dover Publications Inc.
Petrie, W. M. F. & Currelly, C. T. (1906). *Researches in Sinai.* New York, NY: E.P. Dutton and Company.
Petrie, W. M. .F (1906). *Hyksos and Israelite cities.* London, England: Office of the School of Archeology, University College.
Redford, D. B. (Ed.). (2003). *Essential guide to Egyptian mythology.* New York, NY: Berkley Books.
Simpson, F. (1903). *The book of the cat.* London, England: Cassell and Company, Ltd.
Tabor, R. (1991). *Cats: The rise of the cat.* London, England: BBC Books.
Williams, T. (1910). *Aeneid* (Vol. 8). Boston, MA: Houghton Mifflin.
Yurco, F. J. (1990, January/February). The cat and ancient Egypt. *Field Museum of Natural History, 61* (1), 46-54.
Zivie, A. & Chapuis, P. (2008). *The lost tombs of Saqqara.* Cairo, Egypt: American University in Cairo Press.

CHAPTER 3

American Genetic Association. (1917, September). Ancestry of the cat. *Journal of Heredity. 8*(9), 397-399.
Aristophanes. (1822). *Aristophanes (Vol. 2).* (T. Mitchell, Trans.). London, England: J. Murray.
Aristophanes. (2004). *The ecclesianzuae.* Whitefish, MT: Kessinger Publishing.
Aristotle. (1897). *The history of animals.* (R. Cresswell, Trans.). London, England: George Bell and Sons.
Arnott, W. G. & Edmonds, J. M. (1961). The fragments of attic comedy after Meineke, Bergk, and Kock, augmented, newly edited with their contexts, annotated, and completely translated into English verse. *Journal of Hellenic Studies (81)* p. 63.
Beard, M., North, J.A., & Price, S.R.F. (1998). *Religions of Rome: A history.* Cambridge, England: Cambridge University Press.

Bergen, F. D. (1890). Animal and plant lore. *The Popular Science Monthly. 37*, (11). 240-252.

Cameron, M.L. (2009). *Old Etruria and modern Tuscany.* Charleston, SC: Biblio Bazaar.

Castleden, R. (1993). *Minoans: Life in Bronze Age Crete.* New York, NY: Routledge.

Champfleury, M. (1896, 2005). *The cat past and present.* (C. Hoey, Trans.) Teddington, England: Echo Library.

Dennis, G. (1878). *Cities and cemeteries of Etruria, Vol 2.* London, England: J. Murray Publishers.

Depuma, R. D. & Small, J. P. (1994). *Murlo and the Etruscans: Art and society in ancient Etruria.* (Wisconsin Studies in Classics). Madison, WI: University of Wisconsin Press.

Dureau de la Mallu, A. (1829, April-October). Researches in regard to the ancient history of our domestic animals and our common plants. *The Edinburgh New Philosophical Journal* p. 309-317.

Engels, D. W. (2001). *Classical cats: The rise and fall of the sacred cat.* New York, NY: Routledge.

Erman, A. (1907). *A handbook of Egyptian religion.* London, England: Archibald Constable and Co. Ltd.

Forrest, I. (2001). *Isis magic: Cultivating a relationship with the goddess of 10,000 names.* Woodbury, MN: Llewellyn Worldwide.

Gibbons, E. (1900). *The decline and fall of the Roman empire.* (Vols. 1, 5, 7). New York, NY: Thomas Y. Crowell and Co.

Hall, M. P. (1928, 2003). *The secret teachings of all ages.* New York, NY: Penguin.

Hamilton, E. (1896). *The wildcat of Europe, felis catus.* London, England: R. H. Porter.

Jennison, G. (1937). *Animals for show and for pleasure in ancient Rome.* Manchester, England: Manchester University Press.

Leland, C. G. (1899). *Aradia or the gospel of the witches.* London, England: David Nutt.

Mahaffy, J. P. (2007). *Rambles and studies in Greece.* Salt Lake City: UT: Whitaker Press.

Malek, J. (1993). *The cat in ancient Egypt.* London, England: British Museum Press.

Massey, G. (2007). *A book of beginnings* (Vol. 1). New York, NY: Cosimo Inc.

Ovid (1955). *Metamorphoses.*(R. Humphries, Trans.).Bloomington, IN: Indiana University Press.

Pliny (1890). *Natural history of Pliny* (Vol. 4). (J. Bostock & H.T. Riley, Trans.). London, England: George Bell and Sons.

Repplier, A. (1901). *The fireside sphinx.* Cambridge, MA: The Riverside Press.

Rogers, K. M. (2001). *The cat and the human imagination: Feline images from Bast to Garfield.* Ann Arbor, MI: University of Michigan Press.

Ross, J. (1889). *The land of Manfred prince of Tarentum and king of Sicily.* London, England: John Murray.

Schoors, A. & Willems, H. (1998). *Egyptian religion the last thousand years: Studies dedicated to the memory of Jan Quaegebeur.* (Vol. 1). Leuven, Belgium: Peeters Publishers.

Simpson, F. (1903). *The book of the cat.* London, England: Cassell and Company, Ltd.

Turcan, R. (1996). *Cults of the Roman empire.* Hoboken, NJ: Wiley-Blackwell.

Turner, D.C., Bateson, P.G., & Bateson, P. B. (2000). *The domestic cat: The biology of its behavior.* Cambridge, England: Cambridge University Press.

Van Vechten, Carl. (1921, 2004). *The tiger in the house.* Whitefish, MT: Kessinger Publishing.

Witt, R. E. (1971). *Isis in the ancient world.* Baltimore, MD: John Hopkins University Press.

CHAPTER 4

Bast, F. (Ed.). (1995). *The poetical cat.* New York, NY: Farrar Straus & Giroux

Boyce, M. (1977). *A Persian stronghold of Zoroastrianism.* Gloucestershire, England: Clarendon Press.

Champfleury, M. (1896, 2005). *The cat past and present.* (C. Hoey Trans.) Teddington, England: Echo Library.

Chittock, L. & Schimmel, A. (2001). *Cats of Cairo: Egypt's enduring legacy.* New York, NY: Abbeville Press.

Clutton-Brock, J. (1994). *The British museum book of cats.* London, England: British Museum Press.

Engels, D. (2001). *Classical cats: The rise and fall of the sacred cat.* New York, NY: Routledge.

Erman, A. (1907). *A handbook of Egyptian religion.* London, England: Archibald Constable and Co. Ltd.

Etter, C. (1949, 2004). *Ainu folklore: Traditions and culture of the vanishing aborigines of Japan.* Whitefish, MT: Kessinger Publishing.

Gage, M. J. (1893). *Woman, church and state.* New York, NY: The Truth Seeker Company.

Geyer, G. A. (2004). *When cats ruled like kings: On the trail of the sacred cats.* Kansas City, MO: Andrews McMeels Publishing.

Gibbons, E. (1900). *The decline and fall of the Roman empire.* (Vol. 5). New York, NY: Thomas Y. Crowell and Co.

Gooden, M. (1946). *The poet's cat: An anthology.* London, England: Ayer Publishing.

Graves, R. (1966). *The white goddess: A historical grammar of poetic myth.* New York, NY: Farrar, Straus and Giroux.

Lang, J. S. (2004). *1,001 things you always wanted to know about cats.* Hoboken, NJ: John Wiley and Sons.

Legge, J. (Trans.). (1885). The book of rites. Retrieved from http://ctext.org/liji/jiao-te-sheng

Mitford, A.B. (1871, 2010). *The vampire cat of Nabéshima.* New York, NY: Digireads.com Publishing.

Ockley, S. (1847). *The history of the Saracens; comprising the lives of Mohammed and his successors, to the death of Abdalmelik, the eleventh caliph: With an account of their most remarkable battles, sieges, revolts.* London, England: Henry G. Bohn.

Oldfield H., M. (2003). *The cat in magic and myth.* Mineola, NY: Courier Dover Publication.

Omisdsalar, Mahmud, (1990, December 15). Cat I. In mythology and folklore. *Encyclopedia Iranica, 5*(1). 74-77. Retrieved from http://www.iranica.com/articles/cat-in-mythology-and-folklore-khot.

Omori, A., & Doi, K. (1920). *Diaries of court ladies of old Japan.* Boston. MA: Houghton Mifflin Company.

Ouseley, G. J. & Udny, E. F. (1924, 2004). *The gospel of the holy twelve.* Whitefish, MT: Kessinger Publishing.

Probert, W. (1823). *Ancient laws of Cambria: containing the institutional triads of Dyvnwal Moelmud, the laws of Howel the*

Good, Triadical Commentaries, code of education, and the hunting laws of Wales. London, England: W & W Clarke.

Refsing, K. (2002). *Early European writings on Ainu culture, religion and folklore* (Vol. 2). Oxford, England: Routledge Curzon.

Repplier, A. (1901). *The fireside sphinx*. Cambridge, MA: The Riverside Press.

Rowling, M. (1979). *Life in medieval times*. New York, NY: The Berkeley Publishing Group.

Russell, J. B. (1972). *Witchcraft in the Middle Ages*. Ithaca, NY: Cornell University Press.

Simpson, F. (1903). *The book of the cat*. London, England: Cassell and Company.

Spence, L. (1917). *Legendes and romances of Brittany*. New York, NY: Fredrick A. Stokes Co. Publishers.

Summers, M. (1926). *The vampire, his kith and kin: Chapter III the traits and practice of vampirism*. London, England: K. Paul Trench, Trubner.

Thompson, R. C. (1908, 2003). *Semitic magic: Its origins and development*. Whitefish, MT: Kessinger Publishing.

Turner, D. C., Bateson, P., Bateson, P. (2000). *The domestic cat: The biology of its behavior*. Cambridge, England: Cambridge University Press.

Van Vechten, C. (1921). *The tiger in the house*. New York, NY: Alfred A. Knopf, Inc.

Waddell, T. (2003). *Cultural expressions of evil and wickedness: Wrath, sex, crime*. Amsterdam, Netherlands: Rodopi.

Werness, H. B. (2006). *The continuum encyclopedia of animal symbolism in art*. London, England: Continuum International Publishing Group.

West, E. W. (2009). *Pahlavi texts, part 2*. Charleston, SC: BiblioBazaar, LLC.

Williams, J. (1967). *Life in the Middle Ages*. Cambridge, England: Cambridge University Archive.

Winslow, H. M. (1900). *Concerning cats: My own and some others*. Boston, MA: Lothrop Publishing Co.

Zahler, D. (2009). *The black death*. Minneapolis, MN: Twenty- First Century Books.

CHAPTER 5

Aftandilian, D. & Wilson, D. S. (2007). *What are the animals to us? Approaches from science, religion folklore, literature and art.* Knoxville, TN: University of Tennessee Press.

Arnott, M. (Trans.). (1995). *The Aberdeen Bestiary*, (Folio 23v). Aberdeen, Scotland: University of Aberdeen. Retrieved from http://www.abdn.ac.uk/bestiary/translat/23v.hti

Ashton, J. (1890). *Curious creatures in zoology.* London, England: John C. Nimmo.

Baillie-Groham, W.A. & Baillie-Groham, F. (Eds.). (1909). *The master of game by Edward, second Duke of York.* London, England: Chatto and Windus.

Bell, R. (Ed.). (1854). *Annotated edition of the English Poets.* London, England: John W. Park and Son, West Strand.

Bergen, F. (1899). *Animal and plant lore.* Boston, MA: Houghton Mifflin.

Bishop, M. (2001). *The Middle Ages.* Boston, MA: Houghton Mifflin Harcourt.

Bragge, F. (1712). *A full and impartial account of the discovery of sorcery and witchcraft practiced by Jane Wenham.* London, England: E. Curll.

Brehaut, E. (1912). *The encyclopedia of the Dark Ages: Isidore of Seville.* New York, NY: Columbia University.

Burr, G. L. (1914). *The narratives of witchcraft cases 1648-1706.* New York, NY: Charles Scribner's and Sons.

Burton, D. & Grandy, D. (2004*). Magic, mystery and science: The occult in Western civilization.* Bloomington, IN: Indiana University Press.

Calef, R. (1700). *More wonders of the invisible world.* London, England.

Campbell, J. G.(2003).*Witchcraft and second sight in the highlands and islands of Scotland.* Whitefish, MT: Kessinger Publishing.

Champfleury, M. (1896, 2005). The cat past and present. (C. Hoey Trans.). Teddington, England: Echo Library.

Choron, H., Choron, S., & Moore, A. (2007). *Planet cat: A cat-alog.* Boston, MA: Houghton Mifflin Harcourt.

Clutton-Brock, J. (1994). *The British Museum book of cats.* London, England: British Museum Press.

Conway, M. D. (1879, 2003). *Demonology and devillore*, (Vols. 1 and 2). Whitefish, MT: Kessinger Publishing.

Cressy, D. (2000). *Agnes Bowker's cat: Travesties and transgressions in Tudor and Stuart England.* Oxford, England: Oxford University

Press.

Cross, T. P. (1919). *Witchcraft in North Carolina.* Chapel Hill, NC: University of North Carolina Press.

Engels, D. (2001). *Classical cats: The rise and fall of the sacred cat.* London, England: Routledge.

Fiero, G., Pfeffer, W., & Alain, M. (1989). *Three medieval views of women.* New Haven, CT: Yale University Press.

Fragos, E. (Ed.) (2005). *The great cat: Poems about cats.* London, England: Everyman's Library.

Gage, M. J. (1893). *Woman, church and state.* New York, NY: The Truth Seeker Company.

Gay, J. (1822). *The poems of John Gay.* London, England: Press of C. Whittingham.

Hartley, D. (1979). *Lost country life.* New York, NY: Pantheon Books.

Hopkins, M., Stearne, J., & Davies, S. F. (1647, 2007) *The discovery of witches and witchcraft: The writings of the witchfinders.* Brighton, England: Puckrel Publishing.

Howells, W. D. (1872). *Italian journeys.* Boston, MA: J. R. Osgood and Company.

Jonstonus, J. (1678). *A description of the nature of four footed beasts: With their figures engraven in brass.* Printed for Moses Pitt at the Angel, against the little north door of St. Paul's Church. Retrieved from http://digital.library.wisc.edu//711.dl/histscitech.Jonstonus.

Karras, R. M. (2005). *Sexuality in Medieval Europe: Doing unto others.* New York, NY: Routledge.

Kieckhefer, R. (1998). *Forbidden rites: A necromancer's manual of the 15th century.* University Park, PA: Penn State Press.

Kieckhefer, R. (2000). *Magic in the Middle Ages.* Cambridge, England: Cambridge University Press.

Ladinsky, D. (Trans.) (1999). *The gift, poems by Hafiz the great Sufi master.* New York, NY: Penguin Books.

Lea, H. C. (2005). *A history of the inquisition of the Middle Ages,* (Vol. 3). New York, NY: Cosimo, Inc.

Lipton, S. (1999). *Images of intolerance: The representation of Jews and Judaism in the Bible Moralisée.* Berkeley, CA: University of California Press.

Morton, J. (1853). *The Ancren Riwle.* London, England: The Camden Society.

Newman, P. B. (2001). *Daily life in the Middle Ages.* Jefferson, NC: MacFarland.

Notestein, W. (1911). *A history of witchcraft in England from 1558-1718.* Washington, D.C.: The American Historical Association.

Oldfield H., M. (2003). *The cat in magic and myth.* Mineola, NY: Courier Dover Publication.

Paré, A., & Pallister, J. L. (1995). *On Monsters and Marvels.* Chicago, IL: University of Chicago Press.

Paton-Williams, D. (2008). *Katterfelto: Prince of puff.* Leicester, England: Troubador Publishing Ltd.

Pollard, A. W. (Ed.). (1894). *Chaucer's Canterbury Tales.* London, England: Macmillan and Co.

Reeves, C. (1998). *Pleasures and pastimes in Medieval England.* Oxford, England: Oxford University Press.

Repplier, A. (1901). *The fireside sphinx.* Cambridge, MA: The Riverside Press.

Rodenberg, K. (Ed.). (1883). *Epstolæ Sæculi XIII.* Berlin, Germany: Weidmann.

Rogers, K. (2006). *Cat.* Edinburgh, Scotland: Reaktion Books.

Ross, C. H. (1868). *The book of cats.* London, England: Griffith and Farran.

Russell, J. B. (1984). *Witchcraft in the Middle Ages.* Ithaca, NY: Cornell University Press.

Sider, S. (2005). *Handbook to life in Renaissance Europe.* New York, NY: Infobase Publishing.

Simpson, F. (1903). *The book of the cat.* London, England: Cassell and Company, Ltd.

Speranza Wilde, F. (1887). *Ancient legends, mystic charmes, and superstitions of Ireland.* London, England: Ward and Downey.

Stall, S. (2007). *100 cats who changed civilization: History's most influential felines.* Philadelphia, PA: Quirk Books.

Summers, M. (Trans.). (1486, 2009). *Malleus maleficarum.* Charleston, SC: BiblioBazaar, LLC.

Summers, M. (1926). *The history of witchcraft and demonology.* London, England: Kegan, Paul T. Trubner and Co. Ltd.

Taylor, J. M. (1908). *The witchcraft delusion in colonial Connecticut.* London, England: The Grafton Press.

Thompson, R. C. (1908, 2003). *Semitic magic: Its origins and development.* Whitefish, MT: Kessinger Publishing.

Topsell, E. (1658, 1967). *The history of four-footed beasts and serpents and insects* (Vol. 1). New York, NY: Da Capo Press.

Trachtenberg, J. (1939). *Jewish magic and superstition: A study in folk religion.* New York, NY: Behrman's Jewish Book House.

Turner, D. C., Bateson, P., & Bateson, P. (2000). *The domestic cat: The biology of its behavior.* Cambridge, England: Cambridge University Press.

Van Vechten, C. (1921). *The tiger in the house.* Whitefish, MT: Kessinger Publishing.

Von Nettesheim, C. H. A. (1913). *The philosophy of natural magic.* Chicago, IL: Delaurente, Scott and Co.

Waddell, T. (2003). *Cultural expressions of evil and wickedness: Wrath, sex, crime.* Amsterdam, Netherlands: Rodopi.

Warren, J. P. (2006). *Pet ghosts: Animal encounters from beyond the grave.* Pompton Plains, NJ: Career Press.

Whittington, D. (1820). The *history of Dick Whittington Lord Mayor of London; with the adventures of his cat.* Banbury, England: J.G. Rusher.

Williams, J. (1967). *Life in the Middle Ages.* Cambridge, England: University Press Archive.

Zahler, D. (2009). *The black death.* Minneapolis, MN: Twenty-First Century Books.

CHAPTER 6

Beecher, D. (2008). *Renaissance comedy: The Italian masters.* Toronto, Canada: University of Toronto Press.

Boehrer, B. T. (2002). *Shakespeare among the animals: Nature and society in the drama of early modern England.* Basingstoke, England: Palgrave Macmillan.

Brenner, A. (1999). *Ruth and Esther: A feminist companion to the Bible.* New York, NY: Bloomsbury T&T Clark.

Canepa, N. L. (2007). *Giambasttista Basile's the tale of tales, or, entertainment for little ones by Giambattista Basile.* Detroit, MI: Wayne State University Press.

Champfleury, M. (1896, 2005). *Cats past and present.* (C. Hoey, Trans.). Teddington, England: Echo Library.

Cressy, D. (2000). *Travesties and transgressions in Tudor and Stuart England: Tales of discord.* Oxford, England: Oxford University

Press.

de Cervantes Saavedra, M. (1605, 1885). *Don Quixote.*, (J. Ormsby, Trans.). London, England: Macmillan and Co. / Smith, Elder & Co.

Defoe, D. (1722, 1983). *A journal of the plague year.* (A. Burgess, Ed.). New York, NY: Penguin Books.

Engels, D. (2001). *Classical cats: The rise and fall of the sacred cat.* London, England: Routledge.

Evans, E. P. (1906). *The criminal prosecution and capital punishment of animals.* London, England: W. Heinemann.

Fudge, E. (2004). *Renaissance beasts: Of animals, humans, and other wonderful creatures.* Champaign, IL: University of Illinois Press.

Grössinger, C. (1997). *Picturing women in late medieval and renaissance art.* Manchester, England: Manchester University Press.

Hadfield, A. (2007). *Literature, travel and colonial writing in English renaissance 1545-1625.* Oxford, England: Oxford University Press.

Hattaway, M. (2002). *A companion to English renaissance literature and culture.* Hoboken, NJ: Wiley-Blackwell.

Ife, B. (1999). Mad cats and knights errant: Roberto de Nola and Don Quixote. *Journal of the Institute of Romance Studies. 7*, 49-54.

Jardine, D. (1847). *Criminal trials supplying copious illustrations of the important periods of English history during the reigns of Elizabeth and James I.* London, England: M.A. Nattali.

Klein, M. M. (2006). *The empire state: A history of New York.* Ithaca, NY: Cornell University Press.

Landrin, A. (1894). *Le Chat, zoologie, origine, historique, moeurs, habitudes, races, anatomie, maladies, jurisprudence.* Paris, France: G. Carré

Oldfield H., M. (2003). *The cat in magic and myth.* Mineola, NY: Courier Dover Publication.

Paton-Williams, D. (2008). *Katterfelto: Prince of puff.* Leicester, England: Troubador Publishing Ltd.

Patterson, A. (1993). *Reading between the lines.* Milwaukee, WI: University of Wisconsin Press.

Payne, M. & Hunter, J. (2003). *Renaissance literature: An anthology.* Hoboken, NJ: Wiley-Blackwell.

Ruff, J. R. (2001). *Violence in early modern Europe 1500-1800.* Cambridge, England: Cambridge University Press.

Straparola, G. F. (1901). *The facetious nights.* (W.G. Waters, Trans.).

London, England: Society of Bibliophiles.
Ueda, M. &, Bashō, M. (1995). *Bashō and his interpreters: Selected hokku with commentary*. San Francisco, CA: Stanford University Press.
Van Vechten, C. (1921). *The tiger in the house*. New York, NY: Knopf Inc.
Waddell, T. (2003). *Cultural expressions of evil and wickedness: Wrath, sex, crime*. Amsterdam, Netherlands: Rodopi.
Yasuda, K. (1957). *The Japanese haiku: Its essential nature, history, and possibilities in English with selected examples*. Mount Vernon, NY: Peter Pauper Press.

CHAPTER 7

Anonymous. (1769). An epitaph. *Gentleman's Magazine. 39,* 48.
Anonymous. (1775). An epitaph on a favorite cat named Blewet. *London Magazine, 47*, 654-55.
Bayley, J.W. (1821). *The history of antiquities of the tower of London* (Part 1). London, England: T. Cadell.
Bentham, J. (1789,2005) *An introduction to the principles of morals and legislation*. Boston, MA: Adamant Media Corporation.
Bowring, J. (Ed.) (1843). *The works of Jeremy Bentham*. Edinburgh, Scotland: William Tait.
Boswell, J. (1820). *The life of Samuel Johnson*. Oxford, England: Oxford University Press.
Bryant, M. (1999). *The mammoth book of cats*. Philadelphia, PA: Running Press.
Buffon, Georges L. (1792). *Buffon's natural history*. (Vol. 6). (J.S. Barr, Trans.). London, England: J.S. Barr.
Champfleury, M.(1896, 2005). *The cat past and present*. (C. Hoey, Trans). Teddington, England: Echo Library.
Darnton, R. (1984). *The great cat massacre and other episodes in the French cultural history*. New York, NY: Basic Books Inc.
de Paradis de Moncrif, F. (1965). Moncrif's cats. (R. Bretnor, Trans.) New York, NY: A.S. Barnes & Co.
Engels, D. (2001). *Classical cats: the rise and fall of the sacred cat*. London, England: Routledge.
Gooden, M. (1946). *The poet's cat: an anthology*. London, England: Ayer Publishing.
Gosse, E. (1891). *Gossip in the library*. New York, NY: Lovell, Covyell

and Co.

Gray, Thomas. (1902). *Selections from the poetry of Thomas Gray.* (W.L. Phelps, Ed.) Boston, MA: Ginn & Company.

Green, J. (1733). The poet's lamentation for the loss of his cat, which he used to call his muse. *London Magazine*, 2, p. 579.

Hamilton, I. (1997). *Thomas Gray: Selected poems.* London, England: Bloomsbury.

Issa, K. (n.d.). *The haiku and poems of Kobayashi Issa.* Retrieved from http://thegreenleaf.co.uk/hp/issa/00haiku.htm.

Landrin, A. (1894). *Le chat: zoologie, origine, historique, moeurs, habitudes, races, anatomie, maladies, jurisprudence.* Paris, France: Carre.

Lang, J.S. (2004). *1,001 things you always wanted to know about cats.* Hoboken, NJ: John Wiley and Sons.

Milford, H.S. (Ed.). (1905). *The complete poetical works of William Cowper.* London, England: Henry Frowde.

Paton-Williams, D. (2008). *Katterfelto: prince of puff.* London, England: Troubadour Publishing Ltd.

Piggott, S. (1985). *William Stukeley, an eighteenth century antiquary,* New York, NY: Thames and Hudson, New York.

Repplier, A. (1918). *The cat: Being a record of the endearments and invectives lavished by many writers upon an animal much loved and abhorred.* New York, NY: Sturgis and Walton Co.

Rogers, K. (2006). *Cat.* Edinburgh, Scotland: Reaktion Books.

Ross, C.H. (1868). *The book of cats.* Oxford, England: Oxford University Press.

Smart, C. (1763,1939). *Rejoice in the lamb: A song from bedlam.* (W.F. Stead, Ed.). London: England: Jonathan Cape.

Steele, Richard Sir & Addison, J. (1829). *The Tatler and Guardian: complete in one volumne, with notes and general index.* London, England: Jones & Co.

Stockdale, P. (1809/2012). *The memoirs of the life, and writings of Percival Stockdale (Volume 1); Containing many interesting anecdotes of the illustrious men with whom he was connected.* Watertown, MA: General Books LLC.

Van Vechten, C. (1921). *The tiger in the house.* New York, NY: Alfred A. Knopf. Inc.

Westfall, R. S. (1980). *Never at rest, a biography of Issac Newton.* Cambridge, England: Cambridge University Press.

CHAPTER 8

A countess and her cats. (1883, October 6). *The New Zealand Herald.* (Vol. XX, Issue 6829) p. 2-supplement. Retrieved from http://paperspast.natlib.govt.nz/cgi-bin/paperspast?a=d&d=NZH18831006.1.10&e=-------10--1----0--

Aberconway, C. M.(1968). *A dictionary of cat lovers XV century BC – XX century AD.* London, England: Joseph.

Aggeler, W. (1954). *The flowers of evil.* Fresno, CA: Academy Library Guild.

Anonymous. (1820). *Dame Trot and her cat.* London. England: J. Harris and Son.

Aristotle. (1897). *The history of animals.* (Richard Cresswell, Trans.). London, England: George Bell and Sons.

Baille, J. (1840). *Fugitive verses.* London, England: Edward Moxon.

Baudelaire, C.P. (1868). *Oeuvres completes.* Preface (Vol. 1). (T. Gautier). Paris, France: Michel Levy Freres.

Besse, J. (1895, November). L'Assistance publique des bêtes: les chats et les chiens de Paris. *LaVie Contemporaine et Revue Parisienne reunites* (239-256).

Bostridge, M. (2008). *Florence Nightingale: The woman and her legend.* London, England: Viking Books.

Clemens, C. (1931). *My father, Mark Twain.* New York, NY: Harpers.

De Maupassant, G. (1955). *Complete short stories.* Garden City, NY: Doubleday.

Dickens, C. (1853). *Bleak House.* London, England: Bradbury and Evans.

Dickens, C. (1860). *The uncommercial traveller.* London, England: Chapman and Hall.

Elliott, J. W. (1870). *National nursery rhymes and nursery songs.* London, England: George Routledge and Sons.

Frees, H.W. (1929). *Animal land on the air.* New York, NY: Lothrop, Lee & Shepard.

Gautier, Théophile. (1902/2014). *My private menagerie.* Auckland, New Zealand: The Floating Press.

Gavan, Peggy (n.d.) *Rosalie Goodman story*, 1871. Retrieved from http://hatchingcatnyc.com/

Hardy, T. (1994). *The collected poems of Thomas Hardy.* Hertfordshire,

England: Wordsworth Editions, Ltd.

Hartwell, S. (2014). *The case of the Countess De La Torre – A nineteenth century cat hoarder.* Retrieved from http://messybeast.com/1856-cat-hoarder-1.htm.

Hoffmann, E.T.A. (1999/1821). *The life and times of the Tomcat Murr.* London, England: Penguin Books.

Hogg, T. J. (1858). *The life of Percy Bysshe Shelley.* London, England: Edward Moxon.

The Iola Register. (Iola, Kan.), 25 Aug. 1877.

Ireland, C. (2012, June 27). Edward Lear's natural history. *Harvard Gazette.* Retrieved from http://news.harvard.edu/gazette/story/2012/06/edward-lears-natural-history/

Johnson, T. H. (Ed.). (1955). *The complete poems of Emily Dickinson.* New York, NY: Little Brown.

Journal of the Society of Architectural Historians 71, no. 3 (September 2012), 362-385. ISSN 0037-9808, electronic ISSN 2150-5926 © 2012 by the Society of Architectural Historians website, http://www.ucpressjournals.com/reprintInfo.asp.DOI:10.1525/jsah.2012.71.3.362

Keats, J. (1884). *The poetical works of John Keats.* Boston, MA: DeWolfe et al.

Kete, K. (1994). *Beast in the boudoir: Petkeeping in nineteenth-century Paris.* Berkeley, CA: University of California Press.

Lane, J. S. (2004). *1,001 Things you always wanted to know about cats.* Hoboken, NJ: John Wiley and Sons.

Lear, E. (1894). *Nonsense songs, stories, botany and alphabets.* Boston, MA: Roberts Brothers.

Lawton, M. (2003,1925).(with Mary Lawton) *A lifetime with Mark Twain: The memories of Katy Leary for thirty years his faithful and devoted servant.* Amsterdam, Netherlands: Fredonia Books.

Lounsbury, T. R.(Ed.). (1912). *Yale book of American verse.* New Haven, CT: Yale University Press.

Lunn, A. (1953, December 19). The grand tour with Boswell. Interviewing Rousseau and Voltaire. *The Tablet,* p. 9. Retrieved from http://archive.thetablet.co.uk/article/19th-december-1953/9/the-grand-tour-with-boswell.

Milani, M. (1993). *The body language and emotion of cats.* New York, NY:

Harper Paperbacks.

Pierre Loti's cats. (1923, September 29). *The Argus* (Melbourne, Vic.: 1848 - 1957), p. 9. Retrieved from http://nla.gov.au/nla.news-page425145.

Poe, E. A. (1978). *Collected works.* (T.O.Mabbott, Ed.). Cambridge, MA: Belknap Press of Harvard University Press.

Ritvo, H. (1987). *The animal estate: the English and other creatures in the Victorian age.* Boston, MA: Harvard University Press.

Rogers, K. (2006). *Cat.* Edinburgh, Scotland: Reaktion Books.

Rossetti, W. M. (1904). *The Poetical Works of Christina Georgina Rossetti.* London, England: MacMillian and Co. Ltd.

Sharpe, R. S. (c. 1825). *Dame Wiggins of Lee and her seven wonderful cats. a humourous tale.* London, England: Dean and Munday, and A.K. Newman.

Singleton, E. (1895, October 5). Theophile Gautier's cats. *Daily Telegraph*, Issue 7488.

Squire, J. C. (1909). *Poems and Baudelaire flowers.* London, England: The New Age Press, Ltd.

Stedman, E.C. (Ed.). (1895). *A Victorian anthology 1837-1895.* Cambridge, England: Riverside Press.

Swinburne, A. C. (1911). *The poems of Algernon Charles Swinburne* (Vol 6.) London, England: Chatto and Windus.

The countess and her cats. (1884, October 25). *The Aroha News* (New Zealand, Vol.II, Issue 73), p.5 Retrieved from http://paperspast.natlib.govt.nz/cgi-bin/paperspast?a=d&d=TAN18841025.1.5&e=-------10--1----0--.

Toussenel, A. (1852). *Passional zoology or the spirit of the beasts of France.* (M.E. Lazarus, Trans.) (2nd ed.) New York, NY: Fowlers and Wells.

Twain, M. (1980). *The devil's race-track Mark Twain's great dark writings.* Oakland, CA: University of California Press.

Various authors (2010). *Concerning cats: a book of poems by many authors.* Read Books.

Van Herk, M. (1995). *Steinlein of cats and men.* Kattenkabinet, Amsterdam, Netherlands.

Van Vechten, C. (1921). *The tiger in the house.* New York, NY: Alfred A. Knopf, Inc.

Vinegar, A. (September 2012). Chatography. *Journal of the Society of*

Architectural Historians 7/(3). 362-385. Retrieved from http://www.ucpressjournals.com/reprintInfo.asp.DOI:10.1525/jsah.2012.71.3.362

Warner, C. D. (1912). *My summer in a garden.* Boston, MA: Fields, Osgood & Co.

Watson, R. M. (1892). *Concerning cats: A book of poems by many authors.* New York, NY: F.A. Stokes Co.

Wordsworth, W. (n.d.). *The poems of William Wordsworth.* London, England: Edward Moxon.

Zeldin, T. (1981). *France 1848-1945: Anxiety and hypocrisy.* Oxford, England: Oxford University Press.

CHAPTER 9

Bockris, V. (1996). *With William Burroughs: A report from the bunker.* London, England: St. Martin's Griffin.

Brennen, C. F. (2006). *Hemingway's cats: An illustrated biography.* Sarasota, FL: Pineapple Press.

Capote, T. (1958/1993). *Breakfast at Tiffany's.* New York, NY: Vintage Books.

Cat of the day 058: *Harry and Tonto.* (2012, December 17). Cats on film [blog], Retrieved from http://catsonfilm.net/2012/12/17cat-of-the-day-058

Chapman, P. (2004, June 28). Tribute to cat killed by Shackleton in Antarctic. *The Telegraph.*

Churchill should pet cat only if invited, fans say (1941, September 23). *The New York Times* p. 25.

Colville, J. (1986, 1987). *The fringes of power*, 2 vols. London, England: Sceptre.

Copping, Jasper. (2014). *Cats of war: Animals suspected by British of spying on WWI trenches.* Retrieved from http://www.telegraph.co.uk/history/world-war-one/10692910/Cats-of-war-Animals-suspected-by-British-of-spying-on-WW1-trenches.html.

Crossen, C. (2008). *Just asking . . . Doris Lessing the Nobel Laureate talks about cats, dogs and then more about cats.* Retrieved from http://online.wsj.com/news/articles/SB122427970148245879.

Crowther, B. & Gilroy, H. (1965). The screen: Walt Disney's 'Darn

Cat': *Hayley Mills and feline star at Music Hall*, December 3,1965. Retrieved from http://www.nytimes.com/movie/review?res=950DE1DC143EE03ABC4B53DFB467838E679EDE

Downing St. cats create problem of feline protocol. (1940, June 7). *The Washington Post.* p. 6.

Hamblin, G. (1987). *Chartwell memories*, Dallas, Texas, 30 October 1987. Hopkinton, NH: International Churchill Society.

Hamblin, G. (1989). Proceedings of the international Churchill societies 1987. Hopkinton, NH: ICS.

Jameson, William (2004), *Ark Royal: The life of an aircraft carrier at war 1939-41*, Periscope Publishing, p. 372.

Jansson, T. (2003). *The summer book*. London, England: Sort of Books.

Keroauc, J. (1992). *Big Sur.* New York, NY: Penguin Books.

Konishi, K. (2014, July 13) *Haruki Murakami's love for cats comes through in his works.* Retrieved from http://ajw.asahi.com/article/behind_news/people/AJ201407130010.

Lovecraft, H.P. (1949). *Something about cats and other pieces.* North Stratford, NH: Ayer Publishing.

Manchester, W. (1988). *The last lion: Winston Spencer Churchill, vol. 2, alone 1932-1940.* Boston, MA: Little Brown.

Murakami, H. (1985). *On the death of my cat.* Retreived from http://mrmurakamiquotes.tumblr.com/post/100224057049/on-the-death-of-my-cat-by-haruki-murakami .

Reynolds, Q. (1964). *All about Winston Churchill.* London, England: W. H. Allen.

Shackleton, E. (1919). *South.* New York, NY: Signet.

Soames, M. (Ed).(2005, April). Winston and Clementine: The personal letters of the Churchills. *Chartwell Bulletin (7)* p.388, 471. Boston, MA: Houghton Mifflin Company.

Tesla, N. (1939). A story of youth told by age dedicated to miss Pola Fotitch. Retrieved from http://www.pbs.org/tesla/ll/story_youth.html.

Tesla, N. (1939). *Tesla said.* (J. T. Ratzlaff Compiler). Milbrae, CA: Tesla Book Co.

Treisman, D. (2011, August 28). This week in fiction: Haruki Murakami. *The New Yorker.* Retrieved from http://www.newyorker.com/books/page-turner/this-week-in-fiction-haruki-murakami

Wallace, M. (1936, August 9). Colette and a cat. *New York Times Review.*

Women, to win at love, should study cats, says Foujita, Japanese artist. (1930, November 25) *Milwaukee Journal*, p.19 Retrieved from http://news.google.com/newspapers?nid=1499&dat=19301125&id=o5RSAAAAIBAJ&sjid=5SEEAAAAIBAJ&pg=4322,378203.

World War II cat veteran turns 15. (1959, July 4) *Los Angeles Times.* Retrieved from http://framework.latimes.com/2012/11/09/world-war-ii-cat-turns-15/

Yeats, W.B. (1912). *The wild swans at Coole and other poems.* New York, NY: Macmillan.

INDEX

A

B

C

D

E

F

G

J

K

L

M

N

O

P

Q

R

S

T

U

V

W

Y

Z

ABOUT THE AUTHOR

L.A. Vocelle has a Master's of Education and teaching English from George Washington University, Washington, D.C., as well as undergraduate degrees in history and political science. She is the creator and founder of the website The Great Cat, www.thegreatcat.org, and a member of the Cat Writers' Association. She has published several books: *7 Women Artists and their Cat Subjects* (2013), *Ancient Egyptian Cats: A Coloring Book for Adults and Children* (2015) and *Medieval Cats Coloring Book for Cat Lovers* (2016). Her free time is devoted to serving the wishes of her four rescue cats.

Made in United States
Troutdale, OR
12/12/2023

15765907R00257